Communicative Praxis and the Space of Subjectivity

Studies in Phenomenology and
Existential Philosophy

Communicative Praxis and the Space of Subjectivity

CALVIN O. SCHRAG

Indiana University Press
Bloomington and Indianapolis

First Midland Book Edition 1989

Manufactured in the United States of America

Library of Congress Cataloging in Publication Data

Schrag, Calvin O.
Communicative praxis and the space of subjectivity.

(Studies in phenomenology and existential philosophy)
Includes index.
1. Communication—Philosophy.   2. Subectivity.
3. Hermeneutics.   I. Title.   II. Series.
P90.S36   1986   001.51   84-48647
cl. ISBN 0-253-31383-X
pa. ISBN 0-253-20515-8

2 3 4 5 6 93 92 91 90 89

Contents

Preface

A preface provides an author the opportunity to address the reader from the point of view of his authorship. Although etymologically a preface is a prefatory statement of the motivations and circumstances that surround the beginning of a project, there is a widespread practice of using the preface also to inform the reader about what is achieved in the end. A preface is thus at once a "foreword" preceding the text and an "afterword" following its completion; a curious combination of prologue and epilogue; an idiosyncratic blend of that which is first and that which is last; a peculiar mix of a promissory note and its redeemed cash value. Although a preface is placed first in the format, serialized by roman numerals so as to mark it off from the arabic pagination of the main body of the text, it is written last. The writing of such a preface, binding beginning and end, becomes a burdensome task in the moment that the author becomes aware of the elusiveness of all beginnings and ends. Unable to surmount this elusiveness the author gravitates into a quandary as he deliberates on what is to be included and what is to be left out.

Some prefaces are very short and some are quite long. Descartes's preface to his *Meditations* is relatively brief, whereas Hegel's preface to his *Phenomenology of Mind* is notably extensive. Descartes pretty much lets matters rest with an entreaty to the reader that he suspend judgment on the thought experiments in the text until he has worked his way through it. Hegel, on the other hand, uses his preface as a commentary on the account that is rendered in the subsequent chapters. There are other authors, however, who make no reference whatever to the thesis developed in the consummate body of the work, possibly so as not to show their hand before the play of reading begins. In these cases it is assumed that all that is required is a list of acknowledgments including colleagues, institutions, and endowment agencies. It thus becomes readily apparent that there is no standard form to be followed in the writing of a preface. The manuals offer no criteria for success in the prefatory exercise. Given such a state of affairs the most for which the author can hope is that what he says in the preface, however brief or lengthy, will entice the reader to go on.

The discussion that follows is about communicative praxis and about subjectivity. It comprises an effort to find a new space for subjectivity within the praxial space of discourse and action. The texture of communicative praxis is portrayed as an amalgam of discursive and nondiscursive practices, in which the meaning-engendering patterns of the spoken and the written word mix and mingle with meaning-laden actions. The inmixing of discourse and action, however, does not warrant a fusion of them through some species of sublation of the one into the other. Neither the textuality of the spoken and the written word nor the intentionality of action is allowed a status of privilege and primacy. An effort is made to avoid both the modeling of human action after textual analogues and the modeling of language after forms of human behavior. Thus the claim for primacy, either from the side of a philosophy of language or from the side of a philosophy of action, is undermined.

The proposed notion of communicative praxis, which supplies the linchpin for the discussion throughout, takes shape as a three-dimensional or tripartite phenomenon. Discourse and action are *about* something, *by* someone, and *for* someone. Communicative praxis thus displays a referential moment (about a world of human concerns and social practices), a moment of self-implicature (by a speaker, author, or actor), and a rhetorical moment (directedness to the other). The division of the book into three parts roughly corresponds with these three moments that bind the texture of communicative praxis. The topical design in the three divisions is to work out plausible notions of hermeneutical reference, hermeneutical self-implicature, and hermeneutical rhetoric.

Through an exploration of the texture of communicative praxis a new space is cleared for the restoration of the subject. This exploration involves first an exercise of critical hermeneutics, developing as a strategy of deconstruction through which the metaphysical and epistemological space of traditional philosophy of the soul and modern philosophy of mind is disassembled. This disassemblage heralds the "end of philosophy" as conceptual construction and the "death of the subject" as metaphysical substrate and epistemological origin. But it also sets the requirement for a restorative hermeneutics wherewith a transvalued subject is resituated within a new space. After the theoretical constructs of metaphysico-epistemological space are dismantled, the path is cleared for the restoration of subjectivity within the praxial space of discourse and action. The parameters of this praxial space already mark out the presence of the other, displayed in a rhetoric of discourse and a rhetoric of action. The subject that reappears is a decentered and transfigured intersubject, co-emerging with other subjects, courting new descriptions for a new humanism that might in some way direct us in an age in which the philosophical constructs of traditional humanism have ceased to hold our attention.

There are no heroes in the story of communicative praxis which I tell. There are, however, throughout the discussion intermittent critical conversations with Kierkegaard and Nietzsche, Husserl and Heidegger, James and Wittgenstein, Merleau-Ponty and Foucault, Ricoeur and Gadamer, Habermas and Apel, and Derrida and Rorty—to name but the most prominent of my interlocutors. Admittedly, some of these fare better than others, but they all contribute to the conversation and have a voice in my conjugated authorship. As a result of this multifaceted conversation my story of communicative praxis ranges over the familiar terrains of phenomenology, hermeneutics, critical theory, linguistic philosophy, structuralism, and deconstruction. But there is no philosophical position-taking recommended in the end. The format is geared to a probing of interrelated topics in recent thought as they pertain to the integrating thematic of communicative praxis without aspirations to either a perennial philosophy or a laying of the foundations. If a preface were the appropriate place for a prayer, my prayer would take the form of a petition to be delivered from yet another philosophical "ism"! In all this there is admittedly some species of "end of philosophy" thinking at work, particularly as it pertains to philosophy construed as a special body of knowledge that provides the foundational principles for all other bodies of knowledge, a theoretical reconstruction of knowledge in general. This portrayal of philosophy as a special and privileged body of knowledge has been associated with the longstanding portrait of the philosopher as a surveyor of all time and existence, somehow privy to a godlike perspective on the nature of things. In the text that follows, such a portrayal of philosophy and such a portrait of the philosopher are brought under suspicion. If pressed for a one-liner, I would have to reply that my intention is to tell the story of praxis and subjectivity at the end of philosophy thusly construed.

The most difficult part of a preface to write is the paragraph on acknowledgments. To attempt to list all of those who have had a hand in what is said and how it is said would be sheer folly. In the present circumstances this list would have to include not only a multitude of professional philosophers but also a host of practitioners in cognate fields. One of these cognate fields is particularly germane to the present study because it plays such a consequential role in Part III. The study concludes with a "Rhetorical Turn," and to negotiate this turn it was mandatory for me to immerse myself in the historical and current literature on rhetoric and communication theory. The response from rhetoricians and communication theorists to my labors was a continuing source of encouragement and enlightenment, which was sorely needed because this was for me a principally unfurrowed terrain. Even here there are too many to mention, but the contributions of some in this group are rather prominently inscribed in Part III of the present work. These include Michael Hyde and Thomas Farrell of Northwestern University; Walter Fisher of the University of Southern California; Michael McGee of the University of Iowa; Robert Scott of the University of Minnesota; Lawrence Grossberg of the University of Illinois; and Don Burks and Janice Lauer of Purdue University. After listing these colleagues and acknowledging my debt to them it should be made clear in the record that they are in no way accountable for the use (or misuse) that I made of their instruction.

It is also fitting that I make public my gratitude to the participants in my 1978 and 1980 National Endowment for the Humanities Summer Seminars for College Teachers for their keen and sustained criticisms of some of the germinal ideas of this project that were already beginning to take shape at that time. It is not usual practice to acknowledge one's former students in a preface. This is a common oversight that is surely unfortunate, for one learns more from one's students than one is either apt to realize or courageous enough to admit. In particular I would like to name Vilhjálmur Árnason, Michael Emerson, and Alan Schrift, who were my Research Assistants at Purdue University during the spring of 1981–82. They read and judiciously critiqued most of the first-draft chapters. Also I wish to acknowledge my NEH Summer Seminar assistants, Richard Askay and Gayle Ormiston, and express my appreciation to Ruth Porritt for her discernment and perseverance in correcting galley proof.

Finally, an institutional acknowledgment is in order. I must thank the Purdue Center for Humanistic Studies for admitting me as a Fellow for the Fall of 1981–82, freeing me from my routine university obligations and providing a valuable stretch of time for uninterrupted research and reflection.

West Lafayette, Indiana, 1985

Communicative Praxis
and the Space of
Subjectivity

Introduction

A profound and unsettling self-consciousness has infected contemporary philosophical discourse. In the philosophical community there is an almost obsessive preoccupation with the question concerning the type and aim of discourse appropriate for the philosopher's task. Is philosophical discourse to be understood primarily as referential, expressive, persuasive, narrational, poetical, or possibly as a combination of all of these? Are philosophical speech and prose exemplifications of a particular genre, or do they fall out as a panoply of *mixed* discourse? The current republic of professional philosophers, in its various quarters and conclaves, has recognized the importance of language and communication in an unprecedented way. This has opened opportunities for lively exchanges with the sister disciplines of linguistics, literature, rhetoric, and communication. It has also, however, occasioned a measure of disquietude in the philosopher's struggle to understand what he is about when he speaks and writes.

It would seem that philosophers talk and write because they intend to say something *about* something. Their discourse is understood as being in some manner referential. Yet, it is not all that clear what the referenced something of philosophical discourse is. We have all been taught various lessons on the inscrutability and indeterminacy of reference. Cognizant of these instructions can we still maintain that philosophical discourse is about things in the world and about what they are like? Or is philosophical discourse about "problems" that arise from our experience and knowledge of the world? Or is it about "problems" created by other philosophers? G. E. Moore had already pricked our sensitivities on the matter at issue in his autobiographical musing: "I do not think that the world or the sciences would ever have suggested to me any philosophical problems. What has suggested philosophical problems to me is things which other philosophers have said about the world or the sciences."[1] Now what is it that these "other philosophers" have "said about the world or the sciences"? Was their discourse somehow originatively referential? Or were they somehow deluded in thinking that they were saying something about the world but in fact were not, and only managed to create problems for subsequent philosophers who then inherit the task of dissolving them? It is precisely this saying of something "about" something that appears to be the Chinese puzzle, particularly when matters of philosophical discourse are at issue. We seem to be forced into a circle of discourse, a discursive closure, in which writing, philosophical or otherwise, is simply writing about writing. This is a conclusion which Jacques Derrida and some of his followers are happy to accept. Philosophical writing, we are told, is simply writing about what other philosophers

---

[1] *The Philosophy of G. E. Moore,* Paul A. Schilpp, ed. (Cambridge: Cambridge University Press, 1968), p. 14.

have written, from which all references to "presence"—be it the presence of objects, sense-data, or being-itself—should be deleted.

The current self-consciousness of philosophical discourse has also produced an increased awareness of the role and relevance of the hearer in philosophical speech and the reader in philosophical writing. Specific attention has been focused on the speaker/hearer and writer/reader contexts. Philosophical discourse, both spoken and written, it has been urged, is not only *about something;* it is also *for someone.* Rhetoricians and communication theorists have for some time emphasized the importance of the audience and the reader. Philosophy seems at last to have learned something from them. In this shift of concern from the reality talked about in discourse to a concern with the persons addressed there is a concomitant shift from discourse as referential to discourse as persuasive. Here also rhetoricians have been willing to lend a helping hand in refining the art of persuasion. The new emphasis on language and discourse has, not unexpectedly, led to a resurrection of the medieval trivium in which grammar, logic, and rhetoric were accorded their respective and combinatory functions. But the question as to the rhetorical "who" of the audience and reader still remains a matter of some puzzlement. Is this "who" someone to be determined in advance of the discourse? Are hearers and readers discovered in the events of speaking and writing, or are they somehow constituted by these events? What role does the hearer-reader, either as particularized addressee or generalized other, play in the meaning of that which is spoken and written? These are unavoidable questions which arise as discourse seeks to place the audience and the reader within their proper contexts.

Traveling with these questions are those concerning the "who" of the speaker and the author. Discourse is *for* someone. It is also discourse *by* someone. Is the speaker-author properly located anterior to the discourse, after the fact of discourse, or somewhere within the interstitial space of the discourse? What role does the speaker-author play in the achievement of meaning? Is he the central character on stage, or does he remain behind the scenes as the play of meaning goes on? Where within the play of the "conversation of mankind"[2] is the speaker-author announced? What manner of self-implication occurs in the event of speaking and in the labors of textual formation? The question "Who is speaking?" needs to be asked somewhere down the line. According to Foucault this was one of Nietzsche's central questions, to which Mallarmé responded with a "glittering answer" in his reply: "The Word is speaking."[3] Sustained reflection, however, might show that Mallarmé's reply was more like a "littering" answer, heaping up much that needs to be kept distinct and sorted out. Correspondingly, there is the irrepressible question "Who is writing?", and one is invited to reflect with Derrida on the indeterminability of self-reference in an author's signature. Does the signature indicate

---

[2] The phrase is Michael Oakeshott's, but it has been invested with a considerable amount of philosophical capital in Richard Rorty's revolutionary treatise on *Philosophy and the Mirror of Nature* (Princeton: Princeton University Press, 1979), in which philosophy is portrayed as neither more nor less than a voice in the conversation of mankind.

[3] *The Order of Things* (New York: Random House, 1973), p. 382.

some species of signification of the presence of authorial intention and design? What manner of "subject" is implicated in the speaking and writing that comprise the ongoing conversation and *écriture* of mankind? And what shape would discourse about this subject assume? The tendency in the traditon has been to use the intermittent allusions to a speaking and writing subject as illustrations of expressive discourse. As referential discourse is harnessed with the rather awesome demand of hooking up propositions with reality, and as persuasive discourse points us to the audience-reader, so expressive discourse has been assigned the task of delivering the subjectivity of the subject. Unfortunately, the traditional form of this expressive discourse has not achieved the requisite elucidatory power to enable one to see how such a demanding task can be successfully performed.[4]

Yet another facet of the intense self-reflection of philosophers as they ponder the question of what philosophers should think about and how they should proceed with the speaking and writing about that which they think pertains to the pervasive metaphoricity of philosophical language and the insinuation of narrational discourse. Whereas in the past the protocols of the trade have dictated that one assign the topic of metaphor to those doing literature and rhetoric, whose alleged profession was thought to be that of getting things straight on the mechanics of epideictic locution, currently there has been an accelerated interest in the weight of metaphor in philosophical writing as the "transporting" *(meta-phere)* of philosophical thought. There is an original meaning of metaphor that extends beyond its mere epideictic function. Metaphor does not simply adorn our discourse; it *carries* it. In current philosophy and in the new rhetoric alike there has been a recognition of this more substantive role of metaphor in relation to the content of thought. Witness, for example, the weight of the metaphoricity of "revolution" in Kuhn's philosophy of scientific discovery, the thought play in the metaphorical extension of "game" in Wittgenstein's approach to language, and the preeminent role of the metaphor of "textuality" in the hermeneutical reflections of Gadamer and the poststructuralist thought of Derrida. More pointedly, metaphor has become a specific topic as it relates to the nature of philosophical discourse and the problems of reference and meaning in the extensive study by Paul Ricoeur, *The Rule of Metaphor.*[5] This recent concern with the role and rule of metaphor is itself part of a wider interest in the proper placement of narrational discourse in philosophical writing. The flourish of interest in the long-neglected works of Vico and the attention given to the approach to language in the later Heidegger and in the writings of Foucault and Barthes highlight the poetics of narrational discourse as an intrinsic rather than simply extrinsic feature of philosophical speech and writing.

---

[4] James L. Kinneavy in his volume *A Theory of Discourse* (New York: W. W. Norton & Company, 1971), appropriately highlights the need for a new "logic" of expressive discourse. However, somewhat disappointingly, he marks out the approach to such a new logic by remaining rooted in the traditional prejudice of viewing expression as the externalization of internal subjective states and intentions. See particularly chapter 6, "Expressive Discourse."
[5] Trans. Robert Czerny (Toronto: University of Toronto Press, 1977).

This unsettling state of affairs relating to the type and aim of philosophical discourse is closely allied with another concern that has moved to the forefront of the contemporary philosopher's self-understanding of his discipline and task. Reflecting on the nature of his discourse he is also compelled to reflect on where and how he is to start. So large looms this issue before the visage of the contemporary philosophical mind that one author has seen fit to caption his lengthy and detailed probing of the nature and uses of dialectics in philosophical thought with the title *Starting Point: An Introduction to the Dialectic of Existence*.[6] Another writer has made the topic of "beginnings" a unifying thematic in his exploration of the language and thought that inform our projects of writing, reading, and interpreting.[7] Still another lays upon us the requirement of "accepting the contingent character of starting points," urging a constant vigilance that keeps this contingency from taking on alleged features of necessity.[8]

Our starting points seem to borrow heavily from the language and corpus of literature in the tradition in which we stand, as well as from involvement and reflection on the endless spate of personal and social experience. We thus rather quickly learn the truth that we never stand at a beginning but are always somehow already begun, held within a web of delivered discourse, social practices, professional requirements, and the daily decisions of everyday life. It is thus that we do well to recognize the ineradicable situationality of our starting points and avoid the all too facile transformation of them into foundational principles. The urge to lay the foundations anew and uncover the unimpeachable premises of a perennial philosophy, which has been so notably pronounced particularly since the time of Descartes, will need to be curtailed. The resources to satisfy such an urge seem to be progressively deferred as one confronts the proliferation of philosophical writing and the unbounded range of human experience. What set of issues and problems one selects from the delivered literature and what chunk of experience one marks off for analysis have more than a tincture of chance. This in itself, however, need not be taken as counsel for despair. There is still a task to be done. There is something to be gleaned through an understanding of how one moves about in the plethora of discourse and experience, perhaps in some fruitful way. Philosophical reflection and writing may not put us in touch with the bottom of being or the ground of all meaning, but they can disengage us from the facticity of our involvements in word and deed and help us to understand the inscriptions at work in what we say and how we act.

---

[6]Robert D. Cumming (Chicago: The University of Chicago Press, 1979). In this work Cumming offers a fresh approach to the play of dialectics as it proceeds from an existential starting point, resisting the threats of closure by conceptual schemes and the professionalism of academic life.

[7]Edward W. Said, *Beginnings: Intention and Method* (New York: Basic Books, 1975). Said is particularly concerned to distinguish the facticity of our beginnings from the necessity and absoluteness of the metaphysically weighted notion of origins.

[8]Richard Rorty, "Pragmatism, Relativism, and Irrationalism," Presidential Address at the seventy-sixth annual meeting of the American Philosophical Association, Eastern Division, in *Proceedings and Addresses of the American Philosophical Association,* 53 (August 1980), p. 726.

Starting points are often closely allied with claims for primacy. There was a time when the claim for the primacy of sense-data was in vogue. Before that, going way back into the tradition, we were offered claims for the primacy of essences, variously construed. Whereas sense-data were coupled with the faculty of sensation, essences were construed as the proper objects of mind, in both its conceptual and its judicative role. The decision in favor of one or the other of these primacies was motivated mainly by the contingency of standing in the tradition of either the empiricist or the rationalist way of doing philosophy, an option which often was proffered as a forced option in the history of modern philosophy. Since the halcyon days of sense-data theorizing other claims for primacy have made their presence felt. The more recent linguistic turn in philosophy has occasioned the elevation of language to a position of privilege, often in such a way that it is called upon to solve the pesky problems of epistemology that have preoccupied philosophers since the time of Descartes.[9] In still more recent times human action has become a contender for a position of primacy, and we have been urged to view the human self in its agency as being more proximate to the foundations of philosophical reflection. Twentieth century Continental philosophy, in both its existentialist and its phenomenological expression, has displayed its own predilection for primacy in the guise of primacies of existence, perception, and embodiment.

These various claims for primacy have not only provided convenient starting points; they have taken on the more formidable armor of philosophical positions within somewhat arbitrarily defined regions of subject matter—philosophy of mind, philosophy of language, philosophy of action, philosophy of existence, philosophy of perception, and certain combinations thereof. This invitation to position-taking, although at times subtle but overtly consequential, has been a principal factor in the temptation to convert a contingent starting point into one that gradually accumulates the weight of necessity. The tradition, both of the ancients and of the moderns, has nurtured within us a certain fugitive philosophical hope for the security and certainty of a stable Archimedean point, from which our reflections might proceed and to which they could return for the measure of their justification. If we could only assume the proper position on matters of mind, language, perception, or action, then we would finally be able to get things right on the big issues of knowledge and reality. Our deepest epistemological and metaphysical yearnings, we have been told, will achieve fulfillment if we find that correct position or standpoint from which all things become visible.

However, in the more recent past we have also been counseled to assume a more critical attitude toward the traditional "quest for certainty" (Dewey) and to be suspicious about epistemological/metaphysical frameworks of inquiry (Wittgenstein, Heidegger, Derrida, and Rorty). The ensuing radical critiques, deconstructions, and reflections on the "end of philosophy" have occasioned a crisis of philosophical consciousness, in which the present-day philosopher, like the bewildered Barnabas in Franz Kafka's *The Castle,* is no longer certain about his vocation. The proper response to this crisis, we urge, is not a new

---

[9] See particularly Rorty, *Philosophy and the Mirror of Nature,* Ch. VI.

Cartesian effort to establish an unblemished beginning so as to secure the unassailable foundations of knowledge about ourselves and the world, but rather that of achieving an understanding of the interplay in the ongoing forms of life and thought in which we are always already situated. We can indeed talk about the suspension of belief, the bracketing of metaphysical claims, and philosophical reductions, but in doing so we need to be wary about the easy commitment to a new philosophical foundationalism and a new posture of position-taking. The bracketing and reduction at issue, borne by the current consciousness of philosophical crisis, need to be more radical in their consequences. They need to put out of play or set aside not simply particular belief systems or existence claims but also the very notion of philosophy as a professionalized body of knowledge.

The question about the proper starting point is thus no longer a quest for unassailable axioms or unimpeachable epistemological principles but rather a pondering of how one can best enter the ongoing concretion of thought and action, interests and concerns, in such a way that their configurations and disjunctions, directions and misdirections, can be noted and described. Proceeding from such a starting point, the inscriptions of speaking and writing mark out not a constricted focus on elemental units of reality and the conditions for knowing them, but rather an attentiveness to the holistic space in which our ongoing thought and action, language and speech, interplay. We speak of this holistic space as the space of communicative praxis.

Our reflective entry into this holistic space may enable us to see the amalgam of thought, language, and action unfold before our very eyes and lead us to recognize the artificiality of epistemological position-taking in the postures of "philosophy of mind," "philosophy of language," and "philosophy of action." The space in which we move in our shared and singular projects can be said to be hermeneutical rather than epistemological. It is hermeneutical in the originative sense of the term because it is a play and display of understanding, of both a theoretical and a practical sort. Bernhard Waldenfels points us to this holistic and hermeneutical texture of pre-epistemological space with the suggestive title of his provocative book *Der Spielraum des Verhaltens*.[10] In this work the author sketches the comportment of human behavior within the social space of play that is older than either purified theoretical thought or abstracted empirical knowledge. Our holistic notion of the space of communicative praxis calls attention to this contextuality and interplay of thought, language, and action in the comportment of everyday life.

It is this interplay of thought, language, and action that elicits our philosophical interest and gives us a starting point. This interplay is indeed a global phenomenon, evincing similarities to what Heidegger calls the unitary phenomenon of "Being-in-the-world," which comprises his starting point in *Being and Time*. The interplay of thought, language, and action is always contextualized in a world, however vaguely and dimly this world may be understood. Yet, we do not present our starting point, and the hermeneutical requirement that it pro-

---

[10] (Frankfurt am Main: Suhrkamp Verlag, 1980).

jects, in the straightforward ontological fashion of Heidegger. This is partly due
to certain suspicions that we have about Heidegger's "ontological-ontic difference," as it is orchestrated throughout his early works in particular. It is also
due to the more explicitly sociopragmatic posture of our starting point, in
which concerns revolve around not so much a "reminiscence of Being" as a
reminiscence of communicative praxis as a form of life.

Through this reminiscence a more specific direction of questioning rather
quickly comes to the fore. This questioning is directed to the space and stature
of the subject as implicated in the forms of communicative praxis. What is there
to be known of the speaker, the author, and the actor, somehow embedded in
the praxis of speaking, writing, and acting? Factors in the philosophical situation of our day require that we ask this question. Even a cursory acquaintance
with the current directions of philosophical thought will testify that the philosophical vocabulary of subject and subjectivity has fallen upon hard times.
Neither the epistemological nor the ethical subject finds its services to be of
much need in the current market of ideas. Kindred laborers in the vineyards of
knowledge and morality—"mind," "ego," "consciousness," and "moral
self"—are also experiencing problems of unemployment. This depressed state
of affairs for those whose capital is invested in subjectivity is not a regional
phenomenon in the current philosophical economy. The loss of confidence in
the subject has made its way into many different quarters of contemporary
philosophy and is now rather widespread.

Heideggerians and Wittgensteinians, structuralists, neostructuralists, and
poststructuralists, critical theorists and hermeneutical philosophers of various
stripes—have all voiced their suspicions about the philosophical uses of subject
and subjectivity. Martin Heidegger's disenchantment with the subject in his
wide-ranging destruction of the history of metaphysics is by now well known
not only by the exegetes and interpreters of recent Continental thought but also
by interested parties in other traditions. Ludwig Wittgenstein's recommendation that the "I" be thought of essentially as a matter of grammar continues to
be urged upon us by latter-day Wittgensteinians. Claude Lévi-Strauss's call for a
"dissolution" of the human subject so as to make the human sciences possible
as sciences is respectfully heeded by the believing remnant of structuralism.
The celebrated pronouncement of the "Death of Man" by Foucault, which he
sees as the unavoidable sequel to Nietzsche's proclamation of the "Death of
God," continues to be referenced in the literature. Roland Barthes has been
responsible for making the phrase "the Death of the Author" part of the rite of
initiation into certain intellectual circles. Jacques Derrida, the high priest of
poststructuralist thought, proposes a deconstruction of the subject through a
disassemblage of the metaphysics of presence. Richard Rorty, in his recent
work *Philosophy and the Mirror of Nature,* extracts more than a pound of flesh
from the philosophical life of the subject as an epistemological foundation for
the philosophy of mind, and advises us to stick with social practices and the
conversation of mankind.

These dissolutions and deconstructions of subjectivity admittedly issue from
different inquiry standpoints. Lévi-Strauss's program is not that of Heidegger,
and Derrida's interests are not all that consonant with those of Wittgenstein.

However, it is all the more remarkable that given the diversity of perspectives the result relative to the status of the subject should be so similar. The subject in these varied approaches loses the philosophical privilege that it has enjoyed for so long, and particularly since the time of the birth of modern philosophy.

In probing the perspectives of these influential twentieth-century figures we find that their variegated critiques of subjectivity are motivated by a renewed interest in language. They all exhibit, if you will, a linguistic turn, rather broadly interpreted. Lévi-Strauss traces the superstructure of kinship relations and social institutions back to an infrastructure that is modeled after linguistic science. Heidegger's turn toward linguisticality *(Sprachlichkeit)* initiates a move in a different direction—not toward the mathematical models of linguistics as a science but rather toward a pre-objective speaking *(Sagen)*, most decisively illustrated in the voice of poetry. Foucault's archaeology of the human sciences culminates in a shift of focus from the being of man as historical subject to the "being of language." Wittgenstein's later interests revolve around language as a "form of life." Derrida's linguistic turn is grammatological in character, and Rorty's dismantling of philosophy culminates in a hermeneutics of conversation.

In all of these turns and tendencies we can discern the deployment of some species of deconstruction applied to subjectivity. The epistemological subject, either in the dress of a Cartesian thinking subject, a Humean sensing subject, or a Kantian transcendental subject, suffers displacement. The ethical subject as the source of moral judgments loses its efficacy. The existential subject, elucidated in the literature of existentialism, does not fare much better. It too is shorn of its primacy and privilege. Subjectivity in its multiple modalities loses its epistemic, moral, and existential space. The confluence of these deconstructionist critiques in the contemporary disciplines of philosophy and the human sciences has been poignantly referenced by Fred R. Dallmayr as occasioning a "twilight of subjectivity."[11]

It is in the thought of Heidegger and Derrida that this twilight of subjectivity is most sharply highlighted and the fate of the subject most scrupulously detailed. Heidegger charts the demise of the subject as a not unexpected expiration that occurs at the end of the history of Western metaphysics. The subject is portrayed as a residue in a metaphysical constructionism in which the question of being remains stuck in a categorial analysis that moves out from the pictorial view of being as "presence-at-hand" *(Vorhandensein)*. In this constructionism the subject itself becomes peculiarly objectified, a substance among other substances, an instance of finite beings in general. In tracing the history of this conceptual construct Heidegger reminds us that the word *subiectum* is a translation of the Greek *hypokeimenon* and "names that-which-lies-before, which, as ground, gathers everything onto itself."[12] As such, Heidegger continues, "this metaphysical meaning of the concept of subject has first of all

---

[11] *Twilight of Subjectivity: Contributions to a Post-Individualist Theory of Politics* (Amherst: University of Massachusetts Press, 1981).

[12] "The Age of the World Picture," in *The Question Concerning Technology and Other Essays,* trans. William Lovitt (New York: Harper & Row, 1977), p. 128.

no specific relation to man and none at all to the I."[13] Heidegger proposes to disentangle this oxymoronic result of the subject becoming object, in the guise of an objective precondition or basis, by replacing it in his earlier works with *Dasein* and in his later works with the "event of appropriation" *(Ereignis).* This replacement is required because of the misdirected consequences of man becoming the first or inaugural *subiectum,* that existent in which all existence is grounded and through which it achieves its representational truth. Man becomes the center from which existence as a whole is viewed. It is thus that a pictorial and representational view of the world travels with the construction of man as subject. The world of nature and history alike are pictured and represented by a representing subject, inviting the "aberration of subjectivism in the sense of individualism."[14] Heidegger sees this subjectivism and individualism as the central ingredient of that anthropocentric humanism that has informed at every step the metaphysics of the modern age, expressed not only in the epistemological designs of grounding all knowledge in a cognitive subject, but also in the ethical designs of a domination and control of nature and history by a willful subject.

Derrida's project of "deconstruction" can be properly understood as a radicalization of Heidegger's "destruction" of the history of ontology as metaphysics.[15] As a consequence of this radicalization subjectivity recedes even further toward the indefinable edges of a twilight zone. Heidegger's project needs to be radicalized, according to Derrida, because his critical reflections still proceed from the logocentrism of a philosophy of presence. Derrida applauds Heidegger's project for having effectively deconstructed both the objectivism and the subjectivism of metaphysics, but he is of the mind that in Heidegger's effort to mark out the terrain of fundamental ontology as the proper ground of metaphysics he falls back upon the requirement for an elusive and fugitive presence—and no matter at this point whether one speaks of the presence of *Dasein* or the presence of *Ereignis.* In Derrida's reading of Heidegger the central question remains the *Seinsfrage,* and it is a pursuit of an answer to this question, says Derrida, that belies an uncritical acceptance of the primacy of presence, an accepted presupposition that has informed Western philosophical reflection from its very beginning. Heidegger has attacked only the aberrations resulting from a metaphysical picturing of presence. But this attack, according to Derrida, takes as its guiding motif the "forgetfulness of Being" and proceeds from a desire to regain a paradise lost, when a more *originative* sense of presence was in full bloom.

The heavily accented themes of "destruction" and "deconstruction" in the current philosophical literature, rehearsed by Heidegger and Derrida sym-

---

[13] *Ibid.*

[14] *Ibid.,* p. 133.

[15] Although for the most part, and particularly in *Being and Time,* Heidegger uses the language of "destruction" *(Destruktion)* in defining his strategy for the dismantling of the history of metaphysics, in his *Die Grundprobleme der Phänomenologie* and *Zur Seinsfrage* he also speaks of "deconstruction" *(Abbau)* as an auxiliary notion. See *Grundprobleme* (Frankfurt: Vittorio Klostermann, 1975), p. 31, and *Zur Seinsfrage* (Frankfurt: Vittorio Klostermann, 1956), p. 36.

pathizers, have conspired to produce a veritable revolution of philosophical *Denkwege*—at least in the tradition of contemporary Continental thought. The impact of this revolution is noticeable not only in the discipline of formal philosophy but also in the various human sciences and in literary theory and criticism. That which interests us in this current revolution of deconstructive critique is both its positive achievements and its limitations. The deconstructionists have made us duly suspicious of the proliferation of metaphysical structures and epistemological givens, and they have heightened our sensitivity to the uses and misuses of language. They have called our attention to the self-arrogations of philosophy as a special discipline and the often exaggerated claims for what it proposes to deliver. Deconstruction, in its most radical expression, is a move toward the "end of philosophy," in which philosophy is construed as foundational knowledge of reality.

Yet, one cannot but notice that something funny happens on the way to the deconstructionist forum. In the various projects of the deconstruction of the subject a discernible trace of subjectivity remains, whilst the deconstruction is in progress and after it is completed. There are markings that point to an involved speaker, a situated author, and an engaged actor at work. After Lévi-Strauss has dissolved the finite, historical subject so as to make room for the infrastructure of universal mind, he still has to contend with the "identity of its occasional bearers."[16] Now Lévi-Strauss assures us that the social scientist remains "unconcerned" about the identity of these occasional bearers. But whether Lévi-Strauss's idealized social scientist remains concerned or unconcerned about them, their speech and action is not so easily displaced, and one is forced to ask about their peculiar inscriptions. In Heidegger's destruction-deconstruction of the history of metaphysics the subject is not so much eliminated as it is resituated within an existential analytic of man's way to be. We are apprised of this when Heidegger tells us: "Philosophy must perhaps start from the 'subject' and return to the 'subject' in its ultimate questions, and yet for all that it may not pose its questions in a one-sidedly subjectivistic manner."[17] Heidegger sets the challenge for recovering the subject while avoiding the metaphysical and epistemological snares of subjectivity. When Derrida was directly confronted on the issue of the role of the subject in the discussion that followed the presentation of his essay "Structure, Sign and Play in the Discourse of the Human Sciences," he replied:

> The subject is absolutely indispensable. I don't destroy the subject; I situate it. That is to say, I believe that at a certain level both of experience and of philosophical and

---

[16] "If the final goal of anthropology is to contribute to a better knowledge of objectivized thought and its mechanisms, then in the end it does not make much difference whether the thought of Latin American natives finds its form in the operation of my thought or if mine finds its in the operation of theirs. What does matter is that the human mind, unconcerned with the identity of its occasional bearers, manifests in that operation a structure which becomes more and more intelligible to the degree that the doubly reflexive movement of two thoughts, working on one another, makes progress." Claude Lévi-Strauss, "Overture to *le cru et le cuit*," trans. J. H. McMahon in *Structuralism*, ed. Jacques Ehrmann (New York: Doubleday, 1970), p. 49.

[17] *The Basic Problems of Phenomenology*, trans. Albert Hofstadter (Bloomington: Indiana University Press, 1982), p. 155.

scientific discourse one cannot get along without the notion of subject. It is a question of knowing where it comes from and how it functions.[18]

The point that interests us at this juncture is that in these varied projects of dissolution, destruction, and deconstruction of the subject by Lévi-Strauss, Heidegger, and Derrida, traces of subjectivity remain. We thus learn at a rather early stage that the principal lesson to be gleaned from the strategy of deconstruction is that no complete deconstruction is possible. This, however, by no means legitimates a hurried reinstating of some classical notion of self, subject, or ego, saddled with the interrelated metaphysical and epistemological requirement of providing foundations, accounting for identities, and supplying elusive objects of self-reference. The trace of subjectivity that remains leads us into another direction and into another space—a space opened up by communicative praxis. The emerging subjectivity within this space will be that of a subject transfigured and transformed, a *decentered* subjectivity, bearing the wisdom gleaned from the arduous venture of deconstruction as a task never completed but rather to be performed time and again.

If the deconstruction of the subject is an announcement of the first revolution in current philosophical and scientific thinking, the recovery and restoration of the subject within the folds of the space of communicative praxis sets in motion the second revolution, for which the time is now ripe. This second revolution will make possible the recognition of the subject in the hermeneutical self-implicature of the speaker and actor within a form of life as decentered subjectivity, and will provide the directions for detailing its genealogy and its patterns of individual and social formation. From all this we might be able to understand just a little better its origin, its peculiar temporality, its interpretive history, and the accretion and projection of its multiple profiles. In this second revolution particular attention will need to be given to the figures, modes, and aims of discourse for it is within discourse that the subject is implicated. But it is not in discourse alone that the hermeneutical tracking of the subject takes place. There is the extensive panoply of nondiscursive practices which also gestures in the direction of an implicated subject. The space of subjectivity encompasses not only discourse but also action. Subjectivity finds its birth certificate within the wider space of communicative praxis, which includes not only language and speech but also action, both individual and social.

Our emphasis on the amalgam of discourse and action in the space of communicative praxis needs to be highlighted because it bears directly on a widespread misdirection in contemporary philosophy. This misdirection has to do with an excessive and self-limiting preoccupation with discourse and discursive practices. There are two facets of this misdirection. One has to do with a movement in the analysis of discourse itself. The other involves a neglect of the intentionality of nondiscursive and nonlinguistic practices.

The turn to discourse, which seems to be a mark of the current age, has gravitated into a crisis-situation of linguistic closure within the world of dis-

---

[18] *The Languages of Criticism and the Sciences of Man: The Structuralist Controversy,* eds. Richard Macksey and Eugenio Donato (Baltimore: Johns Hopkins University Press, 1970), p. 271.

course. Speech and language, as the polar ingredients of discourse, have been vying for ascendancy and a position of privilege since the time of Ferdinand de Saussure. Saussure, and subsequent structuralists, pushed into the direction of a linguistics of formal language. Speech act theorists moved in the direction of a linguistics of speech. In various philosophical neighborhoods disputation about whether language or speech is primary and foundational continues at an accelerated pace. Can language be properly viewed as the infrastructure that informs and regulates the superstructure of speech as a social phenomenon? Do the synchronic and timeless features of the formal aspects of language explain the diachronic and time-bound performances of speech as it is spoken? Is there an innate competence that informs the concrete speech act? Or are matters the other way around, affording a primacy to speech acts which have their intrinsic intentionality, and relegating the formal structure of language to a second order level of abstraction from the deployment of meaning in actual speech usage? Disputations on these questions have contributed to much of the tension between the structuralists and the empiricists, the formalists and the later Wittgensteinians, the transcendental phenomenologists and the Heideggerians. And then there is the genial mediator, Paul Ricoeur, who proposes an intersection of speech and language within a centered and unified event of discourse, proceeding from a speaking subject. This move on the part of Ricoeur is quickly countered by the poststructuralist master of deconstruction, Jacques Derrida, who in his grammatological countermove decenters the point of intersection and disassembles the subject. The twists and turns in the ensuing poststructuralist debates tend to revolve around the inherited problematic of the speech/ language dichotomy, circling within a linguistic closure of discourse.

The other facet of misdirection in the contemporary turn to discourse, closely allied with the first, pertains to the progressive isolation of discourse from nondiscursive human action and from the fabric of world-oriented experience more generally. This isolation has invited a species of linguistic dogmatism in which the hookup of speech and language, or the subordination of the one to the other, which is most often the case, provides the conceptual frame for settling matters on final grounding and ultimate epistemological foundations. Theory of discourse and linguistics are called upon to answer the riddles of knowledge for which traditional epistemology lacked the resources. Discourse becomes the Rosetta Stone, supplying the key to decipher the hieroglyphs of epistemology. Like the metaphysical dogmatism which Kant critiqued, and the empiricist dogmatism of positivism which Wittgenstein attacked, this linguistic-epistemological dogmatism also requires critical assessment. Our critical assessment will proceed via a move to a more encompassing and global space than that which is defined by the foundationalist markings of linguistic science as an epistemology. We name this encompassing space the holistic, hermeneutical space of communicative praxis. It is thus that our effort to articulate the amalgam of discourse and action is guided by our methodological decision to explore the terrain of communicative praxis. In this exploration we will avoid the reduction of nondiscursive practices to the models and metaphors of discourse. We will take into account the important role of speech and language in the life of communicative praxis, but we will also attend to the intentionality of human action and institutions as expressive behavior. In this exploration we will from time to time accentuate the experiential features of discourse and action alike, but this appeal to the experiential will need to find new forms of description, because the limitations of the empiricist notion of experience have by now become evident to all.

Part I
The Texture of
Communicative Praxis

CHAPTER ONE

Figures of Discourse

The philosophical use of heavily sedimented terms like "communication" and "praxis" presents a plethora of semantical problems. Our conjunction of these terms in the couplet "communicative praxis" would seem to compound these problems. Although the meaning and propriety of these terms, and their supporting lexical associates, can only be exemplified by their use in the continuing discussion, some rationale needs to be provided at the outset for our choice of them for the deployment of our inquiry. Both terms have informed the life and literature of human culture for a very long time. They have been used in a variety of contexts and within a rather broad spectrum of disciplines. However, they have not yet found a secure place in the lexicon of formal philosophy. Indeed, there may be philosophical lexicons in which neither one would survive the last cut. Both terms, and particularly "communication," have also found widespread employment in the everyday language of personal and world affairs. As a consequence, their uses are markedly varied and betray a pervading slackness in the commerce of professional and public life. An effort needs to be made to take up this slack so as to bring them within the bounds of our inquiry. We propose to do this in such a manner that their own boundaries will not be unduly restricted.

The term "praxis," although by no means employed by all working philosophers, does have a rather long history of service to the discipline. Aristotle was the first to use it in the interests of a philosophical exchange of ideas, and he must stand at least partly accountable for its impact upon a rather extensive spate of philosophical and social thought in the continuing tradition. Hegel, Feuerbach, and Marx, all in different ways to be sure, sought to bolster and revitalize the economy of praxis. In the twentieth-century literature of existentialism, neo-Marxism, philosophical anthropology, and critical theory, the commerce of ideas issuing from reflections on praxis has been considerable.

It is not our intention to recount and amplify this history of the grammar and concept of praxis. Numerous writings on the influential, although somewhat uneven, history of this notion have recently appeared.[1] The main and underlying interest in Part I of our study is that of probing a possible semantic symbiosis of communication and praxis that might enrich the senses that each has in a more modal perspective, and showing how the interdependence of these two notions might articulate a hermeneutical space in which the intentionalities of discourse and action interplay. We thus find ourselves talking about communicative praxis. The establishment of an interdependence and reciprocity of these two notions within a holistic fabric of sense will require a dissimulation of the conceptual accruals within the body of these two terms and a disassembling of the epistemological and metaphysics frameworks that have governed their significance. This in turn will make possible the retrieval of certain traces of meaning that have been suppressed in their formalized scientific and philosophical usages.

In approaching our topic we are confronted with an evident plurivocity of senses that have become attached to the couplet of concepts that we have made our theme. It should thus come as no surprise that neither philosophers nor practitioners in the various human sciences have been able to agree on the defining features of either communication or praxis. The elucidation of praxis at times proceeds from ruminations on the character and quality of the performing arts, and at other times moves out from an attentiveness to configurations within the socioeconomic life of society. Communication has been defined through the services of the models of cybernetics and approached through the metaphors of hermeneutics. Aristotle's notion of praxis is not that of Marx, and Norbert Wiener's theory of communication seems to have little in common with Karl Jaspers's description of communication as an existential act. We thus run into a rather formidable semantical and conceptual thicket at the very outset of our explorations. Our hope is that the requisite resources will be available to enable us to work our way through it.

The Greek term "praxis," because of its rather widespread current adoption, is seldom translated when it is used in the scholarly literature of philosophy and the human sciences. If indeed it is translated, it is usually rendered as "practice." It could also, however, be translated as

---

[1] Particularly informative are the following works: Richard J. Bernstein, *Praxis and Action* (Philadelphia: University of Pennsylvania Press, 1971); Jürgen Habermas, *Theory and Practice,* trans. John Viertel (Boston: Beacon Press, 1973); Nicholas Lobkowicz, *Theory and Practice: History of a Concept from Aristotle to Marx* (Notre Dame: University of Notre Dame Press, 1967); and Gajo Petrović, *Marx in the Mid-Twentieth Century* (New York: Doubleday & Company, 1967).

"action," "performance," or "accomplishment." The verbal root of praxis, *prasso* (πράσσω), houses the related senses of doing, acting, performing, and accomplishing. Aristotle, in his writings on practical philosophy, took up the slack within the ordinary meanings of the term by installing a more tailored usage. He provided a specific semantical pivot first by contrasting praxis with *theōria,* distinguishing praxis as the sphere of human action and accomplishment from theory as the domain of rigorous science. *Theōria,* which lies along the path of demonstration yielding apodicticity and the achievement of knowledge for its own sake, follows the requirements of *epistēmē.* From this distinction between theory and praxis, however, Aristotle does not draw the conclusion that praxis is irremediably bereft of cognition. Praxis comports its own insight in the guise of a practical wisdom. Aristotle's term for this is *phronēsis,* which although distinguished from the contemplative knowledge of pure theory is a type of knowledge, more broadly conceived, nonetheless. The first determination of the meaning of praxis in Aristotle is thus based on considerations attentive to distinctions in our way of comprehending the world. Praxis displays a different sort of knowing than that which issues from *theōria.*

On the heels of this distinction, however, there follows rather closely another, which plays on the difference between praxis and *poiēsis. Poiēsis* as artifactual production is distinguished both from the sphere of human action and from theoretical philosophizing. That which guides this artifactual production is *technē,* which is assigned a role distinct from those of *epistēmē* and *phronēsis.* Now it is at this juncture that one needs to be particularly wary of the introduction of facile English derivatives, such as "technical," "technique," and "technological." There is admittedly a play of cognates at work here. *Poiēsis* as artifactual production is an activity that produces an object that lies beyond the dynamics of the activity itself. It consists in what Rudiger Bubner has aptly characterized as "object-determined activity."[2] Now a measure of technique is involved in the calculation of the results of such an activity as well as in the mapping of means, such as rules and procedures, to attain the end. The programming of this technique involves various degrees of manipulation and control. Nonetheless, this programming of technique is not of the essence of *technē.* When it is conflated into the essence of *technē* we have an illustration of the aberrations of technicism and technologism.

---

[2] *Modern German Philosophy,* trans. Eric Matthews (Cambridge: Cambridge University Press, 1981), p. 216. Bubner achieves further clarification of what *poiēsis* is about when he writes: "The goal of production lies beyond the activity as such in the realization of something else. Practice, therefore, is structurally distinct from those processes which are directed towards the production of an object external to themselves." *Ibid.*

Now admittedly, such technification and technologization remains an ever-present threat to the creativity of *poiēsis*. When the production of a work of art is reduced to the techniques of its realization, that which is seen to be at work in the work of art is occluded. But the universalization of technique into a technicism is a phenomenon separate from *technē* itself, and can with equal consequence infiltrate the regions of *epistēmē* and *phronēsis*. When theoretical knowledge is reduced to a calculus of quantification in which it is only the anticipation of objectified results that guides the procedures, we witness the intrusion of technicism into the epistemic domain of *theōria*. When the sphere of human action and the practices of human agents are reduced to a composite of feedback control mechanisms in the service of a program of social engineering, we witness the intrusion of technicism into the sphere of praxis and *phronēsis*.[3] It is thus that the phenomenon of technicism cuts across the tripartite distinctions that Aristotle delineated, and poses an enduring threat in the various dimensions of human culture. This threat of a universal technification of human thought and action, as Heidegger has graphically illustrated, is particularly visible in an age whose mind-set has congealed into a scientific-bureaucratic-technological frame.[4]

The determination of the meaning of praxis in Aristotle's philosophy thus proceeds along the lines of its differentiation both from *theōria* and *poiēsis*. However, this is not the only way that the contours of this notion are illustrated. Indeed, the final and possibly most consequential emphasis in Aristotle's definition of praxis falls on its directedness toward the achievement and maintenance of the virtuous life among the citizens who constitute the *polis*. There is an indissoluble linkage between praxis and the *polis* in the thought of Aristotle. The *polis,* as the interwoven fabric of man's ethical and political existence, is displayed by Aristotle as the distinctive *topos* or locality for the exercise of

---

[3] A particularly decisive historical illustration of this technification of praxis can be found in the development of Marxist orthodoxy, which managed to translate Marxian praxis into a framework of instrumental control, motivated by the calculation of objectified social ends and results. For a discussion of this and related themes the reader is referred to Jürgen Habermas, *Knowledge and Human Interests,* trans. Jeremy J. Shapiro (Boston: Beacon Press, 1971), Ch. 3: "The Idea of the Theory of Knowledge as Social Theory." See also Calvin O. Schrag, *Radical Reflection and the Origin of the Human Sciences* (West Lafayette: Purdue University Press, 1980), Ch. 2: "From Philosophical Anthropology to Radical Anthropological Reflection." The shortcoming of Habermas's account is that he tends to gloss the decisive consequence of the rupture between Marx's original, existentially oriented notion of praxis and its subsequent technification in the garden varieties of later Marxist orthodoxy.

[4] See particularly *The Question Concerning Technology and Other Essays,* trans. William Lovitt (New York: Harper & Row, 1977). Also see William Barrett, *The Illusion of Technique: A Search for Meaning in a Technological Civilization* (New York: Doubleday, 1978).

practical wisdom. It is the institutionalized context provided by the *polis* that regulates and vitalizes the interaction of human beings in the ongoing life of society.

For our purposes it is not necessary to address the particular Aristotelian doctrines on ethics and politics that round out his notions of praxis and the *polis*. This would involve the elaboration of certain explicit axiological and metaphysical constructs and frameworks—e.g., the teleological model, a particular doctrine of virtue, and the philosophy of substance. Indeed, at this juncture we would urge a suspension of these constructs and frameworks. Nor need we formulate a comparative analysis of Aristotle's notion of praxis in relation to those of Hegel, Marx, Sartre, and Habermas. Our project may from time to time require some historical considerations of this sort, but at this stage of our investigation we propose an *epochē* of the various comparative position-takings, be they epistemological, metaphysical, or axiological.

The terminology of communication, like that of praxis, does not point us to a homogenous registry of meanings. The lexical entries that comprise its place in the dictionary do not approximate a unifying definition. They provide rather a spate of filial conceptual resemblances involving a rather extended family. Communication, we learn, is the "act or action of imparting or transmitting." But it is also the "facts or information communicated." These two separate entries display the span of tension within the meaning range of the term as it relates to the difference between performing and that which has been performed, between the act and the result of the action, between imparting and the facts or information imparted. The latter in each case suggests a weighting in the direction of a model or mode of production, reminiscent of Aristotle's notion of *technē*. In this context of association communication has to do with that which is produced through a result-anticipated or object-oriented activity. Another entry characterizes communication as "access between persons or places," in which communication falls out as the *means* of communication, exemplified in the commonly referenced "communication media," which nudges communication even further into the means-ends relationship that governs productive processes. Still another entry proposes that communication is the "interchange of thoughts or opinions . . . through a common system of symbols (as language, signs, or gestures)," underscoring the relevance of linguistics, semiology, and the ethnography of nonverbal behavior for an understanding of communication. Further entries include references to "conversation," "talk," "personal dealings," "common participation," and "sexual intercourse," all of which we are advised to consider to be either obsolete or archaic. And finally the contours of communication are marked out as a special discipline, framed as "an art that deals with expressing and exchanging ideas effectively in speech or writing or through the graphic or dramatic arts," yielding a special area of study within the curriculum.[5]

Like the lexical determinations of communication so also the history of its usage in the work-a-day world of personal and public life and in the halls of academe provides us with a curiously diversified portrait of distinctions, bearing the imprints of the special disciplines in which communication has been appropriated. The recent history of the notion exhibits a close association with technology, from telegraph to Telstar, in which the principal signification of the term has to do with cybernetic transmission systems. Often the language of communication is used to emphasize the role of and codes for human interactions in the domain of politics, religion, industry, medicine, education, and community affairs. Again it is seen as the event of person-to-person encounter within the concrete dialogic transaction. In short, it has been presented as a ubiquitous phenomenon pervading the global constellation of personal and public life.[6]

Orchestrated throughout these various registers of human involvement and interaction, this ubiquitous phenomenon marks out the manner and style in which messages are conveyed and imparted, always against the background of the tightly woven fabric of professional and everyday life, with its shared experiences, participative relationships, joint endeavors, and moral concerns. Communication, in its variegated postures, is a performance within the *topos* of human affairs and dealings that comprise our social world, making these affairs and dealings an issue not only by questioning, informing, arguing, and persuading but also by planning, working, playing, gesturing, laughing, crying, and our general body motility. It thus becomes evident that the space of communication is a space that is shared by praxis. Communication has both a linguistic and an actional dimension. There is a rhetoric of speech and there is a rhetoric of action. The communication of messages in the impartation of objective knowledge and the disclosure of intersubjective concerns interdependently illustrates the signifying power of speech and language and the intentionality of action. Communication and praxis intersect within a common space. Communication is a qualification of praxis. It is the manner in which praxis comes to expression. But praxis is also a qualification of communication in that it determines communication as a *performing* and an *accomplish-*

---

[5] The above lexical entries were taken from *Webster's Third New International Dictionary* (Unabridged).

[6] For a discussion of the multifaceted relevance of communication in the different spheres of human life see the collected essays in Michael J. Hyde, ed., *Communication Philosophy and the Technological Age* (Tuscaloosa: University of Alabama Press, 1982) and specifically the editor's introduction: "The Debate Concerning Technology."

ing. We can thus with equal propriety speak of communicative praxis and praxial communication.[7]

Communication and praxis, now to be taken as comprising a unitary and yet multifaceted phenomenon, are pivotal terms in our subsequent explorations. But there is a third term, mediating those of communication and praxis. This third term is "texture." We want to set forth the *texture* of communicative praxis. In the end this may be the most important term because it indicates the bonding of communication and praxis as an intertexture within their common space.

We have already spoken of a *topos* or horizonal field as the wider sociohistorical space in which communication and praxis interplay. Now we speak of texture as the bonding feature of this wider space. In this shift from "field" to "texture" there would appear to be a disturbing shift of metaphors of discourse. The metaphors of horizon and field are visually weighted. This kind of weighting is characteristic of phenomenological philosophy. Phenomenologists speak of horizonal fields of perception, consciousness, and embodiment, and in doing so there is at least a tacit conferral of primacy upon visual phenomena. The fields of perception and embodiment are principally horizons for the *seeing* of the phenomena as experienced. In our shift to the metaphor of texture a somewhat different range of indexical associations is called forth as one slides away from the privilege of seeing and the centrality of the eye. The texture-metaphor appears to enjoy a wider scope of playfulness. There is the texture of the woven tapestry, the cellular texture of plants, the texture of wood and the texture of soil, muscle texture in the human body, harmonic texture, and the texture of poetry and prose. The extension of senses and applications of texture seems to be virtually unbounded.

Now as there has been a tendency in the phenomenological literature to solicit the services of the field-metaphor for a new theory of vision, so in poststructuralism, as well as in certain types of hermeneutical philosophy, there have been heavy demands placed on the metaphors of text and textuality. The sense of texture illustrated in the body of poetry and prose is given a peculiar privilege in the framing of philosophical issues and tasks. Whereas the field-metaphor provided the phenomeno-

---

[7] That which we have referenced as the *topos* or field of communicative praxis, and which we found to have already been at issue in Aristotle's notion of praxis as it related to the *polis,* has received notice in various styles of contemporary philosophy. In the school of critical theory it translates into the sociohistorical formative process of the dialectic of praxis. In the phenomenological literature it surfaces in the discourse about the "life-world" (Husserl) and the "phenomenal field" (Merleau-Ponty). In the thought of American pragmatism it is indexed as "the world as experienced" (James) and as the configuration of habits in public life (Dewey). In the writings of the later Wittgenstein this *topos* of communicative praxis makes its appearance as a "form of life."

logical movement with a proper locale for the *Prinzip aller Prinzipien* in the guise of phenomenologically reduced consciousness, intending and constituting its objects within a perceptual horizon, the text-metaphor of poststructuralism and later hermeneutics finds its foundational principle in the textuality of spoken and written discourse.

In thus speaking of the texture of communicative praxis we find ourselves already tacitly working with the metaphor of textuality. Texture slides into textuality. This metaphorical posturing of the text as the narration of texture opens up new possibilities for an understanding of both communication and praxis. The life of communicative praxis offers itself as a text. It is the prose and the poetry of the world as experienced, written in the script of both thought and action. But these new possibilities within the text-metaphor, leading to redescriptions of both man and his world, contain their own limitations and invite certain aberrations of interpretation if these limitations remain unattended. David Hoy has perceptively pointed us to these limitations in his critique of the tendency in hermeneutics to overextend the metaphor of the text. "Hermeneutics," he writes, "should avoid turning textuality into a universal model, since this would be to take a metaphor as a method. Forgetting that it is a metaphor may even lead to thinking that hermeneutics is offering a new ontology—a monadology of texts."[8] This warning is peculiarly appropriate when the texture of communicative praxis is at issue. Because communicative praxis involves not only the texts of spoken and written discourse but also the concrete actions of individuals and the historically effective life of institutions, its texture encompasses a wider metaphorical range than that of textuality per se. It includes also the texture of human projects, of motivations and decisions, of embodiment, and of wider processes of social formation.

This brings us to a critical and difficult juncture in our preliminary task of sorting out our figures of discourse and sketching the posture of our inquiry. We are brought to a direct and unavoidable encounter with the problem of metaphor. The omnipresence of metaphoricity in our discourse points us to that which is at once our greatest resource and our chief peril. Metaphor is at the same time the *lumen naturale* in our comprehension of the world and the concealment of the world's surplus of meanings. The peril of metaphor has to do with the recurring proclivity to translate metaphors into epistemological claims and metaphysical truths. The plurivocity and slackness that characterize the play

---

[8] David C. Hoy, "Hermeneutics," *Social Research: An International Quarterly of the Social Sciences*, Vol. 47, No. 4, 1980.

of metaphor are taken up in such a manner that metaphorical meaning becomes congealed into necessary starting points and postulated primacies. Within the play of texture the shift to textuality can take on the aura of a first principle and a privileged aperture to the world, or can indeed become the world itself. This is an ever-present danger in certain varieties of both hermeneutical and poststructuralist thought, where one can discern the impulse to have everything become text.[9] Yet, it is also the case that the field-metaphor is at times rather recklessly employed by phenomenological thinkers and tends to solidify into a visually determined patterning of figure and background, inviting a "primacy of perception." This not only restricts the play and profusion of sense in auditory and tactile posturings of experience but also tends to box in the panoply of forms of life that pervade man's sociohistorical development. This is the ever-present danger in the constructionist designs of formal phenomenology. What is thus required is a continuing and demanding internal critique of metaphoricity, installing the requisite vigilance over the play of metaphor so as to detect recurring tendencies toward overextension and epistemological closure.

Although discussions of the nature of metaphor abound in the literature and philosophy of the Western tradition, issues relating to metaphor have become accentuated in our time. The history of the understanding and use of metaphor is by no means that of a serene development of collegial agreement and practice. Rather early in its history metaphor was assigned to the special fields of poetics and rhetoric, in which its principal function was determined by the epideictic or ornamental role of language, as used particularly in poetry and public oratory. Metaphor performed its function in the telling of a story well, or by lending its hand in the service of the art of persuasion, but it was spared the burden of telling us something about the world. Its domain was the aesthetics of language and it remained off limits to the citadel of knowledge and truth.[10] Defined as a trope or a figure of speech, metaphor found its proper station in discourse as a vehicle of naming through the transfer of sense. It was granted the liberty of substituting

---

[9]This impulse is virtually unrestrained in Jacques Derrida's pronouncement: "There is nothing outside of the text [there is no outside-text; *il n'y a pas de hors-texte*]." *Of Grammatology,* trans. Gayatri C. Spivak (Baltimore: The Johns Hopkins University Press, 1974), p. 158.

[10]Derrida, in his "White Mythology," succeeds in stating the matter well as it pertains to the classical understanding and use of metaphor. "Thus metaphor, an effect of *mimēsis* and *homoiosis,* and a manifestation of analogy, will be a means of knowledge: a subordinate, but for all that a certain means of knowledge. We may say of it what is said of poetry; it is more philosophical and more serious than history (*Poetics,* 145 1b5–6), since it not only tells something particular, but expresses what is general, probable, and necessary.

an unaccustomed name for something that was deemed to have a proper name.[11] This restriction of the function of metaphor, coupled with its banishment from the uses of discourse that really count when the weighty matters of the nature of reality are at issue, has contributed to the bifurcation of narrational and referential discourse.

But as citizens banished from their kingdom are wont to return to their homeland, so also metaphor has staged its return, often quietly and unnoticed, to the *polis* of universal discourse. A consequence of this return is that the practitioners of honest to goodness referential discourse in the various branches of science and philosophy often succumb, unwittingly to be sure, to a reckless employment of metaphorical usages. A particularly telling example of this state of affairs can be detailed in the history of the philosophy of mind and cognitive psychology, where the metaphor of spatial storage has been entrusted with an awesome responsibility, particularly in dealing with the phenomenon of memory retrieval and recall. The sense of physical space as a continuum and container of objects is transferred to the human psyche. As a consequence the mind is pictured as a reservoir or cabinet in which ideas or sensations are stored, and remembering is depicted as a mechanism which somehow unlatches the door to the storehouse of accumulated psychic data.[12]

It has only been in relatively recent times that metaphor has been accorded a central place in scientific and philosophical discourse. It might be said that the linguistic turn in contemporary philosophy has culminated in a burdensome self-consciousness of the metaphoricity of language. Thomas Kuhn, Mary Hesse, and Ian Barbour are ranking historians and philosophers of science who immediately come to mind when the issue of models and metaphors in scientific discourse is raised.[13] Paul Ricoeur, Jacques Derrida, Max Black, and Richard Rorty

---

However, it is not as serious as philosophy itself, and will, it seems, keep this intermediate status throughout the history of philosophy. We might better say ancillary status: for metaphor, properly controlled, is in the service of truth, but the master cannot be content with it, and must prefer that form of discourse which shows truth in its fullness." "White Mythology: Metaphor in the Text of Philosophy," *New Literary History,* Vol. VI, No. 1, 1974.

[11] This classical transfer model of metaphor, based on the recognition of a similitude enabling substitution, has its source in Aristotle's consummate definition of metaphor in his *Poetics.* "Metaphor consists in giving the thing a name that belongs to something else; the transference being either from genus to species, or from species to genus, or from species to species, or on grounds of analogy." 1457 b 6–9.

[12] An informative and comprehensive account of the various types of spatial and storehouse metaphors in connection with memory phenomena is given by Henry L. Roediger III in his article "Memory Metaphors in Cognitive Psychology," *Memory & Cognition,* Vol. 8 (3), 1980.

[13] See particularly Kuhn, *The Structure of Scientific Revolutions* (Chicago: University of Chicago Press, 1962); Hesse, *Models and Analogies in Science* (Notre Dame: University

are some of the widely discussed philosophers who have addressed the role of metaphor on the plane of wider philosophical and literary usage.[14] Mary Hesse's observation on the role of metaphor in science is particularly germane to the general point of our concerns when she writes:

> Acceptance of the view that metaphors are meant to be intelligible implies rejection of all views that make metaphor a wholly noncognitive, subjective, emotive, or stylistic use of language. There are exactly parallel views of scientific models that have been held by many contemporary philosophers of science, namely, that models are purely subjective, psychological, and adopted by individuals for private heuristic purposes. But this is wholly to misdescribe their function of science. Models, like metaphors, are intended to communicate.[15]

In rejecting the subjectivist and emotivist bias which has motivated views on metaphor for some time, and in liberating metaphor from a narrowly perceived epideictic function, Hesse at once breaks down the bifurcation of scientific and narrative discourse and makes explicit the communicative backdrop of metaphorical usages. The longstanding separation of science and literature, of referential and narrational discourse, and the myth of two distinct languages are seen to collapse under their own weight. This enables one to comprehend metaphor in its own originative sense of *meta-phere,* understood as a *transporting* and a *delivering*—a transporting and delivering of new descriptions and new perspectives. It is this originative sense of metaphor that Nietzsche surely had in mind when he spoke of truth as "a mobile army of metaphors."[16] And Nietzsche saw clearly enough how this truth slips into illusion and falsity when its metaphorical character is forgotten, and metaphors begin to take on the armor of epistemological claims.

The current reflections on metaphor have brought into sharp relief two interrelated issues of considerable importance. The one has to do

---

of Notre Dame Press, 1966); and Barbour, *Myths, Models and Paradigms* (New York: Harper & Row, 1974).

[14] See particularly Ricoeur, *The Rule of Metaphor,* trans. Robert Czerny (Toronto: University of Toronto Press, 1977); Derrida, *Of Grammatology* and "White Mythology"; Black, *Models and Metaphors* (Ithaca: Cornell University Press, 1962); and Rorty, *Philosophy and the Mirror of Nature* (Princeton: Princeton University Press, 1979).

[15] *Models and Analogies,* p. 164–165. Although Hesse has succeeded in freeing metaphor from its bondage to the noncognitive, emotive, and merely decorative, the liberation of metaphor as an autonomous form of disclosure and communication has not been fully attained in her thought. Metaphor remains a supplement to the deductive model of scientific explanation, achieving reference only through a circuitous linkage with the explanandum of the primary system.

[16] "On Truth and Lie in an Extra-Moral Sense" (in Walter Kaufmann, *The Portable Nietzsche;* New York: The Viking Press, 1954, p. 46).

with the difference between the literal and the figurative, and the other involves the problem of metaphorical reference. These issues have been dealt with extensively by Derrida and Ricoeur. Derrida works out the issue of the contrast between the literal and the figurative through a critical engagement with Rousseau's *Essay on the Origin of Languages,* while Ricoeur spars with his formidable mentor, Martin Heidegger. The result in both cases, at least in the first round of their respective debates, is remarkably similar. They agree on the need for a deconstruction of the traditional opposition of the figurative to the literal.

Derrida gives notice of Rousseau's intention to place the origin of language in the domain of the figurative, but then points out that Rousseau's analytical procedures evince a curious serendipity which forces him back to the *arché* of literal meaning. The frame which dictates this move is the familiar limning of language with the signifier/signified polarity. Metaphor, prejudged as idea, is the signified meaning. It is that which the trope expresses or indicates. But it is also the sign which signifies, functioning as a representation of an object or an affect within the mind. It is in this play of the representative idea, which can be called upon to function either as signifier or signified, depending upon the circumstances, that grounds Rousseau's explanation of the life of metaphor. Metaphor thus remains for Rousseau "the relation between signifier and signified within the order of ideas and things."[17] It is this foundation or anchorage within the framework of signifier/signified and the accompanying representation of ideas and affects that Derrida proposes to deconstruct so that the play of the sign in metaphorical discourse can proceed unfettered.

Ricoeur also wends his way through a dismantling of the counterpositioning of the literal and the figurative as the privileged stance of metaphorical meaning. As Ricoeur correctly observes, the tradition defined the metaphorical as the transfer of sense from the proper (i.e., literal) to the figurative. This was accompanied by a metaphysical weighting of the proper, leading to a devaluing of the figurative and to talk of the "merely" metaphorical. Heidegger grasped this point clearly enough, and it is this that lies behind his well-known dictum: "The metaphorical exists only within the metaphysical." Having effected his own project of the deconstruction of metaphysical thought, this dictum becomes for Heidegger the springboard for a straightforward denuncia-

---

[17] *Of Grammatology,* p. 275. Compare: "Thus, even while apparently affirming that the original language was figurative, Rousseau upholds the literal [*propre*]: as *arche* and as *telos.* At the origin, since the first idea of passion, its first representer, is literally expressed. In the end, because the enlightened spirit stabilizes the literal meaning. He does it by a process of knowledge and *in terms of truth.* One will have remarked that in the last analysis, it is also in these terms that Rousseau treats the problem. He is situated there by an entire naive philosophy of the idea-sign." *Ibid.,*p. 277.

tion of metaphor. It is at this juncture that Ricoeur seeks to correct Heidegger and salvage the rule of metaphor by dispelling the metaphysical anchorage of the literal through a more precise semantics. In this move the distinction between the literal and the figurative, although it remains in force, no longer accords a metaphysical privilege and primary status to the literal. The literal sense is no more than a lexical decision, and it is discourse itself in its heterogenous usages that marks out the difference between the literal and the figurative.[18]

In Derrida's displacement of the signifier/signified couplet, enabling a free play of metaphorical meaning, and in Ricoeur's defusing of the metaphysical charge of the literal, there is a concomitant dismantling of traditional theories of reference which purport in some way to hook up with what is really there in the world. But here the similarities between the projects of Derrida and Ricoeur end. Whereas Derrida is content to let referential discourse collapse under its own weight in the rhapsodic play of metaphor, Ricoeur seeks to salvage an intentionality of metaphorical reference. His attempt pursues the route of broadening the space of reference so that it is no longer restricted to the denotation of scientific statements. This leads him to a notion of "displayed reference," postured as a second-level denotation that follows in the wake of the suspension of the first-level denotation of scientific discourse.[19] Ricoeur's notion of displayed reference travels with a reformulated notion of discourse as work, which falls out as a kind of baptism of the text by production and labor. This expanded posture of discourse requires a reformulation of the postulate of reference as delivered by Frege. The "structure of the work" is substituted for the Fregean notion of "sense," and the "world of the work" is substituted for the Fregean notion of "reference." Displayed reference is thus accomplished through the transition from the structure of work to the world of work. Reference displays the world, in terms of its arrangement, genre, and style, as it is articulated by the production and the labor that informs the work.[20]

In following the probings of Derrida and Ricoeur on the role and rule of metaphor we thus see how the bifurcation of the literal and the figurative, and the consequent metaphysical attachments to the literal,

---

[18] "We did admit of course that the metaphorical use of a word could always be opposed to its literal use; but literal does not mean proper in the sense of originary, but simply current, 'usual'. The literal sense is the one that is lexicalized. There is thus no need for a metaphysics of the proper to justify the difference between literal and figurative. It is use in discourse that specifies the difference between literal and metaphorical, and not some sort of prestige attributed to the primitive or the original." *The Rule of Metaphor,* pp. 290–91.

[19] *Ibid.,* p. 221.

[20] *Ibid.,* p. 220.

can be displaced. This displacement in turn requires a realignment of scientific and literary modes of discourse, which in the thought of Ricoeur follows the path of a reformulation of the postulate of reference. The undergirding motivation in Ricoeur's project needs to be applauded. Metaphorical discourse is surely discourse *about* something, and to speak of it as being about the world of work would seem to be adequate for the purposes at hand. Yet, there may be some question as to whether the Fregean sense-reference distinction provides the appropriate backdrop for an elucidation of that peculiar referentiality illustrated in metaphorical discourse. It would be our contention that this distinction still trades too heavily on the stock of traditional epistemological-linguistic commitments as they pertain to the use of sense and reference in the interests of epistemological warranting and justification.[21] The consequences of this for Ricoeur's notion of the metaphoricity of the text remain somewhat embarrassing. Even though the text is transmuted into discourse as work, problematic generalizations from the epistemological-linguistic sphere remain in force. Reference finds its touchstone in the text and in discourse as a linguistic accomplishment, and the display of meaning in human actions and institutional processes of sociohistorical formation is glossed and subordinated to textual and linguistic inscriptions.[22]

The text-analogue by itself remains insufficient for displaying the lived-through meanings and comprehensions of the world registered in the fabric of human action and social practices. Principally because of this we urge a vigilance over our root-metaphor of texture so as to keep it from solidifying into a mantle of textuality. Textuality is indeed one of the implicatory senses in our proposal for an exploration of the texture of communicative praxis, but it is an implicatory sense that is balanced with the senses of the texture of human action and the texture of institutional practices.

Our middle term, "texture," thus propels us in the direction of neither a primacy of the text, nor a primacy of perception, nor a primacy of action. The texture of communicative praxis gathers the display of meanings within the text of everyday speech and the text of the written word, but it also encompasses the play and display of meanings within the field of perception and the fabric of human action. Our figures of discourse are thus forced to acknowledge the presence,

---

[21] The peculiar destiny of the concepts of sense and reference has been detailed with remarkable critical insight in Rorty, *Philosophy and the Mirror of Nature*. See particularly Part II: "Mirroring."

[22] This point is tellingly made by John B. Thompson, *Critical Hermeneutics: A Study in the Thought of Paul Ricoeur and Jürgen Habermas* (Cambridge: Cambridge University Press, 1981), p. 125.

integrity, and intentionality of figures of action. The region of nondiscursive practices resists reduction to the realm of the discursive.[23] Thus we need to be wary of the facile reductionisms and claims for primacy that tend to make their way into "philosophy of language" and "hermeneutics of textuality." But one also needs to guard against the opposite tendency to look for the bottom of being in "philosophy of action." The interwovenness of communicative praxis is an interweaving of discourse and action, language and nondiscursive practices, speech and perception, yielding a holistic space of expressive intentionality. It is this holistic space of expression that must now become our topic for exploration.

---

[23] Hubert Dreyfus and Paul Rabinow have given particular attention to the relation of discursive and nondiscursive practices in their recent book *Michel Foucault: Beyond Structuralism and Hermeneutics* (Chicago: The University of Chicago Press, 1982). They argue that Foucault intermittently recognizes that nondiscursive factors (such as political decisions, economic processes, techniques of public assistance, and institutional fields) provide the background for and inform discursive practices, but that in the end he comes precisely to the opposite conclusion, subordinating nondiscursive practices to the autonomy of discourse. It is at this juncture that Dreyfus and Rabinow extoll the virtues of the thought of Heidegger, Wittgenstein, Kuhn, and Searle, all of whom came to see at different stages of their intellectual development that "social practices produce and govern action and discourse and give it serious content." Continuing, Dreyfus and Rabinow speak of this general position as a "broadly hermeneutic view" in which "the regularities of discursive practice are influential, but are themselves explained by understanding the purposes served by specific discursive practices in everyday meaningful activities." (pp. 77–78)

CHAPTER TWO

Communicative Praxis
as Expression

The elucidation of the principal figures of discourse in our proposed project brought us in the previous chapter to an attentive focus on the workings of expression in communicative praxis. The display of meanings in discourse and action unfolds within a holistic space of expression. Texture, we saw, is the mediating figure between communication and praxis, guiding the interplay of discourse and action, language and perception, speech and embodiment. Our task now is to explicate the expressive fibers of meaning within this texture of communicative praxis. The metaphorical play in the polysemy of texture, it was urged in the previous discussion, prohibits any solidification of either the text-analogue or the action-analogue as privileged and foundational.

This figuration of texture, suspended between the text of discourse and the textural features of action, illustrates a peculiar reference. We noted that Ricoeur names this peculiar reference "displayed reference." We shall also speak of it in varying contexts as "nonobjectifying" and "hermeneutical" reference, distinguishing it from the garden varieties of epistemological theories of reference. Freed from the fates of non-cognitivism and subjectivism, to which positivism had consigned it, metaphor assumes a role in referential discourse. However, this referential discourse, it should be underscored, is not that of an epistemologically oriented design, shouldered with the responsibility of delivering either empirical or transcendental contents. It is the reference operative in our conversation about the world and in our being about our every-day activities, displaying variegated patterns of communicative praxis. In this reference, which displays an intertexture of meanings, we are able to discern an inmixing of two types of discourse, referential and narrational, that have often been enjoined to go their separate ways. The advent of this inmixing transmutes the established classificatory models of reference and narration alike. Reference is no longer depicted as the mirroring of honest-to-goodness entities in the external world, as the reaching of the real; and narration is no longer prejudged simply as the telling of a story properly adorned with stylistic accoutrements. Narration already refers in its telling of a story *about* something; and reference in its displaying is inseparable from *how* the displaying proceeds.

In this chapter we are introducing a linkage to another traditionally isolated mode of discourse, that of expression. We are grafting reference and narration onto expression. In the effecting of this graft, however, the institutionalized markings of expression, like those of reference and narration, are recharted. Two principal consequences of such a recharting need to be noted.

The first is that expression is no longer defined as a vehicle for subjective states and as a signifier of an interior mind. The scaffolding of the modes of discourse in such a manner that reference becomes the blueprint of reality, narration the blueprint of style, and expression the blueprint of subjective states and conditions in the mind of the speaker and writer is precisely the scaffolding that needs to be disassembled so as to make visible the fraternization of the various modes of discourse that we use as we make our way about in the world. The language of expression is the language of showing, of setting forth, of making manifest. Wittgenstein's masterful use of the strategy of showing, as it outstrips the technique of defining, is a lesson well learned by the expressivity of discourse.

The second consequence of our coupling of expression with the metaphoricity of texture and its displayed reference has to do with the announcement of its role in the dynamics of human action, in the patterning of social practices, and in the institutional life of a culture. The recognition of the importance of expression as it relates to the postures of praxis thus provides a further sheet anchor against its closure within a linguistic paradigm, in which all problems in philosophy are defined as problems within language and within discourse. Discourse travels with the intentionality and display of meaning in non-discursive practices. Discourse and action are thus amalgamated but not reduced one to the other.

Our elucidation of the expressivity of communicative praxis as an amalgam of discourse and action begins with a discussion of expressive performance displayed from the side of discourse.[1] Discourse is here understood as a multifaceted event, comprised of speaking, writing, and

---

[1]There is a sense in which our sketch of the expressivity of communicative praxis can properly be taken as a response to James Kinneavy's request for "a new logic of expression," which he calls for in his book *A Theory of Discourse* (Englewood Cliffs: Prentice-Hall, 1971: pp. 418–423). It should be noted, however, that our new logic of expression follows a somewhat different route than that which Kinneavy himself adumbrates. Kinneavy continues the traditional line of viewing expression essentially within

language. Speaking not only has to do with the multiple forms of verbal communication, but also includes the deployment of gestural meaning and articulations through body motility. The ethnography of nonverbal behavior in gestures, facial expressions, and body language falls within the purview of what we call speech performances. Writing includes not only the usual spate of prose and poetry, but also the inscriptions of signs and symbols on historical markers, signatures on paintings, and identifying labels on artifacts. Language comprises both particular social systems of discourse, either spoken or written (e.g., English, French, German, Greek, and Latin), and a more general system of linguistic structures and rules (phonemic, syntactic, and lexical) that informs both semiology and semantics, signs and propositions. All of these features of speaking, writing, and language are relevant to discourse as an event of communicative praxis. They interplay within the event of discourse and determine it precisely *as event*—as a holistic phenomenon that antedates both the abstraction of speech acts as empirical data and the abstraction of language as a linguistic system of formalized rules.

We move into our topic beginning with the performative character of speech as a speech act, for it is here that the amalgam of discourse and action is most clearly discernible. Even more specifically, we focus on speech performance as gesture, facial proxemics, and body motility, where language, action, and embodiment can be seen as collaborators in a joint venture of expression. The shaking of the fist in the encounter between two business associates is at once the performing of an act and a medium of discourse, expressing the anger and frustration of betrayal. The grimace and the smile express readily understood meanings in our social relations. The stooped shoulders and the inhibited movement of the body evince a general attitude toward the world, announcing certain depressing conditions of life.[2]

---

the framework of subject-oriented philosophy. He sees the common concern motivating the interest in expression to be "the reassertion of the importance of the individual, of subjectivity, of personal value in an academic, cultural, and social environment which tended to ignore the personal and the subjective," p. 396. Particularly unfortunate in this regard is his use of Merleau-Ponty in support of this common concern, failing to recognize the critical importance of Merleau-Ponty's "third dimension," situated between mind and nature, subjectivity and objectivity, which provides a new context for the expressive performances of perception, embodiment, and valuation. See particularly "The Philosopher and His Shadow," *Signs*, trans. R. McCleary (Evanston: Northwestern University Press, 1964). Also, and this may be the root of the problem in Kinneavy's discourse on discourse, he invests too much capital in the already overly taxed communication triangle of reality-speaker-audience, and in the too facile correspondence of this triad with the topology of referential, expressive, and persuasive discourse.

[2] Erwin W. Straus has given close attention to the expressiveness of body motility in the use of the hands, standing, and walking. According to Straus, the social use of space by

Not only gestures and body motility, however, but also speech in the narrower sense of locutionary and illocutionary articulation is inseparable from the phenomenon of human action. To speak is to perform a speech act, in which movements of mouth and larynx are concordant with the "voicing" of concerns, attitudes, feelings, and concepts. Speaking is an event or an occurrence in which something happens or is undergone. Writing, too, as an allied genre of discourse, is an undertaking, a performance, a project, a species of labor, through which forms of expression are inscribed, calling forth the interpretive response of reading. The expressions in the various manners and modes of speaking and in the labor of writing are indissolubly linked with the expressiveness of action, and again we see how discourse and action are interwoven within the unitary phenomenon of communicative praxis.

Guided by our interest in uncovering an amalgam of discourse and action within the texture of communicative praxis, we have moved out from expressive speech as act and event, surging up in the domain of human action as gesture, facial proxemics, body motility, locutionary and illocutionary performances, and the labor of writing. Meaning undergoes a realization in action. This realization proceeds, we maintain, by dint of expression. The speech act as event is an event of expression. Now this moment of expression in gestural and locutionary articulation is attuned to wider configurations and solicitations in the history and structure of language, which provide a background for the particular acts of gestural and verbal expression. Although expressive speech is indissolubly linked with action, the gestural expression is not isomorphic to the episodic behavioral manifestation as empirically defined, nor are the locutionary and illocutionary forces of verbal utterances locked into the singularity of an isolated empirical datum. The speech act, as gestural and verbal utterance, carries a linguistic and social history.[3]

---

the body provides an opening to the world as experienced. See particularly the discussion in "The Upright Posture," in Maurice Natanson, ed., *Essays in Phenomenology* (The Hague: Martinus Nijhoff, 1966), where Straus writes: "Confidence and timidity, elation and depression, stability and insecurity—all are expressed in gait," p. 175.

[3] Although John Searle, in his influential work *Speech Acts: An Essay in the Philosophy of Language* (Cambridge: Cambridge University Press, 1970), has succeeded in providing the proper launching pad for an investigation of the texture of discourse, his descriptivist program remains unduly restricted because he continues to buy into a traditional empiricist framework of inquiry, which construes the expressive performance of the speech act as an empirical datum. He never fully recognizes the need for a transmutation of empiricistic behaviorism into a more global structure of human comportment. What is required to correct this residual empiricism in Searle's philosophy is attentiveness to Merleau-Ponty's seminal explorations of the lived-body as expression and speech (see particularly *Phenomenology of Perception*, trans. Colin Smith [New York: The Humanities Press, 1962], Part I., Ch. 6). Searle's continuing adherence to the empiricist frame-

It is thus that any description of the speech act must take cognizance of language as a social institution and a linguistic system. The act or performance of saying embodied in the speech act is effected through the resources of a spoken tongue that solicits a linguistic system of phonemic, lexical, and syntactic rules. The institutionalized spoken tongue, in conjunct with its linguistic rules, provides a history of sedimented signs and socially imbued meanings which come to expression in the speech act. The expressiveness of the speech act is thus never simply the articulation of private meaning by an autonomous speaker but is rather a display of a social semantics borne by the public language that is spoken. In the individual speech act, linguistic forms and systems, with their own peculiar sedimentations, are set forth, informing that which is expressed. Although the act of speaking can properly be understood as the incarnation of a spoken tongue and its linguistic system within a particular event, the words after they have been spoken return to the system as a part of its history. In speaking, the system of linguistic rules slides into history and then returns bearing historical inscriptions. We thus need to recognize a feature of linguistic transcendence in the constant reconversion within the play of language and speech, sedimented structure and particular act, system and event, which make up the texture of expressive discourse.[4]

Since the time of Saussure it has become rather common to indicate this play within the configuration of expressive discourse in terms of the distinction between language (le langue) and speech (la parole). Although this distinction holds the unfortunate potential of congealing into a bogus dichotomy, inviting the temptation for an appeal to the one or the other as providing a platform of primacy, it does offer limited resources for pointing one in the direction of a broader texture of expression than that delivered through a preoccupation with singular speech acts. In expressive discourse a complex of social meanings embedded within a linguistic system is put into play. These sedimented social meanings, in both the spoken and the written word, transcend

work occasions particular difficulties in his attempt to derive normative and evaluative judgments from descriptive propositions. With the empiricist's distinction between the normative and the descriptive in force, Searle remains unsuccessful in surmounting the "naturalistic fallacy" charge. An incisive discussion of the limitations of speech act theory as espoused by Austin and Searle is found in Richard L. Lanigan's book *Speech Act Phenomenology* (The Hague; Martinus Njhoff, 1977). Lanigan finds the principal limitations of speech act theory to reside in its inability to come to grips with the existential dialectic of sociality and embodiment as it figures in communicative interaction. He then proceeds to reassess the potentialities and limitations of speech act theory within the broader space of a comprehensive theory of human communication.

[4]Paul Ricoeur has given particular attention to the play of system and event in his philosophy of language. See particularly *"La structure, le mot, l événement," Man World*, Vol. I, No. I, 1968.

the episodical speech act, and may indeed come to expression unbeknownst to the speaker or author. Language embodies a competence of expressive discourse that is never fully actualized in particular speech acts; and speech embodies that performance without which language would never be spoken. Competence and performance are thus never discrete elements of discourse but rather twin halves of an undivided processual event.

Our explication of the fabric of communicative praxis as a texture of expression began with an examination of the expressive function displayed from the side of discourse. The necessary complement to our examination of expressive discourse is an explication of expressive action. Discourse and action, as we have already noted, are interrelated moments in the life of communicative praxis. Hence, the metaphors of discourse, such as word, script, and text, must always be balanced with metaphors of action, such as work, labor, and play, if the texture of communicative praxis is to be properly displayed.

Events of action, like events of discourse, are expressive. Human actions make manifest the preoccupations and purposes in our personal and social behavior. The doing of a kind deed, the exercise of a voting privilege, and the involvement in a community project are expressive of self and social understanding, bearing the imprint of a configuration of perceiving, feeling, willing, imagining, conceiving, and valuing. These activities and involvements of man as *homo praxis* are at once communicative performances, conveying messages sent to the wider public domain. As already noted, the amalgam of discourse and action makes it difficult to draw clear demarcations as to where the one begins and the other leaves off, as illustrated principally in the deployment of gestural communication. A gesture is at once an action and a mode of discourse. In the activities of caressing, waving farewell, and shaking the hand of a returning colleague something is said in its being done. The "speech" of gestures is embedded in action.

Expression, however, is also at work in the more common illustrations of personal and corporate action, which are not so explicitly tied to the expressive function of the speech act as are gestures. The activities and daily routine of a modern day wage earner, working on an assembly line, express the purposes and goals in the life of an average laborer in an industrial society as he seeks to provide for himself and his family. The activities at once express the socioeconomic patterns of a technological and industrialized culture as well as certain levels of self-understanding on the part of the worker. It may indeed be the case that the level of self-understanding expressed through the routines of his laboring activities is qualitatively low, the laborer never achieving explicit self-consciousness of himself as a laborer in the latter half of the twentieth century. It may also be the case, as some Marxists have argued, that the species of self-consciousness that remains in force is a self-consciousness under the conditions of alienation. But whatever the stripe or species of self-understanding or self-consciousness that is registered in labor as human action, it comes to expression through the laboring activity itself. False and authentic consciousness alike are ensconced in the situated milieu of the laborer and in the particular activities required for the task to be done. It is in the doing of the task, as much as in the speaking of the word, that the various permutations of self-consciousness are made manifest.

There are also the phenomena of collegial decisions and corporate actions. An institution, such as a university, a corporation, or a nation-state, is said to act by carrying out a certain policy, procedure, or program. The United States acted in its annexation of the Philippines in 1898 and in its declaration of war against Japan in 1941. Admittedly these "acts" of annexation and war are general designators of a composite and concatenation of acts in the plural, yet these general designators do point us to an interweaving of national interests that come to expression in the actions undertaken and executed. A curious mixture of an imperialistic stance and a national vocational consciousness is expressed in the annexation of the Philippines. The threat of a foreign power coupled with a distinctive political slant on the world is expressed in the taking up of arms. Commonly referenced corporate actions, no less than individual action within a more restricted social space, are fibers of expression within the texture of communicative praxis.

This posture of expression, suspended between the nonabsolute poles of individual and corporate action, is positioned within a holistic horizon of praxial space that encompasses the particular actions of individuals and institutions, but also extends beyond them. There are explicit motivations and conscious actions entertained and performed by agents in solitude and in society. The individual, through his acting, endows his behavior with a meaning which he already understands, either in a theoretical or pretheoretical manner. This endowment or conferral of meaning issues from a self-awareness of motivational factors and a conscious projection of goals to be realized and purposes to be achieved. This is the mark of the individual actor or agent as a purposive self, and the mark of a goal-directed institution. But there are also actions that express meanings hidden and submerged, scarred by self-deception and infected with ideology. Expression is at work even if the action undertaken by the individual or the corporate unit is not the result of a conscious and reflective intending to accomplish a particular purpose. Expression surpasses the intentions of particular actors and institutions, announcing patterns of ideation and valuation that remain opaquely entrenched within the habitual behavior of everyday life and the delivered processes of social formation.

Expressive action should thus not be restricted to the deliverance of meaning through conscious motivation and reflective, deliberate acts. The sources of human motivation, and the layers of meaning that encircle them, are drawn from a wider context and a wider space, in which acquired habits, established customs, and historical trends mix and mingle. This is why any science of human behavior is called upon to do a double duty. It needs to attend to the conscious motivations and calculated actions on the part of social agents, but it also needs to employ at the appropriate stages of its investigations the resources of a hermeneutic of tacit and repressed meanings. It was surely a notable achievement on the part of Freud to recognize the prevalence of a psychopathology of everyday life in which the expressiveness of human action has a motivational level that operates beneath the layer of a consciously engineered style of life. He also must be credited with the recognition of the need for a psychoanalytical hermeneutic wherewith to decipher the latent significations that play in the unconscious. It may indeed be the case, as Ricoeur has persuasively argued, that Freud's mistake was that of restricting his hermeneutic to an interpretive de-masking and demystification, but the realization of the requirement to attend to the oblique and circuitous expressivity of repressed drives and motivations was an important contribution not only to psychoana-lytical theory and practice but to the human sciences more generally.[5] In a similar vein the contributions of Sartre's theory of self-deception and Marx's teaching on the insinuation of ideological constellations into the fabric of human praxis need to be acknowledged and to be taken into account by any science of human behavior. Unconscious motivations, self-deception, and submerged ideologies intertwine within the texture of communicative praxis, and their circuitous ave-nues of expression need to be detailed and described.

Our examination of the expressivity of action in its dual capacity of announcing both manifest and latent meanings again brings us to the point of intersection between the ways of discourse and the ways of action. As the singular speech act in the expressivity of discourse is at once the articulation of specific meanings as intended and the history of discourse as a complex of conventional usages and linguistic rules,

---

[5]Ricoeur develops his extensive critique of Freud's understanding and use of her-meneutics in his book *Freud and Philosophy: An Essay on Interpretation,* trans. Denis Savage (New Haven: Yale University Press, 1970). A somewhat more positive appropria-tion of Freud's psychoanalytical model is found in Jürgen Habermas, *Knowledge and Human Interests,* trans. Jeremy J. Sharpiro (Boston: Beacon Press, 1971). Habermas uses Freud's metapsychological ruminations to help him map out the region of emancipatory interests in which the technical interests of Marxism and the communicative-practical interests of Dilthey and the hermeneutical tradition undergo a quasi-Hegelian *Aufhebung.*

unbeknownst to the speaker, so the individual actor through his action expresses both manifest meanings consciously intended and latent meanings resting on the edge of consciousness. There is more to the expressivity of discourse than the episodical speech act, and there is more to the expressivity of action than the projects of individual actors and institutions.

Both expressive discourse and expressive action draw upon a surplus of meanings that overflows the intentions of particular speakers and particular actors. This surplus resides, first of all, in the established habits and customs and the sedimented grammatical forms and linguistic rules of language as a system. These habits, customs, and rules always inform communicative praxis and condition the style and intentionality of the particular speech act and the individual action. They comprise a coefficient of sedimentation in the historicity of communicative praxis, in which word and act are always embedded. This is the case even when speech and action assume a critical or a creative stance, inaugurating a change of custom and a modification of rules. That which has become sedimented can indeed be transfigured and transvalued, but it can never be outstripped. This points to the feature of an unavoidable facticity in the weight of tradition within the texture of communicative praxis. It is this facticity of tradition that receives the paramount emphasis in Gadamer's program of philosophical hermeneutics.[6]

Although the unavoidable facticity and formative influence of the tradition need to be acknowledged in an investigation of the communicative performance of discourse and action, the texture of communicative praxis is disfigured at the moment that one confers a privilege and primacy on delivered habits, customs, and rules.[7] There is no

---

[6]See *Philosophical Hermeneutics,* trans. David E. Linge (Berkeley: University of California Press, 1976) and *Truth and Method,* trans. Garnett Barden and John Cumming (London: Sheed & Ward, 1975).

[7]This problematic appeal to primacy is illustrated in both the ontological hermeneutics of Gadamer and the linguistic hermeneutics of Peter Winch. In Gadamer's hermeneutics the appeal to primacy takes the form of a privileged positioning of the tradition. The tradition for Gadamer is the source of the prejudgments of understanding which at once inform and legitimate the hermeneutical enterprise. It indeed provides the "authority" for reflective interpretation. Now admittedly the recovery of the prejudgments and insights of the tradition proceeds not by dint of a species of empathic identification but rather via the hard struggle of the "fusion of historical horizons," which provides for a measure of play of creativity. Yet, the critical moment in interpretive understanding is suppressed in Gadamer's hermeneutical program, and requires the corrective of a more radical reflection. In Winch's linguistic hermeneutics the appeal to primacy takes the form of a rule apriorism in which the sociohistorical sources of rule constructivism are glossed. For a critique of Winch's rule-governed linguistic hermeneutics see Calvin O. Schrag, *Radical Reflection and the Origin of the Human Sciences* (West Lafayette: Purdue University Press, 1980), pp. 109–113, and John B. Thompson, *Critical Hermeneutics: A Study in the Thought of Paul Ricoeur and Jürgen Habermas* (Cambridge: Cambridge University Press, 1981), pp. 121–123.

pristine origin of expression to be found in some period of innocence of untrammeled custom or in some layer of ideality of pure linguistic rules, secured either ontologically or transcendentally. Although bearing the inscriptions of the delivered text of language and the delivered practices of custom, speech and action also possess the resources to say that which has not yet been said and do that which has not yet been done. Not only is there a surplus of sedimented meaning structures, there is a surplus of possible worlds and unexplored horizons in which the delivered facticities can be transmuted. The surplus of expressive meanings has its source in the surfeit of sedimentation and in the power of the possible. It is this that determines the texture of communicative praxis as an "open texture." The semantics of discourse cannot be fully formalized through an idealized structure of language, and the intentionality of action resists the destiny of a determining past. They both enjoy the openness of a creative advance.

Our discussion of communicative praxis as expression has already at this juncture shown how discourse and action intercalate in an ongoing adventure of expression. We have also attempted to show why the fabric of expression in discourse needs to involve more than singular speech acts, and why the fabric of expression in action stretches beyond references to individual projects. A wider space, encompassing the history and system of language and the spate of social practices in the scopious play of sociohistorical formation, must be acknowledged for its relevance to the global texture of communicative praxis. A schematic depiction of the results of our exploration up to this point might be sketched as follows:

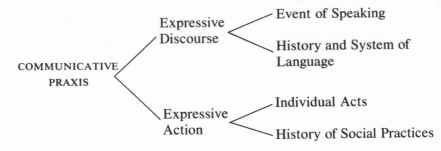

Along the way in our explication of the texture of expressivity we have already brushed against certain time-honored assumptions and beliefs regarding the source and functioning of expression. We have alluded to the traditional view of expression as a vehicle of subjective states and a channeling of interior contents. If the path of exploration that we have marked out above is to be followed, then the traditional view of expression will need to be undermined and set aside. The undermining will proceed by way of a testing and contesting of the metaphorical extension of the interior/exterior dichotomy in the explanation of matters of mind, consciousness, communication, thought, and action.

The use of the interior/exterior dichotomy in the construction of theories of mind and theories of knowledge may be a peculiar legacy of modern philosophy since the time of Descartes. Admittedly, a franchise for the philosophical employment of this dichotomy would seem to have been issued even before the fateful turn effected by modern thought. Yet the fact remains that it was principally in the development of modern epistemology and philosophy of mind, as practiced by both the empiricists and the rationalists, that the metaphorical use of the distinction between the interior and the exterior produced such far-reaching philosophical consequences. Cartesian philosophy pictured the mind as a sphere of interiority which housed the intrapsychic states of consciousness. Epistemological inquiry, as its purposes were defined by Descartes, assumed as its principal task that of accounting for the commerce, or lack thereof, between the internal states of consciousness (sensations and thoughts) and an external world. The empiricists rejuggled the status and function of sensation and thought, but appropriated the metaphor of interiority as applied to mind and continued to define the task of philosophy essentially as epistemological inquiry. Empiricist and rationalist alike were called upon to probe the interior domain of mental contents and their epistemic connection with an external world in the hope of securing the unimpeachable foundations of knowledge. Although the two traditions came up with different starting points, one appealing to the primacy of sensations and the other to the primacy of concepts, the utility of the root-metaphor through which events were parceled out as being inside or outside remained both untested and uncontested.

The effects of the continued employment of the metaphor of interiority/exteriority as somehow at the root of all our philosophical problem-solving soon became discernible in the literature on expression. Proceeding from the requirement of a clean separation between that which is inside and that which is outside, expression assumed the form and function of an articulation of internal states of consciousness, in which were gathered a rather wide-ranging collection of sensations, feelings, volitions, images, and concepts. Expression became defined as the struggle of interiority straining for externalization. It was viewed as the odyssey of privacy yearning to break out into the public domain. In this arbitrary and reckless extension of the language of interior and exterior to the domains of the private and the public, the space of communicative praxis suffered its most acute disfiguration. The textural space of communicative praxis, which bonds the singular speech act with the history and system of language and integrates the actions of the individual with the panoply of social practices, is not folded over in such a manner as to produce a private interior and a public exterior. The distinction between the private and the public is a relatively late arrival. If installed at all in talk about the space of communicative praxis, it must be said that this space is at once private and public—in a manner reminiscent of James's talk of the subjective and the objective correlation of experience, of which he said "we have every right to speak of it as subjective and objective both at once."[8]

The solidification of the metaphor of interiority into a methodological principle has had its peculiar consequences for the placement of gestures and body motility in the workings of expression. The methodological polarization of interior and exterior functions as a blade that severs the gesture as an event of expression from the expressed meaning. The gesture itself slides to the outside while the meaning finds its locus in the inside, within the interior of consciousness. The unavoidable question at this juncture is whether the schematization of that which is observable on the outside as distinct from that which occurs in the inside does not effectively occlude the density of the gesture as an upsurge of meaning. We use the language of inside and outside quite unproblematically when we distinguish that which is inside a bottle of scotch from the label that appears on the outside, or again when we distinguish the functions of an interior decorator from those of a landscape designer. It is surely not the case that the words "inside" and "outside" or "interior" and "exterior" should be deleted from the lexicon. But it surely is the case that one should be vigilant over their extension into the domains of expression and meaning. Specifically, one needs to be on guard against construing the human body as simply another external object in the world, given as a composition of *partes extra partes*. We can speak of this as the objectivist prejudice of the human body. But one equally needs to be on guard against construing the mind as some species of mental entity within the body. This is the subjectivist prejudice of the human mind. When these prejudices are combined, meaning falls out as a property of an interior mind and the expressive gesture is objectivized as a brute, nonintentional, external, behavioral datum.

What we would urge at this juncture, following among others the seminal suggestions of Merleau-Ponty, is a new description of the human body, not as a mere composition of parts, but as a configuration of thought and action that displays an attitude toward the world and a

---

[8] *Essays in Radical Empiricism* (New York: Longmans, Green and Company, 1940), p. 10.

field from which projects are entertained and tasks accomplished. This new description allows us to comprehend gestures, not as external signs of internal meanings, but as expressions which contain the meanings in the act of expressing. The shaking of the fist is not an external sign pointing to anger as a recessed meaning in the mind. The meaning of being angry is inseparable from the gesture itself. The caress is not an atomistic bit of behavior that points to the feeling of affection. The act of caressing is the embodied display of affection. Likewise facial expressions are not instruments for the externalization of inner states or conditions. The grimace is not an external sign of pain. It is the event of being in pain. Descriptions of this sort may contribute to an attenuation of the metaphorical extension of interiority/exteriority to the life of meaning and expression.

Traveling with these new descriptions of human embodiment and gestural communication, descriptions that undermine the bifurcation of expression and meaning, is a new perspective on the expressivity of verbal discourse. Verbal discourse, like gestures, has often been depicted through an instrumentation of the familiar dichotomy in which words become exterior signs of inner thoughts. Words somehow signify internal meanings. Wittgenstein had already called our attention to the mischievous implications of the split between the interior and the exterior when applied to thought and language, and spoke of their inseparability. "Thinking," he says, "is not an incorporeal process which lends life and sense to speaking, and which it would be possible to detach from speaking."[9] Verbal discourse, like gestures, envelops the meaning within the discourse. The spoken word is not an exterior garment that clothes an inner thought. The spoken word is the performance of thought.

In moving from expressive discourse to expressive action, from word

---

[9] *Philosophical Investigations,* trans. G. E. M. Anscombe (New York: Macmillan, 1953), no. 339, p. 109e. Heidegger offers a similar suggestion when he writes: "Words and language are not wrappings in which things are packed for the commerce of those who write and speak. It is in words and language that things first come into being and are." *An Introduction to Metaphysics,* trans. Ralph Manheim (New York: Doubleday, 1959), p. 11. On this particular issue the views of Wittgenstein and Heidegger need to be rather sharply contrasted with the position espoused by Husserl. Husserl subscribes to a notion of communicative speech acts as "indicators" or "signs" of internal thoughts and inner experiences. In doing so he appropriates, without question, the interior/exterior dichotomy as applied to communicative performances. "If one surveys these interconnections, one sees at once that all expressions in *communicative* speech function as *indications.* They serve the hearer as signs of the 'thoughts' of the speaker, i.e., of his sense-giving inner experiences, as well as of the other inner experiences which are part of his communicative intention. This function of verbal expressions we shall call their *intimating function.* The content of such intimation consists in the inner experiences intimated." *Logical Investigations,* Vol. I, trans. J. N. Findlay (London: Routledge & Kegan Paul, 1970), p. 277.

to deed, we find a similar texture of expression illustrated. Actions and deeds, like words, have often been construed as exterior markings which signal a concatenation of interior mental states and processes and their accompanying meanings and purposes. The meaning of the action is encapsulated within the interior life of the individual. The overt action is then viewed as a trigger in a transmitting system which occasions the externalization of the private ongoings in the mind. Again, we propose a suspension of this framework, modeled after cybernetic functioning, to permit the phenomenon of expressive action to show itself in the context of its lived-through dynamics. This context is that of the social practices and institutional life to which the individual action adheres, and it is within this context that the trace of meaning as purposive action is to be found. Charles Taylor, in his essay "Interpretation and the Sciences of Man," has offered some suggestions that point us in the right direction on this issue. Examining the specific social practices of voting and negotiation, he concludes: "The meanings and norms implied in these practices are not just in the minds of the actors but are out there in the practices themselves, practices which cannot be conceived as a set of individual actions, but which are essentially modes of social relation, of mutual action."[10] Human actions tell the story of the social practices of which they are organically a part. Wittgenstein had already instructed us well on this matter when he wrote:

> How could human behaviour be described? Surely only by sketching the actions of a variety of humans, as they are all mixed up together. What determines our judgment, our concepts and reactions, is not what *one* man is doing *now*, an individual action, but the whole hurly-burly of human actions, the background against which we see any action.[11]

Human actions are fibers embedded in the texture of social practices and display a contextualized sense. The meanings which they bear reside in the socialized manner or style of their performance rather than in a psychic basement of the mind as interior agency.

Although the meaning of an action is inseparable from its expression, this meaning may not be immediately transparent. Because the meaning is always that of an intertexture, playing among the circumstances in which it is performed and within the wider space of institutional practices and social history, factors of sub rosa power relations and repressed motivations and ideologies often inform the display of meaning

---

[10] "Interpretation and the Sciences of Man," *The Review of Metaphysics*, Vol. XXV, No. 1, Issue 97, 1971, p. 27.

[11] *Zettel*, edited by G. E. M. Anscombe and G. H. von Wright (Oxford: Basil Blackwell, 1967), entry 567, p. 99ᵉ.

in action. As we have already shown, the expressivity of action transcends the intentions of particular agents, requiring a hermeneutic of tacit and repressed meaning. It is principally because of this that the analysis of the concept of meaningful action into the conscious and willful following of a rule, as proposed by Peter Winch, for example, encounters some consequential limitations. Actions are meaningful also if they involve a suspension or even an explicit abrogation, either voluntarily or involuntarily, of a socially sedimented rule. A voter who casts two ballots rather than one, violating a rule of sanctified democratic procedure, is not because of this involved in a meaningless act. A researcher who executes a project unknowingly contributing to the political infrastructural power configuration in his society does not engage in a set of activities that can be deemed meaningless. His actions tell a story about prevalent social power relations that invade his academic life. A salient point to be distilled from all this is that the expressivity of action does not congeal into a universalized essence of action, defined either by a system of rules, a noematic structure, or an interior intention in the mind of the actor—a point perceptively made by John B. Thompson in his ruminations on the project of a "critical hermeneutics."[12]

We have urged in this discussion that the metaphorical extension of the interior/exterior dichotomy into the arenas of discourse and action be set aside so that the expressivity in the texture of communicative praxis can be elucidated by staying with the dynamics of its performative intentionality. Our dismantling of this dichotomy and the consequent consolidation of expression and meaning provide a new way of narrating the story of how we live our personal and social life in speaking and acting. To be noted as a consequence of this project is a dislodging of certain prejudices that have become enshrined not only in the literature of philosophy of language and philosophy of action but also in that of rhetoric and communication. Textbooks on rhetoric and communication theory have a longstanding tradition of construing expression as having to do with matters of privacy and communication as having to do with the public. Expression is viewed as referring, in some odd and circuitous manner of reference, to a process taking place within a solitary mental life; and communication has the burden of making public the private thoughts and meanings housed within the friendly

---

[12]*Critical Hermeneutics,* p. 142. Thompson's proposal that the meanings of action be specified by the way in which they are described is basically on target, particularly if it is emphasized that the plurivocity of descriptions move about within the *open texture* of communicative praxis as an amalgam of discourse and action. One needs, however, to be wary about an unsuspected recourse to a theory of description regulated by a nomothetic postulate of explanation.

confines of an inner mental sphere. This facile bifurcation of the private and the public is erased in our displacement of the philosophical employment of the interior/exterior schema. The articulated meanings of individual speech acts and gestures are at once displays of the intentions of particular speakers and the inscriptions of sense in the history of publically spoken language. The expressive speech of particular speakers is inseparable from the wider context of the language community, as the expressive action of particular agents is inseparable from the public history of social practices. The private and the public are not separate domains, positioned as incorrigible givens, nor do expression and communication fall out as custodians of these domains.

In this chapter we have made an effort to detail the expressive texture of communicative praxis as an amalgam of discourse and action, interweaving the event of speaking and the history and system of language on the one hand, and individual actions and the history of social practices and institutions on the other. We have emphasized the open texture of communicative praxis, which extends the reach of expressive meaning beyond the intentions and the conscious appropriation of rules by particular speakers and actors, and which keeps in view the relevance of the various forms of self-deception, ideology, and unconscious motivation that infect the ongoing conversation and social practices of mankind. We have disassembled the philosophical use of the dichotomy of interior and exterior. Communicative praxis as the ongoing process of expressive speech and expressive action has neither an interior nor an exterior, viewed as separable domains. Expressive meaning is woven into the fibers of verbal speech acts, gestures, body motility, personal goals, social practices, institutions, and historical trends. Never coming to rest as an essential feature of this and that, meaning is stitched into the global and processual texture of communicative praxis in such a way that its holdings can only be determined by taking an inventory of the times. Now the odyssey of this expressive meaning in the life of self and society, when its course is charted by reflection and the designs of understanding and explanation, encounters certain complexities arising from the desire to comprehend the truth of its manifold manifestations. It is to these ensuing complexities that we are forced to turn in the next chapter.

CHAPTER THREE

Distanciation, Idealization, and Recollection

The discussion of expression and meaning in the preceding chapter left us with a problem. The problem was occasioned by our explicit linkage of expression and meaning, which we worked out through a detailing of the collaborative maneuvers of expressive discourse and expressive action. The central issue in this problem concerns the roles of reflection, thematization, and critique, all of which seem to require a carriage of distanciation. Might it be that in our preceding discussion we have inscribed meaning too indelibly on the facticity of our participatory involvements in discourse and social practices, blocking the moments of reflection, thematization, and critique? Have we not congested the passage to an understanding of what goes on in our speaking and acting, and consequently locked ourselves into a brute facticity of participatory experience? Is there not some manner or posture of distanciation required both for a reflective comprehension of the patterns of communicative praxis and for a critique of the sedimented prejudices that inhabit the metaphors of expressive discourse and the customs and institutions of expressive action? This is the cluster of questions that we now inherit from our preceding discussion of communicative praxis and expressive meaning.

The central problem at issue is the very same one that Ricoeur and Habermas have raised in their critical responses to Gadamer's hermeneutical philosophy. Ricoeur defines the problem as that of an unresolved tension in Gadamer's thought between our participatory belonging to the tradition and the posture of distanciation required for the achievement of objective knowledge in the human sciences. The route of Gadamerian hermeneutics, according to Ricoeur, marks out an unacceptable alternative between participation and distanciation. It is this unacceptable alternative that Ricoeur promises to overcome.[1] Habermas's attack on Gadamer is more direct. He criticizes Gadamer for investing the linguistic and cultural tradition with an authority and an ultimate sanction, failing to recognize that all language and culture are infected with ideology and that a principle of ideality is needed to provide a standpoint from which to critique the aberrations of ideology and the constellations of power that distort communication. Habermas finds this principle of ideality in the "ideal speech situation," which functions as a necessary condition for "control-free" communication.[2]

We propose, however, to open our discussion of the issue at an earlier stage of the contemporary debate of the matters at hand. Merleau-Ponty, in the context of related concerns, had already forced us to ask the question about the role of distanciation in his observation "that our existence is too tightly held in the world to be able to know itself as such at the moment of its involvement, and that it requires the field of ideality to become acquainted with and to prevail over its facticity."[3] We have accentuated the facticity of our involvement in the life of communicative praxis and its history of expressive meaning in discourse and action. Wherein reside the available resources of reflection wherewith to prevail over this facticity? Merleau-Ponty's appeal to a "field of ideality" to account for the requisite distanciation from our existential involvements provides us with a new challenge for an elucidation of expressive meaning as embedded in the facticity of speaking and acting. We are called upon to consider the detailing of a distinction within the global fabric of meaning, sorting out in some manner the expressive meaning in performative speech and action from meaning refracted through a field of ideality.

It is the status and function of this field of ideality that must now solicit our attention. Merleau-Ponty positions this field through the resources of a critical use of the language of essence. He speaks of the

---

[1] See particularly his essay "The Hermeneutical Function of Distanciation," in *Paul Ricoeur: Hermeneutics and the Human Sciences,* ed. and trans. John B. Thompson (Cambridge: Cambridge University Press, 1981), where he writes: "The description has led us to an antinomy which seems to be the mainspring of Gadamer's work, namely the opposition between alienating distanciation and belonging. This opposition is an antinomy because it establishes an untenable alternative; on the one hand, alienating distanciation is the attitude that renders possible the objectification which reigns in the human sciences; but on the other hand, this distanciation, which is the condition of the scientific status of the sciences, is at the same time the fall that destroys the fundamental and primordial relation whereby we belong to and participate in the historical reality which we claim to construct as an object" (p. 131).

[2] See Habermas's reply to Gadamer in his "Summation and Response," *Continuum,* Vol. 8, No. 1, 1970.

[3] *Phenomenology of Perception,* trans. Colin Smith (New York: The Humanities Press, 1962), p. xv.

requirement of a field of ideality as "the need to proceed by way of essences."[4] Clearly, in the background of this language and claim is Merleau-Ponty's effort toward a critical appropriation of Husserl's *Wesensschau*. This need for essences, however, is hurriedly qualified by Merleau-Ponty, indicating that his appropriation of the language of essence exhibits an accentuated critical turn. Essences are not objects; essences are means rather than ends; and essences are to be placed back into existence.[5] In an even more critical vein Merleau-Ponty urges us to consider the possibility that our intuition of an essence is nothing more "than a prejudice rooted in language."[6] Now what precisely remains after such a succession of weighty mutations and warnings may indeed be up for grabs. It is a moot question whether one is here not witnessing the proverbial death by a thousand qualifications. Could one suppose, entertaining a somewhat audacious interpretation, that this is precisely what Merleau-Ponty intended? It must be remembered that although Merleau-Ponty took his project to be a *mitdenken* with the programmatic of Husserl's phenomenology, in which a doctrine of essence remained rather firmly entrenched, Merleau-Ponty's definition of his philosophical role was anything but that of a mere filial successor to Husserl's phenomenologcial idealism. On the final tally Merleau-Ponty's existential phenomenology is more concordant with Heidegger's *analytic of Existenz* than with Husserl's *Wessenswissenschaft*. And long before talk about deconstruction became fashionable Merleau-Ponty deployed his own strategy of deconstruction by disassembling the epistemological buttresses that supported the theory of essence from the ancients to Husserl. Yet, Merleau-Ponty continues to speak of a requirement for a field of ideality, and it is our task to see in what manner such a field might be displayed within the texture of communicative praxis.

We must not lose sight of our problem, created by our interweaving of expression and meaning in the everyday praxis of living speech and

---

[4] *Ibid.*, p. xiv.
[5] *Ibid.*, pp. vii, xiv–xv.
[6] Commenting on the danger of self-deception in the deployment of a Husserlian "eidetic intuition" Merleau-Ponty emphasizes the need to proceed with caution in our "idealizing" constructions. "It is possible for me to believe that I am seeing an essence when, in fact, it is not an essence at all but merely a concept rooted in language, a prejudice whose apparent coherence reduces merely to the fact that I have become used to it through habit. The best way of guarding against this danger would be to admit that, although a knowledge of facts is never sufficient for grasping an essence and though the construction of 'idealizing fictions' is always necessary, I can never be sure that my vision of an essence is anything more than a prejudice rooted in language—if it does not enable me to hold together all the facts which are known and which may be brought into relation with it." *The Primacy of Perception,* ed. James M. Edie (Evanston: Northwestern University Press, 1964), p. 75.

action. Does not an account and critique of the lived-through expressive meaning in our daily praxis require some tincture of theoretical reflection, enabling a conceptual comprehension and evaluation of that which we live through? And does this not involve the introduction of another level of meaning, possibly a strata of ideal meaning, operative in our theoretical musings, through which the patterns of praxis are identified, connected, constituted, represented, and thus cognitively known? Now before anything can be achieved in a pursuit of these questions, it is necessary to play with the questions themselves. In our day we surely do not need to be reminded of the importance of the way that a question is posed and formulated. Questions have a way of directing the inquiry, often tacitly presupposing that which is to be questioned. Our questions as formulated above would seem to place us on rather familiar turf. They appear to be peddling pretty standard epistemological ware, asking for a bit of theory that might offer criteria for epistemic reference, supply principles of identity, sort out incorrigible givens, and legislate forms of representation. In short, we seem to have landed on the epistemological terrain of modern theory of meaning, including both the Fregean (and subsequent analytical) and the Husserlian (and subsequent phenomenological) traditions. The philosophical problematic of sense and reference (Frege) as well as the tripartite scaffolding of indication, expression, and pre-expressive sense (Husserl) continue to trade on an appeal to givens, marks of identity and reference, presentational thoughts or essences, and procedures of representation. This epistemological grid of presentation/representation and identification/reidentification not only leads to puzzles and aporias of sundry stripes, as Wittgenstein and Heidegger have almost effortlessly shown, it also disfigures the texture of communicative praxis. The presentation and representation of thoughts and essences, and the identification and reidentification of phenomenal properties, remain alien to the texture of communicative praxis as an ongoing form of life.

So our exploration of the role of reflection and idealization will need to be redirected. The move to a region or field of ideality designed to deliver the needed distanciation from praxis so as to render a trustworthy account of it, if indeed such a move is to be made, cannot profitably follow either the route of a classical doctrine of essence or that of modern epistemologies of meaning. Such uses of theory to enlighten praxis tend to mistake that which is accounted for with the account itself. What the present task requires is a radical critique of meaning both as a metaphysical postulate and as an epistemological achievement. This radical critique is accompanied by a provisional nihilism, as both Nietzsche and Heidegger had already clearly seen. Heidegger performs such a critique in his "destruction" of the history of Western metaphysics and epistemology, which takes shape as the move from the question as to "the *meaning* of Being" to the question as to the "*truth of Being.*" The early writings of Heidegger comprise an effort to think the question of the meaning of Being to its denouement and displacement while making use of the resources of transcendental philosophy. The celebrated turn in Heidegger's philosophy marks a redirection of inquiry. After the turn he no longer places the question of meaning at the center of the inquiry, but speaks instead of the happening of truth as disclosure or unconcealment, for which he still finds the resources of the Greek notion of *aletheia* (Αλήθεια) to be helpful. The "truth of Being" is an event in the life of "commemorative thinking" *(andenkendes Denken)* rather than the product of "representational thinking" *(vorstellendes Denken);* it is revelatory rather than referential; and its language is that of poetic dwelling rather than that of correspondence of judgments with states of affairs.[7]

Derrida's deconstruction of the theory of meaning is more radical than that of either Nietzsche or Heidegger, and his provisional nihilism begins to take on a feature of permanence. Chiding Heidegger for his logocentrism and his quest for the ever-deferred presence of Being, Derrida advises us to stick with the play of *écriture*. Writing, according to Derrida, displays neither logos nor telos but only itself, in a grammatological play of signs that overrides every signifier and every signified. There is in writing neither meaning nor truth; no articulation of sense and reference; and no discourse of the presence of Being. Not only is there in this project of deconstruction a dismantling of all traditional theories of meaning and truth, including the Heideggerian notion of truth as disclosure, there is nothing to take their place. Nothing is disclosed in writing for there is nothing to disclose. It is in this respect that Derrida's nihilism can be seen as fulfilled rather than provisional. But the very notion of a fulfilled nihilism contains a paradox, for that which is fulfilled can no longer be a *nihil-absolutum*. Derrida's writing itself falls out as an accomplishment, a form of praxis, that effects a change in our attitudes toward the various genres of inscription—philosophical, scientific, and literary.[8]

---

[7] See particularly his short essays "The Way Back into the Ground of Metaphysics," trans. Walter Kaufmann in *Existentialism from Dostoevsky to Sartre* (New York: Meridian Books, Inc., 1956), and "Building, Dwelling, Thinking," trans. Albert Hofstadter in *Martin Heidegger: Poetry, Language, Thought* (New York: Harper & Row, 1971).

[8] David Wood has addressed this general issue in his article "Derrida and the Paradoxes of Reflection," and has concluded that an ineliminable paradox resides in the very metaphorical heart of deconstructionist strategy. More specifically, he has attempted to show how Derrida's project of *écriture* leads quite inevitably to the reinstallment of presence, as well as a more general metaphysical posture. "Whatever he [Derrida] says about the merely strategic value of his writing, the function of control, of internal reflexive

The strategy in our critical hermeneutics of communicative praxis, as should by this time be evident, is not that of a blanket displacement of meaning as such, construed in every sense you please. The dismantling of the metaphysico-epistemological framework in which meaning arises as a protocol of pure theory, so energetically carried through by Heidegger and Derrida, is indeed applauded; but this only illustrates the negative moment in our critical hermeneutics. There is also a positive moment, inaugurating the resituation of meaning within the hermeneutical and holistic space of communicative praxis. The deconstruction of meaning as a property of entities, be they objective essences or subjective thoughts, first provides the appropriate aperture for the discernment of a pre-epistemological texture of meaning operative in the everyday life of conversation and social practice.

This pre-epistemological texture of meaning, we have suggested, is displayed in the expressive discourse and expressive action of communicative praxis. Meaning and expression make up an intertexture of intentionality in the facticity of the spoken word and the enacted deed. The expressivity of a verbal speech act, a gesture, and a form of social behavior is the accomplishment and performance of meaning. Words and deeds are not outer garments which adorn inner meanings; they are the meanings as displayed. But we have now been confronted with the special demand of accounting for that moment of reflection in which the facticity of our expressive speech and behavior is set at a distance and becomes a theme for analysis, understanding, and explanation. We have been advised by Merleau-Ponty that this requires a field of ideality. But we have resisted the portrayal of this field of ideality as either a determination of essence or a field of epistemological postulates in the service of a theoretical reconstruction of meaning. Our only option would thus seem to be that of locating this ideality within a folding over of the fabric of communicative praxis itself. The performance of a reduction on the world of discourse and action as experienced, if indeed there is still some utility in the language of *epochē* and reduction, will be discerned to be at work within the interstices of our linguisticality and historicity. Reflection will involve not a move to another standpoint but ways of moving about in our everyday engagements. Distanciation makes possible the understanding and evaluation of our participation,

interpretations, 'vigilance', ultimately responsibility, seems to me to be a transference to the field of writing of an ideal relationship between subject (writer) and object (writing) which is nothing short of metaphysical. It is as if having admitted the ineliminability of absense, alterity, otherness in writing, that all the old values of directness, contact, and dare one say it, presence (the presence of the author to his reader) can be reinstated at another level." *Journal of the British Society for Phenomenology*, Vol. II, No. 3, 1980, p. 231.

not from a vantage point beyond it, but from the changing perspectives within it. As a consequence, meaning falls out as a duality of expression and signification.

This brings us to our decisive point about meaning. Expressive meaning qualified by reflection and distanciation slides into *signitive* meaning. Our introduction of signitive meaning does not mark out another level, either higher or lower, nor does it indicate a domain alongside that of expressive meaning. It is rather a further detailing of the configurative process of expressive meaning as leavened by reflective distanciation and critical disengagement, illustrating a play of idealities within discourse and action, through which a repetition of expressed meaning is effected. The first point to be underscored about the deployment of signitive meaning is that it adheres to the space of communicative praxis; the shift from expressive to signitive meaning is more that of a consummate reciprocity unfolding within the holistic fabric of the hermeneutical space of communicative praxis than of a progression from one level to another. The second point to be underscored is that signitive meaning involves a play of idealities which are themselves situated within the history of discourse and action. The third point is that signitive meaning is borne by recollection and repeatability; signitive meaning enables us to talk about various particularized configurations of expressive speech and expressive action as being in some sense the same.

The role of idealization in signitive meaning requires particular attention because the language of ideality is so freighted with metaphysical and epistemological sedimentations that its very use in a hermeneutics of communicative praxis becomes suspect. It gathers within its philosophical history the metaphysical difference of universal ideas and particular entities, the axiological difference of ideal structures and actual states of affairs, and the epistemological difference of transcendental conditions for knowledge and putative facts as known. The singular merit of Merleau-Ponty's suggestive probings of the "field of ideality," as that which at once acquaints us with and enables us to prevail over the facticity of our concrete involvements with nature and history, is that they initiated a disassemblage of these sedimented metaphysical, axiological, and epistemological constructs. Admittedly, Merleau-Ponty is still interested in a salvage operation of rescuing a vestigial sense and relevance of Husserl's celebrated phenomenological reduction, from which "the most important lesson" to be learned is "the impossibility of a complete reduction."[9] In this lesson it is difficult to sort out that which has been appropriated from Husserl's rather

---

[9]*Phenomenology of Perception,* p. xiv.

intricate program of phenomenological, transcendental, and eidetic reduction, and that which has been subject to deconstructionist critique. It is relatively clear, however, that the field of ideality of which Merleau-Ponty speaks is in no sense separable from the existential posture of perception which provides the central topic in Merleau-Ponty's existential phenomenology. The field of ideality is ensconced within the interstices of the field of perception. Whereas according to Husserl the ideality of the perceptual noema or cogitatum, the perceived object as meant, is given as a meaning only after the performance of a reduction that yields the transcendental field of subjectivity, structured by the intentionality of the ego-cogito-cogitatum complex, for Merleau-Ponty idealized noemata are inserted into the density of a functioning, precognitive intentionality that already comprehends the world.

Merleau-Ponty's interest in the field of ideality was motivated principally by his concern to provide a phenomenological description of the structure and dynamics of perception. However, insofar as speech and language were seen by him as being part of the phenomenal field, his explorations led him straightway to a search for the functioning of ideality in linguistic performance.[10] But it was in the thought of his fellow countryman Paul Ricoeur, in his confrontation and dialogue with the growing company of structuralists during the sixties and seventies, that the distanciation of discourse and the ideality of language became an all-absorbing problematic. For Ricoeur, the text becomes the paradigm of distanciation in communication, displaying a primitive type of distanciation in the surpassing of the event of saying by the meaning of what is said, which can then be inscribed in writing. From this primitive type of distanciation a procession of other forms follows: the surpassing of the intentions of the original speaker by the inscribed expression; the surpassing of the original audience through textual embodiment; and the surpassing of the limits of ostensive reference to things by a metaphorical reference to the world of the text.[11]

Ricoeur works out his theory of distanciation, and the associated notion of meaning in communicative discourse, through a continuing conversation with the Lebanese linguist Émile Benveniste and the German logician Gottlob Frege. From each he inherits a set of distinctions. Benveniste supplies the distinction between the lexical sign as the basic unit of language and the sentence as the basic unit of discourse. Frege supplies the distinction between sense *(Sinn)* as the ideal object

---

[10] Some interpreters of Merleau-Ponty's thought, such as for example James Edie, have argued that Merleau-Ponty's interests, and particularly in the later phases of his philosophical development, were geared specifically in the direction of the philosophy of language. See the chapter "Merleau-Ponty's Structuralism" in Edie's book *Speaking and Meaning* (Bloomington: Indiana University Press, 1976).

[11] *Paul Ricoeur: Hermeneutics and the Human Sciences,* pp. 131–144.

intended by the proposition and reference *(Bedeutung)* as the claim to reach reality. Language, functioning on the syntactical level, is a complex of phonological and lexical signs which relate only to each other. Discourse, functioning on the semantical level, sees the sentence escape its linguistic closure as it becomes the saying of something *by* a speaker, *for* a hearer, *about* something. The syntactics of language provides only a prior condition for the semantics of discourse, in which the exchange of messages by a speaker about the world takes place. Language provides the system of signs. Discourse provides the "eventful" performance.[12]

Ricoeur's next move is to graft this distinction by Benveniste between linguistics and discourse onto Frege's distinction between sense and reference. The ideal objects of sense, like phonological and lexical signs, are purely immanent. They are the meanings intended by propositions, but these meanings remain within the sphere of immanence. They have no truth value. Reference, properly understood, is the truth value of the proposition, enabling one to pick out that which is real. The Fregean notion of reference can thus be used to distinguish discourse from the immanental play of signs within language. "Language," says Ricoeur, "has no relation with reality, its words returning to other words in the endless circle of the dictionary. Only discourse, we shall say, intends things, applies itself to reality, expresses the world."[13] Although we find Ricoeur's analysis of the interplay of sign-system and event in the performance of discourse to be a considerable contribution, and his transmutation of Frege's notion of ostensive reference into a metaphorical reference to the world of the text highly suggestive, we are compelled to propose certain emendations in Ricoeur's overall project. The one has to do with his narrow understanding of "sign," which imposes undue restrictions on what we call signitive meaning. The other has to do with the issue of the origin of idealities displayed in the texture of signitive meaning.

To restrict sign to the sign-system of linguistics (phonology and lexicography), or even to use linguistics as a basis for the understanding of semiological problems (the view of Saussure, which at least in part has been taken over by Ricoeur), unduly delimits the range and power of signification. The sign overflows its linguistic determination. Along

---

[12] "The signs of language refer only to other signs in the interior of the same system so that language no more has a world than it has a time and a subject, whereas discourse is always about something. Discourse refers to a world which it claims to describe, express or represent. . . . While language is only a prior condition of communication for which it provides the codes, it is in discourse that all messages are exchanged. So discourse not only has a world, but it has an other, another person, an interlocutor to whom it is addressed." *Ibid.*, p. 133.

[13] *Ibid.*, p. 140.

with the linguistic signs of phonology and lexicography there are natural signs, like sedimented fossil imprints in rocks and the canals of Mars, which indicate the existence of a prehistoric world and the possible presence of intelligent life on our planetary neighbor; there are various types of artifactual signs, such as the mark of a branding iron, the trademark on a piece of furniture, and the signature on a painting; there are signs in the medium of body motility, such as the signals by the official on the athletic field and the policeman controlling traffic; and there are signs indicating a sacramental view of the world, such as the partaking of bread and wine in a religious ceremony. Not only are linguistic signs but a region within a broader field of semiology; each of the signs within the panoply of communicative behavior needs to be studied and understood within its particular context of associations.

The notion of sign implicated in our approach to signitive meaning has broader parameters than those delimited by linguistics. The signification operative on the phonological and lexical level borrows its structure and dynamics from a more encompassing semiological field. But there is a yet more global context surrounding linguistics and semiology alike, traces of which are discernible in the workings of signification in each of these special sciences. This wider global context is the holistic space of hermeneutics. Linguistics slides into semiology and semiology slides into hermeneutics. This passage from linguistics to hermeneutics via semiology determines the sign as it is operative in signitive meaning as *hermeneutical sign*. Signification becomes qualified by interpretation. Signs, on whatever level and in whatever context of associations, do not simply indicate a sense. They indicate a sense already infused with interpretation. Not only are the signs that regulate the political and religious life of a community infused with an interpreting social memory and a projection of a future quality of life, the lexical signs of linguistics are themselves inscribed against the backdrop of interpretation. Interpretation is at work both in the writing and in the reading of the dictionary. The decision to include some words and exclude others, the decision to flag some senses of an included word as being archaic and other senses as current, and the decision to close the entries and consider the text complete, are all decisions carried through in the context of interpretation. This does not mean, however, that the various special branches of linguistics and semiology (phonology, lexicography, grammar, and semiotics) cannot treat the indicating function of signs within the context of the methodological requirements and prescriptions of these branches as special sciences. These special disciplines retain their legitimate and important function. Neither linguistics nor semiology is dethroned as a special science. The point at issue is rather that the odyssey of signitive meaning illustrates an expanded texture of the sign, interwoven within the interstices of hermeneutical space. The sign, inscribed and deciphered, *is taken as* indicating such and such. To this extent Nietzsche was correct when he said that there are no facts but only interpretations.[14]

The second issue prompted by Ricoeur's essay "The Hermeneutical Function of Distanciation" involves the question of the origin of the idealities displayed in signitive meaning. In discussing the first issue we recommended a broader context for the understanding and use of sign than that suggested by Ricoeur in his dialogue with the structuralists. In discussing the second issue we undertake a reconsideration of the role of idealization in the formation process of signitive meaning to see if the strategy of investigation might be shifted further away from the paradigm of epistemological inquiry that has dominated modern reflections on the meaning of meaning. Discourse as a variegated composite of speaking, writing, and language illustrates the role of idealization on a variety of levels—phonemic, lexical, syntactical, semantical, and textual. Phonemes, the words in the lexicon, forms of grammar, rules that govern the semantics of the sentence, and textual paradigms are all part of a web of ideality. In the performance of speech and writing one finds oneself already working with these idealities. They are, as it were, "called upon" in our communicative activities as we make our way about in the world. Like Mount Everest, simply there to be climbed, phonemic distinctions, rules of grammar, and ideal semantical objects intended by propositions seem to have a somewhat similar status. One is tempted to speak of them as "givens." Now we urge that it is precisely this temptation, fostered by the modern epistemological paradigm, that needs to be resisted, and that an effort be made to resituate these idealities more squarely within the ongoing formative process of communicative praxis. If one indeed persists in speaking of idealities as "givens," then it must be added that they are given *in* praxis and not *to* praxis.

In dislodging the question of the origin of the idealities in discourse from the epistemological paradigm, we are setting aside the legislated either/or in the dichotomies of the conceptual versus the empirical and the a priori versus the a posteriori, as well as disengaging the positing of external givens.[15] Our question "How does ideality take its rise within

---

[14] *The Will to Power,* trans. Walter Kaufmann and R. J. Hollingdale (New York: Random House, 1967), section 481.

[15] At this juncture we are in basic agreement with Wilfred Sellars's own version of the deconstruction of the "myth of the given" and his persistent attack on the given as an ineluctable feature of epistemological foundationalism. See particularly his essay "Empiricism and the Philosophy of Mind" in his book *Science, Perception and Reality* (New York: The Humanities Press, 1963). The route which leads us to a critical deconstruction of the given is admittedly different from that followed by Sellars, but the results are

the closely knit unitary phenomenon of communicative praxis?" should not be confused with the question "What is the empirical basis for the idealities of discourse?" The latter question continues a commerce with an epistemological programmatic of delivering foundational referents and privileged representations. Our notion of communicative praxis is not designed to deliver yet another empirical foundation for the panoply of idealities in the patterning of everyday speech and action. Nor does our project move in the direction of an a priori of discourse in the form of invariant rules and ideal objectivities that structure the manifold of empirically discrete instances of speaking and acting. Ideal objects, as Husserl already saw, but unfortunately not clearly enough, do not have their origin in some *topos ouranos* and then become actualized through a fall into language and history.[16]

Our question regarding the role of idealization in signitive meaning takes the form of a quest for the solicitation of idealities within the preobjective and presubjective intentionality of expressive speech and action. Before speaking is thematized as an empirical speech act in contradistinction to the logical system of language, it unfolds as an

---

remarkably similar in their presentation of challenges to any future epistemological theory. We do, however, harbor some reservations about Sellars's implied restrictive meaning of myth in his phrase "myth of the given." Myth is itself a positive feature in the history of expressive speech and expressive action. The notion of the given that is at issue is not so much a myth as it is a sedimented philosophical protocol that needs to be set aside.

[16] In some of his later works, and particularly in his seminal essay "The Origin of Geometry," Husserl began to resist the implications of his earlier transcendental idealism and pointed to a historical inscription of ideal objectivities within the density of a concrete life-world. Although still committed to his attack on a historicism that dissolved all experienced contents into the merely relative, in the latter period of the *Crisis* and the essay on geometry Husserl initiates a move to a more vibrant notion of historicity. The momentous import of this later work is that the relevance of history for both the data and the method of phenomenology is made manifest. Derrida perceives the import of this shift when he observes that "when, in the period of the *Crisis,* history itself breaks through into phenomenology, a new space of questioning is opened, one that will be difficult to maintain in the regional limits which were so long prescribed for it." *Edmund Husserl's Origin of Geometry: An Introduction,* trans. John P. Leavey (Stony Brook, New York: Nicolas Hays, Ltd., 1978), p. 29. Yet, Husserl's project, even in this later mature work of his, ultimately founders. It founders because his standpoint is never fully liberated from that of an absolute transcendental consciousness and the intentional acts of the ego. History breaks through into phenomenology but it is not given its due as the bearer of meaning. The origin of meaning is still sought for within the folds of a transcendental intrasubjectivity, the result of a constituting act of intentional consciousness. Admittedly, this intentional consciousness is now seen as laboring *with* other intentional consciousnesses in a *"lebendige Bewegung des Miteinander." (Die Krisis der europäischen Wissenschaften und die transzendentale Phänomenologie,* herausgegeben von Walter Biemel, *Husserliana* VI: The Hague: Martinus Nijhoff, 1954, p. 380.) In the end, however, this referenced "being-with" borrows the intentionality of its communal life from the constituting performance of the ego in its solitary mental life. The "problem" of Husserl's fifth *Cartesian Meditation* continues to haunt him even in his later works.

expressive performance with a historical breadth and a temporalization that knits together a speaking, an already spoken, and a yet to be spoken. The temporal present of the speech act is not a knife-edge that cuts into an atomic instant of time, but rather a Jamesian "saddleback" that overlaps the past and the present. This historical and temporal breadth of the experienced present occasions the workings of an idealization that occurs in advance of any construction of time and history as a serial succession of instants and pre-exists the reification of speech acts as empirical data. The speech act as empirical datum is an abstraction and objectification of the moment of speaking (which is never an instantaneous present), as the system of language is an abstraction and objectification of the already spoken. The deconstruction of the empiricist–a posteriori and rationalist–a priori paradigms, and the recognition of a new inscription of historical time, make visible a broader texture of experience than that espoused by the empiricist tradition. The facticity of human involvement, infused with ideality as a result of the stance of distanciation, offers a broadened context and a more vibrant sense of experience and history. The odyssey of signitive meaning, borne by distanciation, charts its course through an interplay of speech and language as a play *within* rather than *against* history. This history, it needs to be underscored, is not an abstracted *eidos,* but history as experienced.[17]

We are looking for that window on the world from which we might get a glimpse of ideality from the side of the temporality and historicity that envelop every speech performance. This temporality of expressive speech is to be construed neither as the empirical succession of abstracted time points nor as a transcendental frame for representation. It is the temporality of meaning-sedimentation and meaning-formation, proceeding by dint of a projection of possibilities, patterning discourse as the interplay of the ideality of competence and the facticity of performance. It was the remarkable achievement of Heidegger's analytic of *Dasein* in *Being and Time* to point us in the direction of metaphysically deconstructed notions of temporality and historicity. However, at this stage of his philosophical development his projected deconstruction was still engineered from the standpoint of transcendental interests. Within a transcendental standpoint, even Heidegger's existentialized version of it, ideality is destined to take the shape of transcendental conditions. For this reason, as Heidegger himself realized, his

---

[17]This expanded notion of experience, as an alternative to the atomistic and epistemologically oriented view of experience in traditional empiricism, has been developed in some detail in an earlier work by the author. See Calvin O. Schrag, *Experience and Being: Prolegomena to a Future Ontology* (Evanston: Northwestern University Press, 1969).

analytic came up short in the effort to locate the origin of ideality in the temporality and historicity of communicative praxis.

One of the more audacious current attempts to shape ideality as a transcendental condition is exemplified in Habermas's notion of the ideal speech situation. The ideal speech situation is a projected control-free communicative exchange in which all participants are given an equal voice in submitting arguments, providing either refutations or justifying reasons. This ideal speech situation clearly is not an empirical state of affairs, either past, present, or future. It functions rather as a Kantian regulative principle, which motivates one's anticipation of a form of undistorted communication that can never be actualized but which nonetheless guides the concrete situation of communicative praxis. Traveling with this ideal speech situation is a pragmatic, consensual theory of truth. Truth is the accountability of theory and practice in the face of a projected consensus by a community of speakers and investigators.[18]

Certain problems in Habermas's attempt to provide a transcendental ground for ideality rather quickly come to the fore. In defining the ideal speech situation as bonded by the play of argumentation and counterargumentation, anticipating consensual agreement, Habermas suppresses the performance of discourse in its nonargumentative form. The expressive power of gestures, the function of illocutionary and perlocutionary acts, and the disclosing performance of mythopoetic language, are all effectively occluded.[19] There is also the question as to whether the anticipation of an ideal speech situation, grounding a universal pragmatics, indeed reflects a transcultural norm. The marks of ideality seem to borrow their determinations from the existential speech situation, in its varying cultural settings. But even more to the point at issue is Habermas's indebtedness to the transcendental/empirical doublet in formulating his standpoint of inquiry. Still working with a traditional notion of what counts as empirical or factual, Habermas is forced to install a transcendental region of ideality to account for the moment of critique and the drive toward consensus. It is precisely this transcendental/empirical doublet that falls away in the strategy of

---

[18] For a comprehensive discussion of Habermas's thought, including its various stages, the reader is referred to Thomas McCarthy, *The Critical Theory of Jürgen Habermas* (Cambridge: The MIT Press, 1981).

[19] For a more extended criticism of this consequence in the thought of both Habermas and Apel the reader is referred to the author's *Radical Reflection and the Origin of the Human Sciences* (West Lafayette: Purdue University Press, 1980), pp. 21–24. A similar criticism is offered by Mary Hesse when she chides Habermas for "the high human significance given to argumentation and rational justification as compared with other possible contenders, for example intuitive, artistic and spiritual faculties." *Revolutions and Reconstructions in the Philosophy of Science* (Bloomington: Indiana University Press, 1980), p. 220.

deconstructionist critique, yielding a more inaugural sense of experience and reason, as well as time and history.

Comprehended within this pre-epistemological context of experience, time, and history, antedating the construction of the empirical/transcendental dichotomy, which positions a manifold of pulverized, atomized, and sightless experience against the cognitive efficacy of ideas and ideals, the ideality within signitive meaning suffers both a retentional and a protentional qualification. Ideality is never simply a pure presence delivered from the past. Such was the peculiar consequence of Hegel's idealism, which located ideality within the body of essence understood as "that which has been" *(Wesen ist was gewesen ist)*. This led to a species of historicism which solidified that which has been as the locus of signitive meaning. Only after the events of the day have passed does the owl of Minerva begin its nightly flight of assessment and comprehension. Hegel's idealism remained incapable of recognizing the claim of the future upon the structure and dynamics of signification. This claim of the future, we maintain, is inscribed on the temporality of discourse. The fabric of discourse has both retentional and protentional threads. The spoken language, activated in the speech act and in writing, retains the ideality of sedimented linguistic elements (phonological and lexical) and semantical rules. One speaks and writes *because of* the retentional replay of ideality. But one speaks and writes also *in order to* express new configurations of meaning in the articulation of that which has not yet been said and written. This protentional push to the "not yet" of the future is a decisive moment in the life of discourse itself.

Thus far our attention has been focused principally on the signitive meaning and the play of idealities illustrated in discourse. Ideality, however, also pervades the deeds and actions of humanity. The idealities of expressive action, although not separable from discourse, do nonetheless assume different configurations by virtue of their direct insinuation into personal, social, and institutional behavior. In the facticity of communicative praxis these idealities are displayed in the formation of personal ideals, in the typification of social action, in institutional goals, and in the specific ethical norms that direct the course of human life. Yet, in addressing the ideality of individual and institutional action one must avoid a facile bifurcation of the idealities of discourse and the idealities of action. Not only is there an implied ethic of discourse in the language of promise-making and in the "giving of one's word," normative ideals are already at work in the signitive meaning of discourse as it strives for agreement and consensus. This is the salvageable insight of Habermas's appeal to ideality as a condition for discourse, after his use of the transcendental/empirical doublet has been set aside. However, it is in the field of human action that the sedimentation of ethical idealities is most clearly visible. What we do as individuals and institutions is shaped by the insinuation of ideals of action. Some of these ideals are very much in the forefront of consciousness; others are more recessed, eclipsed by a social forgetfulness or by the intrusion of self-deception and ideology. Idealization leaves its mark not only on the conscious envisagement of ideals but also on the twists and turns of self-deception and on the sedimentation of ideology. Hence, idealization requires its own critique, but this is a critique that can proceed only by tradeoffs within the play of idealities, demanding a choice of some as more preferable and more satisfactory than others. The critique proceeds from the side of our involvements in history, not from a vantage point above it.

The signitive meaning through which the facticity of expressive action moves to self-understanding, self-comprehension, and self-critique is borne by the play of idealities, which, like those of discourse, are embedded in the historicity of retentional and protentional dispositions. From the "ego ideal" in personal motivation and self-actualization to the social and institutional ideals of democracy, equality, and justice, the traces of ideality remain discernible. The ideals which guide self-actualization, as well as those that direct the course of society, are "forms of praxis." As forms of praxis they answer neither to a Platonic requirement, in which the becoming of praxis is a moving image of some transcendent idea, nor to a transcendental requirement, in which form is an *a priori condition* for action. The reality of praxis as a form resides in the forming process itself, which proceeds by way of an appropriation of established patterns of custom and habit and a distanciation and critical disengagement wherewith the established patterns are redescribed, modified, or straightway displaced. The idealities of action, like the idealities of discourse, exemplify both the sedimentation of past constellations of praxis and the open texture of new descriptions and new valuations. They suffer the historicity of a formation process, which determines their signitive meanings not as atemporal essences or clear and distinct ideas but as meaning structures calibrated by the restrospection of retention and the prospection of protention.

This retentional/protentional spanning within the texture of signitive meaning provides a new context for the placement of distanciation, reflection, and critique within the life of communicative praxis.[20] The

---

[20] Although we have continued to make use of the Husserlian terminology of retention and protention it should be remembered that Husserl worked out this distinction through an investigation of inner time-consciousness and thus remained committed to the primacy and privilege of the cogito. In our display of the texture of communicative praxis this primacy has been displaced and the retentional and protentional vectors have been situated within the space of sociohistorical formation.

new context is that of recollection, but recollection of a special sort. The notion of recollection itself is of course as old as the philosophy of Plato, and very likely older. Used by Plato to account for the apprehension of meanings that are neither fully known nor completely unknown in advance, *anamnesis* provided the path to an untrammeled rationality of mind united with the eternal forms. Although we have made an effort to disentangle our notion of signitive meaning from the classical metaphysical doctrine of essence, and its accompanying views of knowledge, we find in Plato's notion of recollection an originative suggestiveness, the resources of which still need to be exploited. A deconstruction of Plato's metaphysics, as Heidegger has shown, can bring to light the traces of an originative thinking which for the most part has been suppressed within the development of theo-metaphysical construction.[21]

The topic of recollection has been given particular attention by some of the leading representatives of recent Continental thought. Differing interpretations of recollection are at play in Husserl's "re-presenting" *(Vergegenwärtigung)*, Heidegger's "repetition" *(Wiederholung)* and "commemorative thinking" *(andenkendes Denken)*, Gadamer's "fusion of horizons," Ricoeur's "reminiscence of being," Foucault's "archaeology," Adorno's "memory of an archaic impulse," Derrida's "reiteration," and undoubtedly much more. Clearly in all of these cases the traditional Greek notion of recollection has been transmuted, but also the linkage of recollection with some species of signitive meaning remains explicit.

Too often, however, in the numerous modern and contemporary discussions of the philosophical importance of recollection, the seminal insights and prophetic voice of Søren Kierkegaard are forgotten. It is Kierkegaard who stands behind the paramount role played by recollection in modern thought. It was he who effected the decisive transmutation of the Greek notion of recollection into the modern notion of repetition.

---

[21] Fred R. Dallmayr, in his recent book *Twilight of Subjectivity: Contributions to a Post-Individualistic Theory* (Amherst: University of Massachusetts Press, 1981), has sketched the possibility for a critical appropriation of Plato's notion of recollection via a transposition of its revelatory function into the key of imaginative insight and poetic wisdom. "I consider it preferable, following Plato's suggestion in the *Meno*, to approximate cognition more closely to the process of *recollection*. In contrast, however, to interpretations which equate the Platonic notion with a priori principles of reflection or with a return to an unspoiled rationality I am inclined to the reverse view: one which sees recollection as a probing of opacity or as an effort to decipher the signals of a precognitive or prereflective practice—a practice which is not synonymous with individual or collective designs and which seems less akin to reason than to imagination (or to the poetic wisdom discussed by Vico)" (p. 251).

Repetition is a decisive expression for what "recollection" was for the Greeks. Just as they taught that all knowledge is a recollection, so will modern philosophy teach that the whole of life is a repetition. The only modern philosopher who had an inkling of this was Leibnitz. Repetition and recollection are the same movement, only in opposite directions; for what is recollected has been, is repeated backwards, whereas repetition properly so called is recollected forwards.[22]

With this notion of repetition, as fleshed out by Kierkegaard, a new sense of historicity breaks through into the milieu of modern thought. Hegel had already introduced history to the philosophical world, but within his system of idealism history remained in custody to the designs of the Absolute Idea. It was this essentializing of history that Kierkegaard brought under attack in his existential revolt, and curiously enough he found the resources for doing so in the Greek notion of recollection. However, it is the transmutation of recollection into repetition around which everything turns. In Kierkegaard's teaching that the whole of life is repetition the decisive feature is that meaning reclaims the past only through the projection of future possibilities as repetition is "recollected forwards." Now Kierkegaard's interest in the notion of repetition was motivated principally by ethico-religious concerns, but implicit in this notion were suggestions for a new posturing of meaning that extended beyond the domains of ethics and religion as Kierkegaard understood them. More specifically, the notion of repetition carried implications for an existential ontology, which Heidegger was quick to see and quick to appropriate. It is thus that, from one perspective at least, Heidegger's philosophy, and particularly that of the *Being and Time* period, can properly be understood as an ontologization and secularization of Kierkegaard's concrete ethico-religious concepts.[23]

Heidegger's ontologization of Kierkegaard's notion of repetition in *Being and Time* is a consequence of his effort to work out a fundamental ontology, proceeding from an analytic of *Dasein*. In this fundamental ontology, *Wiederholung*, as the repetition or reclamation of meaning, plays a crucial role. Repetition is the performance of projective understanding, within the holistic and ecstatic temporality of *Dasein*, reclaiming the preconceptual and preontological understanding of

---

[22] *Repetition: An Essay in Experimental Psychology*, trans. Walter Lowrie (Princeton: Princeton University Press, 1946), pp. 3–4. John D. Caputo, in his article "Hermeneutics as the Recovery of Man" (*Man and World*, Vol. 15, No. 4, 1982), provides an illuminating discussion of Kierkegaard's notion of repetition, and particularly as it informs Heidegger's notion of *Wiederholung*.

[23] For a demonstration of this ontologization by Heidegger of the Kierkegaardian notion of repetition, and related concepts, see the author's *Existence and Freedom: Towards an Ontology of Human Finitude* (Evanston: Northwestern University Press, 1961).

Being that is always manifest in one's everyday discourse and involvement in the world. Through this ontologization of the Kierkegaardian notion of repetition the Platonic concept of *anamnesis* suffers a consequential transformation and reapplication. That which is recalled is no longer the pure presence of the proper objects of *epistēmē* but rather a precognitive understanding of *Dasein's* being-in-the-world. Admittedly, this performance of reclamation in Heidegger's fundamental ontology still enlists the services of a transcendental form of questioning. The understanding that reclaims the meaning of Being is that of a comprehension of the existential-ontological possibilities within the panoply of everyday concerns. It proceeds via a description and interpretation of the existential-ontological structures present in concrete, existentiell-ontic experience. The existential-ontological structures, which Heidegger names "existentials" *(Existenzialen)* so as to distinguish them from "categories," replace the transcendental concepts that function as a priori and logical conditions in classical transcendental philosophy. Transcendental philosophy, when it is thought through and its inner resources are worked out, becomes existentialized. This is the momentous achievement of Heidegger's *Being and Time*.

But the analytic of Heidegger's fundamental ontology in *Being and Time* was designed only as a preparatory project in the study of the question of Being. And this preparatory project was itself reshaped through the shift of thinking in the celebrated *Kehre* of Heidegger's later philosophy. In this later philosophy the word "Being" itself undergoes erasure and is rewritten as B̶e̶i̶n̶g̶.[24] Being is effectively displaced as a transcendentally signified meaning, and the ontological-ontic difference and the designs of a fundamental ontology are surmounted. The *Kehre* announces a shift from the problematic of meaning, transcendentally formulated, to truth as disclosure through the language of poetical reminiscence. Repetition is transmuted into "commemorative thinking" *(andenkendes Denken)*. Heidegger realized that the question as to the meaning of Being *(Sinn des Seins)*, with its quest for ontological structures, was still too epistemologically oriented, and proposed in his later writings a shift to the disclosive power of language, particularly as illustrated in poetical speaking and writing.

This shift in the later philosophy of Heidegger has been characterized by Richard Rorty as a shift from systematic to edifying philosophy, exemplified not only in the later thought of Heidegger but also in the later Wittgenstein and in the elucidations and maieutic artistry of Nietzsche and Kierkegaard. It was as though the curious destiny of Heidegger's *Kehre* was to be at once a "return" to the edifying use of

---

[24]*Zur Seinsfrage* (Frankfurt: Vittorio Klostermann, 1956), pp. 30–36.

repetition in the seminal reflections of Kierkegaard. As edifying philosophers, Kierkegaard and the later Heidegger, according to Rorty, no longer propose world views and arguments which somehow mirror the nature of things, but rather become participants in a conversation that offers satires, parodies, and aphorisms. They display a revolutionary stance, in which the constructs of systematic philosophers are disassembled and the infirmities in the vocabulary of professional philosophy are exposed. This involves a shift away from the representational language of formal philosophical discourse and a move in the direction of poetically inspired elucidations. It flags an appetition for the new and the unsaid, and accentuates the role of imaginative redescription. "Edifying philosophers want to keep space open for the sense of wonder which poets can sometimes cause—wonder that there is something new under the sun, something which is *not* an accurate representation of what was already there, something which (at least for the moment) cannot be explained and can barely be described."[25]

Our placement of the notions of recollection and repetition as pivotal notions in recent philosophy, and our more extensive discussion of their role in the philosophies of Kierkegaard and Heidegger, have been undertaken to provide the proper context in which to address two critical issues that travel with our new approach to signitive meaning. The issues are old ones. They are the issues of identity and reference. Our hope is that something new might be said about them.

Our effort to find the traces of signitive meaning within the workings of a distanciation, idealization, and recollection, wherewith one's participatory life in discourse and action is penetrated and comprehended, has brought us to a decisive juncture. We have encountered the requirement to move beyond expressive meaning so as to provide a posture of critical understanding and reflective assessment of the facticity of our involvements. This move beyond expressive meaning we have named the move to meaning in the mode of signification, attended by a new emphasis on the hermeneutical functioning of the "sign" as a mediator between the retentionality and protentionality of historical experience. The mantle of idealities in signitive meaning allows for the repeatability of meanings that issue from expressive discourse and action and in turn legitimates talk of their sameness within the history of communicative praxis. It is this issue of sameness that becomes an unavoidable problem for any theory of signitive meaning.

Our intention is to liberate this issue from the inquiry standpoint of modern epistemological theory, in which the issue has been defined as

---

[25] Richard Rorty, *Philosophy and the Mirror of Nature* (Princeton: Princeton University Press, 1979), p. 370.

the "problem of identity," propelling a search for stable and invariant meanings as the proper objects of knowledge. This search for identical meanings has been directly linked with unexamined assumptions regarding the representational function of thought and language. The recollection of signitive meaning in communicative praxis, we maintain, exhibits a texture quite different from that of a representation of a past presence, identified through an act of pure cognition. Recollection is not representation, and sameness is not identity. The same signitive meaning can be found in various configurations of expressive discourse and action, bearing the imprint of repeatable phonemic and grammatical elements, semantical objectivities, and idealizations of personal and institutional life. The "sameness" of signitive meaning, however, is not the self-identity of an idea, essence, or noema, unmolested by time and becoming, perpetually in "reserve," like the inactive militia, and up for recall as dictated by the turn of events.

Husserl's theory of meaning provides an instructive lesson in the functioning of repetition as the vehicle of signification, although what one learns from this lesson has principally a negative effect. *Bedeutung,* according to Husserl, is delivered through the signifying power of expression, which proceeds by way of a reproduction of a presentation in the act of "re-presenting" *(Vergegenwärtigung).* In this operation of re-presenting, an invariant, atemporal, ideal noema is called forth. Meaning as a noematic structure is delivered through an act and process of re-presenting. Noemata fall out as "privileged representations" that mirror the eidetic nature of things.[26]

According to Husserl, names offer the clearest examples of the representational character of signitive meaning. Napoleon as "the victor of Jena" and Napoleon as "the vanquished at Waterloo," as different meanings naming the same object, are noematic idealities, whose presence can be repeated, called up time and again.[27] They provide partial perspectives of the more encompassing meaning of Napoleon as a historical figure, to which of course other perspectival noemata, such as "the initiator of the French legal code," can be added. The lesson to be learned from this exercise of collating profiles in the search for the "true" meaning which somehow mirrors the reality of Napoleon is that the procedure of representation collapses under its own weight. The real presence of that which is represented dissolves into a temporalized and historicized sedimentation and accrual of interpretive horizons.

---

[26] For a discussion of the epistemological weight placed on representation, in both classical phenomenology and analytical philosophy, see Rorty's chapter on "Privileged Representations" in *Philosophy and the Mirror of Nature.*

[27] *Logical Investigations,* trans. J. N. Findlay (London: Routledge & Kegan Paul, 1970), p. 287.

"Napoleon" signifies not the abstracted profiles of his "presented" deeds and actions, but his reception by the community of interpreters of his day and by subsequent historians. Involved in this reception and interpretation are not only his explicit utterances and accomplished deeds, but also his tacit intentions, unconscious motivations, and the inscriptions of ideology in his thought and action. The significance of "Napoleon" is thus the result of the play of interpretations and reinterpretations, the fusion of variant horizons, and the accretion of historical profiles. The texture of the signitive meaning of Napoleon as a model for the Civil War general George McClellan ("the Little Napoleon") is not that of a representation of a given presence in the person and life of Napoleon but rather an interpreted text of historical inscriptions. The sedimented signitive meanings of the traits and deeds of Napoleon congealed into noematic structures and ideal types have their origin in the descriptions, interpretations, and assessments within the communicative practices of the responding community of inquirers. Recollection is the reminiscence and reenactment of these communications and practices.

The problem of meaning in the epistemological literature has been accompanied by the problem of reference. What the epistemologist cannot do with meaning he hopes to do with reference. Often the two are proposed as the proverbial two sides of the same coin. Both Frege and Husserl saw reference as the fulfillment of meaning. Meaning delivers the "what," and reference delivers the "that" to which meaning is somehow attached. And reference, like meaning, according to the modern epistemological paradigm, remains within the purview of representation. An epistemic claim, according to this paradigm, if properly engineered, will hook into the referent, be it an object, a state of affairs, or a semantical construct, in such a way that apodicticity will result. Again, our notion of recollective signitive meaning undermines, at least as a privileged and necessary starting point, this epistemologically laden concept of reference. As a consequence of our reposturing of the sign as hermeneutical, reference is the taking of something *as* something (be it a perceptual object, a phenomenal property, or a historical event), *as* a figure against a background, *as* a text within a context, *as* a happening within a horizon of happenings. The epistemological construct of a region of "pure facts" and untarnished givens is disassembled. That which is recalled in communicative praxis is expressive discourse and action infused with interpretation, bearing the inscriptions of speakers and actors, and the response to this speech and action by the community of inquirers.

Reference as the taking of something as something in the performatives of discourse and action remains unproblematic so long as one desists from requiring of it a representation of reality. One takes something as something by making it a topic of discourse, a motivation for action, a goal to be accomplished, a utensil to be used, a deed to be valued, an artistic performance to be appreciated. Reference displays, as it were before our very eyes, the topics in our conversations and the happenings in our social practices. Rorty appropriately cautions us against confusing "talking about" with "reference"; the former "is a common-sensical notion" while the latter is "a term of philosophical art."[28] In our communicative praxis we talk about rather wide-ranging topics—fictional characters, mythical creatures, historical personages and events, DNA, perceptual objects, works of art, and political policies. The bane of the epistemological notion of reference is that it seeks to confine us to the isolable elements of the "really real," principally physical objects or phenomenal properties. The discourse of communicative praxis, imbued as it is with an unavoidable polysemy and metaphoricity, is geared not to the establishment of a correspondence of word and reality mediated by representation, but rather to a disclosure of patterns of sedimented perspectives and open horizons. The reference of signitive meaning is a performance of disclosure rather than an identification of things and properties as the basal elements of reality. What is talked about and disclosed is "the world," "work," "experience," or even "being," but not any of these as candidates for metaphysical or transcendental "signifiers" and "signifieds." They mark out the topology of communicative praxis and circumscribe the holistic space of our expressive participation and involvement in speaking and acting.

Our intention has been to show how the recollection operative in signitive meaning is a reminiscence of forms and patterns in communicative praxis rather than a recall of isolable essences and properties. This has occasioned a shift away from the epistemological paradigm of modern philosophy and its preoccupation with theories of meaning and reference that purport to lead us ever closer to epistemological foundations. This recollection, we have seen, following the suggestions of Kierkegaard and Heidegger, exhibits a protentional directionality. It is a recollection which, as Kierkegaard says, is "recollected forwards." And again we see how temporality and historicity are allies rather than foes of signitive meaning. The epistemologists of meaning and reference, frightened by temporality, sought the security of a pure presence, anchored either in an invariant essence or a fixed phenomenal property, which could be reproduced in an act of representation that defined the instant of knowledge. In a hermeneutical display of meaning the "dis-

---

[28] *Philosophy and the Mirror of Nature*, p. 289.

tance" from the past is acknowledged not as a coefficient of adversity for understanding but as an open horizon for a fusion and redescription of the varied configurations of discourse and action—a horizon which contains, in the words of Rorty, "the potential infinity of vocabularies in which the world can be described."[29] By virtue of the combined movements of distanciation, reflection, and critique the patterns of discourse and action can be described and redescribed in multiple ways. Through these descriptions and redescriptions the facticity of our involvements in the life of expressive speech and action is comprehended and understood. The web of facticity that situates our communicative praxis is penetrated by recollective thinking.

---

[29] *Ibid.*, p. 367.

CHAPTER FOUR

Understanding and Explanation
as Ways of Interpretation

Our preceding discussion of expressive and signitive meaning has
brought us into the clearing of the hermeneutical demand. This demand, as the demand for interpretation, falls out as a double requirement of understanding and explanation. In probing the texture of
communicative praxis we have found within its intertexture a display of
both expressive and signitive meaning. Our participation in the discourse and social practices in which we are historically stationed is a
display of expressive meaning. This display of meaning within the
facticity of speaking and acting defines our inherence in the world. This
is meaning as it is lived and relived in the quotidian performances of
everyday life. But there is also resident within the dynamics of communicative praxis the moment of signification. We not only express meaning in our lived-through communicative praxis, we also signify it. We
not only participate in various forms of life, we comprehend them by
penetrating them with thought. This requires, as we have seen in the
previous chapter, a distanciation from the performances of communicative praxis so as to render them comprehendible. Through this
distanciation expressive meaning slides into signitive meaning as communicative praxis folds over, becomes reflexive, in such a way that a
repeatability of sense is occasioned. We were thus led to an examination of distanciation, idealization, and recollection and the part they
play in the ongoing dynamics of discourse and action. Our uses of
language and our engagements in social practices invite a comprehension of them through reflection and critique. In all this we observed the
announcement of hermeneutics as a *critical* hermeneutics.

These previous discussions now bring us to the hermeneutical demand as a dual requirement of understanding and explanation. The
slide of expressive meaning into signitive meaning by way of distancia-

tion opens up the space of the workings of understanding and explanation. We speak of these as constituting a dual or double requirement because they are jointly implicated in the project of interpretation which the communal play of meaning solicits. Understanding and explanation are coemergent forms of communicative praxis that are prompted by the demand to comprehend the configurations of sense inscribed on it. As we will attempt to show, the postures of understanding and explanation, although providing distinguishable moments and traces, are inseparably bonded in the workings of interpretation and comprehension. They are, in the piquant locution of Thomas Hardy, "twin-halves of an august event."

The arts and the sciences, since their deliverance to mankind by Prometheus, have been challenged to respond to the inscriptions in the texts of human discourse and in the texture of social practices. There have been recurring tendencies, however, and particularly in modern and contemporary thought, to divide the labor between the arts and sciences in such a way that the former are assigned to a mentalistic order of understanding and the latter to a physicalistic order of explanation. Discourse about mind, we are told, falls within the province of understanding, which apparently humanists do best, while discourse about matter falls within the province of explanation, guarded, and at times somewhat jealously, by the practitioners of scientific inquiry. This bifurcation of understanding and explanation, congealed into separate disciplines, has effectively concealed their common origin in the play of communicative praxis. The sorting out of the humanities as the special custodians of the meanings set forth by communicative praxis is colored by more than a tincture of arbitrariness. Natural science, seen as a *doing* of science and a process of discovery, is as much a venture of communicative praxis as is any special humanistic endeavor. The arts and the sciences in their originative postures are joint ventures of "making sense together," to borrow from the title of John O'Neill's provocative book on the science and the art of doing sociology.[1]

This ongoing process of making sense together, in response to the hermeneutical demand for interpreting the text of human discourse and the texture of human action, is patterned as a double performance of understanding and explanation. In this double performance we find a mixed discourse of expression, persuasion, reference, and narration, as we observe the employment of metaphors, models, and myths. Because of this mixture of modes, aims, and genres of discourse in understanding and explanation alike, we need to be particularly wary of the

---

[1]*Making Sense Together: An Introduction to Wild Sociology* (New York: Harper & Row, 1974).

insinuation of the tempting and facile dichotomies of logic and metaphor, model and myth, reference and evocation, the scientific and the humanistic. These dichotomies, in conjunction with the continuing legacy of the Cartesian split between *res extensa* and *res cogitans*, have become solidified through the petrification of epistemological and metaphysical interests. The destiny of these dichotomies as illustrated in more recent philosophical position-taking has congealed into an acrimonious methodological dispute between the proponents of explanation and the friends of understanding.

Wilhelm Dilthey, as is well known, was very much in the center of this dispute and debate, and unwittingly may have contributed to its intensification. His program for humanistic studies *(Geisteswissenschaft)* was guided by the distinction between *verstehen* and *erklären,* which separated the contents of the *Geisteswissenchaften* from those of the *Naturwissenschaften.* "Nature we explain; man we understand," says Dilthey in one of his most often quoted declarations.[2] Now if space would permit, it could be successfully argued that this one-liner by Dilthey is a somewhat overly exaggerated peroration of his mature hermeneutical reflection. Yet, it cannot be denied that Dilthey was profoundly responsible for the installation of the dichotomy of nature and spirit as it pertained to the tasks of explanation and understanding, and it is doubtful whether the resources of his own reflection were adequate for overcoming this unacceptable opposition.

For the most part, the controversy in recent times between the friends of understanding and the proponents of explanation has been staged as a methodological debate in which understanding and explanation are presented as candidates of opposing parties with alternative platforms for a theory of cognition. They both promise a surefire epistemological access to the facts of the case at issue. But these methodological and epistemological interests travel with metaphysical presuppositions, either tacit or explicit. The epistemological dualism of understanding and explanation works hand in glove with the metaphysical dualism of spirit and nature, which tends to be reduced to a dualism of the mental and the physical. The facts of mental phenomena are then judged to be different *toto caelo* from the facts of physical phenomena.

Within this dualistic framework, of both an epistemological and a metaphysical sort, the controversy surrounding the claims of understanding and explanation has assumed a variety of forms. There are the die-hard reductionists who claim that all facts can be gathered into one epistemological net, either that of understanding or that of explanation.

---

[2] *Gesammelte Schriften,* Vol. 5: *Die Geistige Welt* (Stuttgart: B. G. Teubner, 1951), p. 144.

This claim exhibits a desire to undermine the dualism by either reducing that which is understood to that which is eventually explained or spreading the mantle of understanding so broadly that it effectively covers all strategies of explanation, causal and structural. For the most part, however, the friends of understanding and the proponents of explanation have worked out another *modus vivendi* and have placed the locus of controversy elsewhere. Members of the *verstehende* school take on a disposition of philosophical tolerance in acknowledging the importance of explanation in rendering an account of the forces and patterns in nature while maintaining that the facts of human consciousness, mind, or spirit are properly understood rather than explained. And the proponents of explanation nurture their generosity in making room for understanding. The controversy then begins to center on the relative weight and cognitive importance to be attached to these two ways of knowing. Even some of the more adamant positivists recognized the contribution of understanding to scientific inquiry, but it was made clear to all those in the neighborhood that the role of understanding in cognitive matters was very limited. At best, understanding was a kind of prescientific, psychological intuition of how to set up a problem and formulate a hypothesis, which would then await its solution through the use of the resources of explanation. Useful for generating the proper heuristic frame of mind, understanding provided the anteroom through which one passes on one's way to the logico-empirical evidence that is delivered through strict verificationist procedures.

This display of generosity on the part of the friends of understanding and the proponents of explanation, straining to find in the opposing camp something to recommend after all, may exemplify a nobility of spirit that is commendable in its own right. Unfortunately, however, this may in the end add up only to an unnecessary expenditure of moral energy. What we wish to urge is that the traditional and longstanding controversy between the contestants in the fray proceeds from a format of inquiry and investigation that is itself suspect. This format of inquiry continues to be informed by ruminations on epistemological grounding and a spate of disguised metaphysical claims. Both epistemological and metaphysical constructionism, which define understanding and explanation as alternative species of knowledge and install an ontological cleavage of spirit and nature, disfigure the texture of communicative praxis. The hermeneutical project of making sense together, on the part of the human and natural sciences alike, installing the double requirement of understanding and explanation, occasions not the continuation of an epistemological problematic but rather a displacement of it. What the times require is a radical reflection on the status of epistemology as an autonomous discipline and a resituation of understanding and explanation into the wider space of communicative praxis. The criteriological rules constructed out of a presumed subject/object epistemic relation need to be suspended. There is thus a required negative moment of deconstruction and radical *epoché* that first makes possible any positive descriptions of the interplay of understanding and explanation within the folds of communicative praxis.

This wider space of hermeneutical ruminations, inviting a fresh approach to the understanding/explanation controversy, has already been opened up by the new slants on interpretation in the thought of Heidegger, Gadamer, and Ricoeur, and in Rorty's more radical move "beyond epistemology." Our response to this decisive turn in the reposturing of hermeneutics takes the form of a critical engagement with those responsible for the turn, and must itself be seen as a performance of communicative praxis in the ongoing conversation of mankind. We have already set the stage for our nonepistemological reclamation of the resources of understanding and explanation in our disassembling of the interior/exterior dichotomy in our discussion in chapter 2. The overextension of the metaphorical range of "interior" and "exterior," we have seen, has produced irreparable damage to the fabric of meaning. In our elucidation of the expressive meaning of discourse and action we sought to undermine this longstanding dichotomy applied to the interior contents of a solitary mental life cut off from its external behavioral manifestations, leading to the bifurcation of the private-expressive and the public-communicative domains. Now we are in position to see how the traditional rift between understanding and explanation also buys into the interior/exterior schematization. As an epistemic vector, understanding has been assigned the task of defining what transpires on the inside—inside the mind of a speaker, an author, or an agent performing a social activity—while explanation provides the proper reading of external and objective states of affairs. If this untested presuppositional complex is simply accepted, then it becomes inevitable that understanding and explanation will remain in opposition as alternative avenues to alternative sets of data, and methodological-epistemological disputes will become the order of the day. But it is precisely this presupposed and pointless opposition of interior and exterior, subjective and objective, that needs be set aside.

The displacement of this dichotomy becomes particularly relevant in regard to the proper placement of the author's and the actor's intentions in the much discussed "intentional fallacy" issue. This was the reef on which all romanticist hermeneutics, inspired chiefly by Schleiermacher, foundered. Construing understanding as a project of entering the mind of the author, romanticist hermeneutics glossed the communicative praxis operative in the text itself and choked off the surplus of meaning that overflows the intentions and motives of particular speakers and actors. Dilthey, in spite of his intermittent lapses into a romanticism of empathic identification, recognized with his notion of *Besserverstehen* that the author's intention does not have the last word on the matter of understanding. Proceeding from the performance of poetic imagination and creation, which comprised Dilthey's model for the expressive life of human culture in general, his notion of "better-understanding" was able to account for the surplus of meaning that surrounds the intentions of a particular artist or author, making it possible for those who are historically distanced from him to understand his work better than he did himself.[3]

The individual accomplishments of particular authors and particular actors are themselves situated along a horizon of both sedimented and possible meanings that remain open to new inscriptions of sense in another time and place. Our understanding of these accomplishments is always a response to their efficacy in shaping emergent trends and their reception by the community through which they achieve their significance. The reception and internal critique by the community of interpreters supplement the intentions of the original authors and actors and open dimensions of meaning that were unknown to them. Understanding is borne by the participatory praxis in this reception and critique. Understanding the significance of the American Revolution proceeds not by way of a representation of the ideas and intentions in the minds of the authors of the Constitution and the military and political actors who lived in the geographical space of the late eighteenth century. The meaning of the American Revolution resides in the configuration of the commitments and joint endeavors that responded to the occurrent threats to liberty and that anticipated future safeguards for the emerging nation. Understanding continues this responsiveness and anticipation in a continuing play of new interpretations. It is in this way that the Gadamerian "fusion of horizons" *(Horizontvershmelzung)* is effected. But this fusing of horizons has nothing to do with a dredging of solitary mental interiors. The displacement of the category of interiority for locating the sphere of thought and mind becomes crucial for clearing the path to the ways of understanding and explanation.

---

[3] For an illuminating discussion of this facet of Dilthey's approach to the cultural sciences see Theodore Plantinga, *Historical Understanding in the Thought of Dilthey* (Toronto: University of Toronto Press, 1980), Ch. 6. Paul Ricoeur also has provided a helpful summation of what is at issue in the notion of *Besserverstehen*: "To understand an author better than he could understand himself is to display the power of disclosure implied in his discourse beyond the limited horizon of his own existential situation." *Interpretation Theory: Discourse and the Surplus of Meaning* (Fort Worth: The Texas Christian University Press, 1976), p. 93.

After the path has been cleared through a dismantling of the stock categories of philosophy of mind and epistemology, which have their roots deep in the tradition of modern philosophy, understanding and explanation can be seen in a new perspective as forms of communicative praxis. As forms of praxis they are joint endeavors in the common and ongoing task of interpretation. Interpretation does not provide the mark for distinguishing understanding and explanation. Both the friends of understanding and the proponents of explanation in the traditional epistemological dispute misconstrued the workings of each by identifying interpretation with understanding. This was a confusion which stemmed principally from the tradition of romanticist hermeneutics, which viewed interpretation as a special case of understanding. Contra this tradition we maintain the "hermeneutical as" is already stitched into the project of explanation, and the "apophantical as" is operative in the development of understanding. Understanding and explanation share the space of interpretation.[4] Their distinctive contributions in the texture of communication will need to be located elsewhere.

We propose that the distinctive functions of their contributions be worked out through an exploration of the relative weight placed on the holistic and elemental perspectives of discourse and social practices. Understanding is geared principally to a reading of human thought and action in their configurative shapes and contextual wholes. Explanation fixes its attention on the constitutive elements. Interpretation is the ongoing play between the holistic and the elemental as illustrated in the interrelated progression of understanding and explanation. This duality of the holistic and the elemental in the project of interpretation has suffered the fate of solidifying into a *dualism* through the constructionism of epistemological/metaphysical position-taking, in which the holistic perspective congeals into *holism* (as was the case in idealism) and the elemental perspective congeals into *elementalism* (as was the case in positivism). Within the texture of communicative praxis the holistic and the elemental are intercalating moments within discourse and commingling profiles within the dynamics and structure of human action. They have no claim upon foundationalist principles, of either an epistemological or a metaphysical sort.

Discourse, as spoken and written, invites both a holistic and an elemental comprehension. In the dynamics of the dialogic encounter the sense of the communicated message is grasped as a whole, con-

---

[4]Ricoeur's contribution toward a clarification of this issue has been of considerable value to the semantics of hermeneutics. "The term interpretation," he writes, "may be applied, not to a particular case of understanding, but to the whole process that encompasses explanation and understanding." *Interpretation Theory,* p. 74.

textualized within the situation as defined by its purposes and goals. But this understanding is never complete, often erratic, and sometimes breaks down. When the achievement of genuine understanding is threatened there is a call for explanation, a request to analyze the elemental units (lexical meanings, grammatical usages, and semantical referents) to supplement the labor of understanding. Comprehension is the play between the grasping of the whole in a unitary act of synthesis and an apprehension of the constitutive elements through regressive analysis. The phenomenon of discourse as the intersection of speech and language provides us with a revealing example of such an interplay. The space of discourse encompasses wholes and parts. The holistic fabric cradles the speaker/hearer transaction as a narration by someone about something. In understanding the spoken and the written word there is a grasping of the world of the speaker and the world of the text, in which the word as spoken and written meets with the hearer and the reader in a fusion of perspectives and horizons. But this event of understanding is supplemented by a drive to explanation through a refocusing of attention on the constitutive units of language which always accompany the act of speaking. It is at this juncture that the explanatory force of linguistic science needs to be recognized. Linguistics, in its turn away from the speaking subject to the system and structure of language, offers explanations of phonemic differences, lexical units, and grammatical structures which always travel with discourse as illustrated both in speaking and writing.[5]

Comprehending a discourse thus swings to and fro between the moments of understanding and those of explanation. We have attempted to elucidate these moments through a description of the interfusion of the holistic and the elemental. Understanding and explanation alike "make sense" of the phenomenon of discourse, but they do so from different although complementary perspectives. Most generally put, these complementary perspectives move about in a space marked out by whole-part relationships. However, in one's use of the language of whole and part, which has enjoyed widespread employment in the philosophical tradition, one must proceed with some caution. One should be cautious about an uncritical appropriation of the whole-part relational schema because it is so easily co-opted by the epis-

---

[5] As Ricoeur has correctly observed, the uses of explanation in linguistic science are to be distinguished from those modeled after the causal-scientific paradigm traditionally employed by the natural sciences. "Today the concept of explanation is no longer borrowed from the natural sciences and transferred into a different field, that of written documents. It proceeds from the common sphere of language thanks to the analogical transference from the small units of language (phonemes and lexemes) to the large units beyond the sentence, including narrative, folklore, and myth." *Interpretation Theory*, p. 86.

temological paradigm that has informed philosophical reflection since the time of Descartes. In the tradition of modern epistemology parts function as simple ideas constitutive of complex ideas, or as atomic facts isomorphically connected with atomic and molecular propositions. In such an epistemological scheme of things parts are called upon to do duty in the service of epistemological grounding and the stage is set for a metaphysical elementalism. The elemental congeals into a foundational principle, both epistemologically and metaphysically defined. The counterthrust to this elementalism in the name of epistemological and metaphysical holism does not change matters much, insofar as it remains beholden to a foundationalist inquiry standpoint. This was the error of holism, in both its idealist and its romanticist expressions. Our use of the whole-part relationship, as it is operative within the structure and dynamics of discourse, undermines the epistemological problematic as it figured in the garden varieties of empiricism, rationalism, and romanticism. The whole-part relationship in hermeneutics is marked out by a different space than that which informs the philosophically incoherent pursuit of knowledge about knowledge. The elemental and the holistic, as they are set forth in the phenomenon of discourse, mark out the postures of explanation and understanding as different forms of interpretation and comprehension—different ways of *taking* the phenomenon *as* it bodies forth in communicative praxis.[6]

We have elucidated the interplay of holistic and elemental features in the interpretation and comprehension of discourse. It now must be illustrated how this interplay informs the interpretation and comprehension of human action, which in its amalgamation with discourse comprises the wider fabric of communicative praxis. Actions, like discourse, are understood and explained. An understanding of an action involves a comprehending or grasping of the performance of an action

---

[6]Charles Taylor has provided a version of the hermeneutical posturing of the whole-part relationship in his elucidation of the distinction between "partial" and "contextualized" expressions. "What we are trying to establish is a certain reading of text or expressions, and what we appeal to as our ground for this reading can only be other readings. The circle can also be put in terms of part-whole relations: we are trying to establish a reading for the whole text, and for this we appeal to readings of its partial expressions; and yet because we are dealing with meaning, with making sense, where expressions only make sense or not in relation to others, the readings of partial expressions depend on those of others, and ultimately of the whole." "Interpretation and the Sciences of Man," *The Review of Metaphysics*, Vol. XXV, No. 1, Issue 97, 1971, p. 6. Taylor's analysis, however, remains truncated at that decisive point where explanation begins to bear upon the status of what he calls "partial expressions." It is precisely here that the explanatory function of linguistics and semiology collaborates in a joint endeavor with understanding in making sense together. Unfortunately, his pronounced cleavage between explanation and understanding and the natural and the human sciences makes such a move impossible.

as a synthetic totality. Explanation contributes an apprehension of the constitutive elements within the action and the exercise of forces upon it. Working in concert, understanding and explanation achieve a comprehension of the action as being performed and as already performed. Action shows itself whilst in progress and as already accomplished. Even in attending to an action that has already been completed comprehension requires a resituation of the action within the context of its performative dynamics through a recollective imaginative variation. It is only by virtue of such a resituation and recollection that the action is salvaged from sliding into a solidified brute fact, a datum without intentionality and without motility.

The comprehension of acts of violence and acts of compassion involves both the synthesis of understanding and the analysis of explanation. We make sense out of the individual act of Pierre as he participates in the storming of the Bastille by attending to the action as a holistic envelopment of meanings that enjoy a concrescence in the performance of the action. The motives of his particular action are inseparable from the wider fabric of political, economic, and religious beliefs and practices which informs the background of his specific act. We understand the action within the context of this wider fabric, in which the particularities of his performance are embedded. However, as in the case of understanding a text there is no one-to-one correspondence between the text's meaning and the author's intention, so in understanding what an action means there can be no facile identification of the motive in the mind of the actor with the significance of the action. The meaning of Pierre's act of violence resides as much in the web of social beliefs and practices that surrounds his action as in the individual motives themselves. Indeed there are meanings of the action which may remain hidden from the conscious intending of what Pierre seeks to accomplish in his particular act, not only because he is unaware of the manifold formative influences that issue from his social and historical inherence but also because the meaning of his action remains open to new inscriptions by subsequent responses to the event. The community of interpreters that lives after him has a hand in the telling of the story of what his particular action means.[7]

---

[7] Ricoeur has succeeded in perceptively elucidating this wider fabric of meaning within a holistic, hermeneutical space, and in pointing us to its similarity with textual meaning when he observes: "Even more like a text, of which the meaning has been freed from the initial conditions of its production, human action has a stature that is not limited to its importance for the situation in which it initially occurs, but allows it to be reinscribed in new social contexts. Finally, action, like a text, is an open work, addressed to an indefinite series of possible 'readers'. The judges are not contemporaries, but subsequent history." "Explanation and Understanding," in *The Philosophy of Paul Ricoeur*, Charles E. Reagan and David Stewart, eds. (Boston: The Beacon Press, 1978), pp. 160–61.

The holistic space in which an action is understood thus extends beyond the delivered panoply of beliefs and practices that surrounds its performance to an expanding future of possible new interpretations and new descriptions. The meaning of an action is never an *idée fixe*. The holistic space of interpretation does not offer a comprehension of fully determinate sense. The full determination of sense is perpetually deferred. Yet, within this space of interpretation there is the moment of explanation that yields an analytical determination of the elemental constituents of action interwoven within its holistic fabric. The action of Pierre can be explained as well as understood. And it is explained by analytically sorting out the forces and influences that come to bear on the action in an effort to detail sequences and consequences. This effort at explanation has traditionally made use of appeals to "causes," "laws," and to the "facts" which are in some way accounted for by causal and lawlike processes. Such procedures, so long as they resist the lure of metaphysical and epistemological construction, retain their limited legitimacy. In these appeals an effort is made to dissect the action as an accomplished fact so as to get a perspective on the particular preconditions and forces and the sequential patterning of them. But this is to view the action only in its perspective as a product of the past, in terms of what Alfred Schutz would flag as its "because-motive" as distinguished from its "in-order-to-motive,"[8] and in its dissociation from the context of possible new descriptions by the ongoing community of interpreters. This is why explanation as a method of causal and structural analysis remains partial and incomplete and needs to work jointly with understanding in its reading of the historical inscriptions of actions as configurations within synthetic totalities. Explanation and understanding thus combine resources in a joint endeavor of making sense together. But the distinctive contribution of explanation in the interpretation of human behavior should not be glossed. The behavior of Pierre, as an effective force in the storming of the Bastille, can be explained in terms of the antecedents of existing social ideals, political options of the day, economic deprivation, parental influence, body chemistry, or even unconscious motivation. These various profiles and levels of Pierre's behavior in his act of violence can be mined to yield elements and relations which provide helpful information in the ongoing process of interpretation and comprehension. Contrary to some hermeneuticists, we do not oppose the effort to explain certain levels of human behavior and certain patterns

---

[8] *The Phenomenology of the Social World,* trans. George Walsh and Frederick Lehnert (Evanston: Northwestern University Press, 1967), pp. 86–96.

of human action. Dilthey simply overstated the case when he said, "Nature we explain; man we understand." And he overstated the case because there are perspectives of nature which lend themselves to understanding, and there are perspectives of human action that require the analysis of explanation.

Pursuant to our distinction between the ways of understanding and the ways of explanation, it should be noted that recent attempts to deal with the issue in terms of the distinction between causes and motives, as proposed for example by Elizabeth Anscombe,[9] although suggestive, suffer their own limitations. The positive fallout of such attempts resides in their contribution toward a clarification of the difference between human motivation and nonhuman, causal interaction among things. But this utility is limited because the meaning of cause that informs the language about things is rather straightforwardly and uncritically taken from Hume's program of epistemological skepticism. It is further limited because the meaning of motive remains psychologically defined and is isolated from its embeddedness within the intentionality of social practices and historical inscriptions. It is thus that the proponents of the cause/motive distinction leave us with problematic notions of each, and they succeed in overcoming the metaphysical/epistemological opposition of nature and spirit, the *Naturwissenschaften* and the *Geisteswissenschaften,* only by introducing another opposition, that of two heterogeneous language-games.

The linguistic hermeneutics of Peter Winch's interpretive social science does take us a bit further than does Anscombe's congenial settlement for the coexistence of two language neighborhoods. Winch recognizes clearly enough the explicit hermeneutical stance that is involved in understanding human action, and he does not run together, at least not as quickly as does Anscombe, the senses of "intention" and "intentionality." The distinctive point of Winch's version of linguistically oriented social science is that meaningful action is rule-governed and that we understand an action when we identify the context of rules in which it is embedded.[10] Now being attentive to the orchestration of rules in our speech and action is surely a good thing, and Winch, following Wittgenstein, has made an important contribution in showing how rules are at work in understanding. But what is required is a radicalization of Winch's position through a deconstruction of rules as "givens" for an untrammeled rationality, and a reinsertion of them into the texture of communicative praxis as achievements within a

---

[9] See particularly her book, *Intentions* (Ithaca: Cornell University Press, 1957).
[10] See his book, *The Idea of a Social Science* (New York: The Humanities Press, 1958).

process of historical formation. Linguistic hermeneutics needs to be positioned within the space of a wider cultural and critical hermeneutics.

A more pivotal issue for dealing with the understanding versus explanation controversy, we suggest, has to do with the *factuality* of the alleged facts which understanding purportedly understands and explanation purportedly explains. Ruminations on the meanings of "cause," "law," "motive," "intentions," and "rules" assuredly have their place, and continuing thought-experiments on their proper placement need to be performed. But often covered up in the interminable treatises on the meaning of these concepts and their proper usage are the problematic presuppositions concerning the status of "fact." It seems to be taken for granted that everyone in the vicinity knows what a fact is. The only problem for discussion then becomes whether facts are to be understood or explained. A fact is simply a fact, and apparently that itself is a fact. Facts are prejudged as the ineluctable brute givens of our experience. They are the bare bones of things, acts, or propositions, devoid of all tendons and tissues of interpretation. This bare-bones concept of fact, although a peculiar legacy of empiricism, also colored the project of phenomenology as "pure description." Drawing upon the constructionism at work in the Cartesian tradition, facts are sorted out into separate groupings of facts of nature and mental facts or facts of consciousness. The latter signifies a rather broad spectrum of events of sensing, feeling, willing, imagining, conceiving, and judging. Facts, both those of nature and of mind, are construed as *data*. They are the brute, given data that comprise the furniture of the world. They somehow fall from heaven as *datable* and *determinate*. This, we urge, is already a derivative and abstract construction on "fact" as the primordial facticity of lived-through experience in communicative praxis. Discourse and action are not given as atomistic and serialized brute data of words and deeds, but rather display an interwoven texture of wholes and parts, configurative tissues and partitive profiles, that enjoys a changing scene of meaning-formation. This is the facticity of communicative praxis, with its lived-through speech situations and its participatory action. What are understood and explained in our reflections on and thematizations of this communicative praxis are not separable brute data which come determined, waiting to be picked out, but rather interwoven wholes and parts which we seek to understand holistically and explain through an analysis of their constituted levels and elements. Approaching communicative praxis as a Heideggerian *Ereignis* of discourse and action, rather than as a collection of data, enables us to surmount at once the metaphysical dualism of nature and spirit and the accompanying epistemological dichotomy of understanding and explanation as separate modes of cognition.

Our effort to deformalize facts as data and reinsert fact into the facticity of the world of nature and history as abodes of human dwelling leads to a displacement of the traditional controversy surrounding the identification of "hard" and "soft" data. Humanists and humanistic social scientists have often been enjoined to settle for soft data, leaving the hard, knobby stuff for those who have the requisite quantifying procedures for nailing it down. This has tended to foster an increasing loss of nerve on the part of the humanistically oriented as they observed their soft data becoming progressively compacted through the advance of quantification and measurement. First "nature" had to be given over to the number crunchers, and then successive levels of "spirit"— neurological processes, bodily functioning, perception, and various objectified slices of human action—gradually succumbed to objectifying procedures. Perpetually regrouping after these onslaughts by the hunters for hard data, the humanists found themselves making their "last stand" on the turf of ethics, poetry, and religion—the final citadels of soft data. This scenario, we submit, is a mixture of comedy and tragedy. It illustrates comedy because it depicts the comic unawareness of the background of lived-experiences through which the merchant of hard data lives as he searches for his objective pot of gold. It illustrates tragedy because it leads to a loss of the *humanitas* of the *homo humans* within the very project of the science of man. The appropriate response to this state of affairs is not that of a new definition of the boundaries between hard and soft data, but rather a shift away from the abstract empiricism which supplied the props for this tragicomedy by first legislating this schematized opposition. It is at this juncture that the seminal reflections of Merleau-Ponty in his *Phenomenology of Perception* assume their revolutionary importance. Sensing that there was something fundamentally miscast in an abstract empiricism that construed perception as a mosaic of data—hard, soft, or somewhere in between—Merleau-Ponty instructed us in relearning to see the world from the side of the facticity of our embodiment and our concrete spatial orientation.

Understanding and explanation, in our reading, are situated within communicative praxis as moments of interpretive comprehension, penetrating the density of the facticity of our discourse and action. This follows in the wake of the deconstruction of understanding and explanation as epistemological connectors between events of knowing and data as known. Understanding and explanation are conversational and communal endeavors rather than mental acts of a lonely cognitive subject. And that which is talked about in these communicative practices and endeavors are the configurations in the ongoing play of discourse and action rather than brute facts as data, either "hard" or "soft," abstracted from our experience of things in nature and persons in society.

The resettlement of understanding and explanation as inhabitants of communicative praxis can now be seen as being of a piece with our earlier delineation of the slide of expressive meaning into signitive meaning. Interpretation as the co-working of understanding and explanation is the effort of making sense in a detailing of the configurations of expressive meaning in our speech acts, gestures, social practices, and institutional life, as these configurations solicit a reflection and critique through distanciation, idealization, and recollection. The holistic approach of understanding follows the endless display and surplus of expressive meaning, while the elemental approach of explanation, geared to an analytical development, is occasioned by the intentionality of signitive meaning. The discourse of explanation quickly becomes the discourse of signifier and signified. It makes use of signifiers that comport semantical and logical rules—rules that guide one's structural analyses, inferences, and predictions as the relevance of these rules is defined by the community of investigators. But the meaning of sign and the uses of signification in the project of explanation, as we have argued, continue to move within the wider play of interpretation. Semiology remains linked with hermeneutics. The signified is that which is *taken as* something signified. Hermeneutics becomes "universalized," and it can be properly said that we are condemned to interpretation.

The explicit linkage of understanding with praxis, which we are urging, was already achieved in Gadamer's hermeneutics, seen particularly in his emphasis on "application *(applicatio)* as an integral moment of understanding.[11] David Hoy, in his discussion of Gadamer's hermeneutics, has shown how this close connection between understanding and praxis recalls the Aristotelian notion of *phronēsis*.[12] *Phronēsis,* as a practical wisdom, was already understood by Aristotle as being inseparable from action. However, whereas for Aristotle the notion of the resident insight of practical wisdom within praxis pivoted principally around concerns about moral action, for Gadamer the practical wisdom of praxis is linked more directly to the project of interpretation, which Gadamer, following Heidegger, sees as involving not simply the interpretation of texts but also the more basic interpretation

---

[11] *Truth and Method* (New York: The Seabury Press, 1975), pp. 274–278.
[12] *The Critical Circle: Literature and History in Contemporary Hermeneutics* (Berkeley: University of California Press, 1978), chapter 2: "The Nature of Understanding: Hans-Georg Gadamer's Philosophical Hermeneutics."

of man's being-in-the-world. Thus, praxis for Gadamer becomes universalized in a way in which was not the case for Aristotle. Aristotle still saw the distinction between *theōria* (as a study of the universal and unchanging) and *praxis* (as practical wisdom about the particular and the changing) as articulating a genuine difference. Hence, Gadamer's hurried appropriation of Aristotle may not be as innocent with regard to the consequences as at first appears to be the case.

In his comprehensive study Hoy already points us, although somewhat obliquely, to a problem in Gadamer's use of Aristotle on this issue and to a more general problem in Gadamer's account of the theory/praxis issue. Hoy states the matter well in the following explication:

> The *applicatio* that, Gadamer insists, is involved in understanding is not the same kind of application defined by traditional epistemology. The question is not one of applying concepts or theories to a practical situation or a series of observations. The term is not used, furthermore, in the sense of 'applied sciences' or 'technological application.' Gadamer must explain how understanding occurs at all, not how understanding can be properly applied.[13]

It is modern epistemology and technology that are at fault for the misconstrual of "application." Application is not a derivative and secondary mode of knowing. It is a central and integral feature of understanding and need not wait upon the pronouncements of epistemology. Hoy's assurance that Gadamer does not see application as the instrumentation of theory is to be heeded. The *applicatio* of praxis is not the application of a fund of knowledge delivered by pure theory. What Gadamer learned from Heidegger is that praxis, in the guise of "circumspection" *(umsichtiges Besorgen),* accommodates its own "insight." Praxis is a way of living through life's involvements *and* already understanding them—although in a pre-ontological manner. This is Gadamer's *phronēsis* at work in praxis. Yet, the assurance that Gadamer will have no truck with the modern bifurcation of theoretical thinking and its practical application does not displace all the problems that Gadamer has brought upon himself through his quick appropriation of Aristotelian concepts and principles. Aristotle indeed recognized that the distinction between *theōria* and praxis is not a distinction between knowledge and the lack of it, and admittedly one cannot saddle Aristotle with the modern epistemological bifurcation of theory and practice. Yet, he did put considerable weight on the peculiar contributions of the two types of knowledge involved in the *epistēmē* of *theōria* and the *phronēsis* of praxis. The former is accorded the privilege of

---

[13] *Ibid.*, p. 54.

putting us in touch with "real" essences, and it would certainly be questionable to portray Aristotle's practical knowledge as having nothing to do with his epistemological realism. A more radical break with Aristotle's general epistemological framework is required than Gadamer appears ready to acknowledge.

There are two problems in Gadamer's hermeneutics which travel with the above. One has to do with the repositioning of theory in his philosophical hermeneutics. The other concerns his somewhat cavalier treatment of "method." On the matter of theory, we are left with a refashioning of theoretical reflection along the lines of what Heidegger called "existential-ontological comprehension" in his effort to work out a fundamental ontology—a project which Heidegger himself later abandoned. But even in Heidegger's ruminations on fundamental ontology in his early period it should be noted that his "existentials" have very little to do with the "real essences" allegedly discovered in Aristotle's *theōria*. They have more to do with Kant's transcendental categories, of which they are an existentialized version. This also, however, is left behind in Heidegger's celebrated *Kehre*, a turn which Gadamer appears reluctant to take. Now whether indeed this is the proper turn to take is not to be decided at this time, and Gadamer's decision not to take it does not in itself constitute a criticism. The main point at issue is that the theory/praxis distinction in Gadamer remains pretty much at loose ends, particularly when one begins to probe its possible connections with Aristotle's *theōria*. Now the leverage of our probing is not to persuade Gadamer to find a special place for theory, in some reconstructed Aristotelian mode, but rather to suggest that the whole project of playing theory off against praxis and praxis against theory be set aside, and that our attention rather be directed to a discernment of the workings of distanciation and reflection within the texture of communicative praxis itself. Theory, scientific as well as philosophical, is itself a form of communicative praxis.[14]

---

[14] Hubert L. Dreyfus has provided a fresh approach to the theory-praxis issue by playing with the distinction between "theoretical holism" and "practical holism." He uses this distinction principally to illustrate the difference between the holistic approaches of Quine and Heidegger. Theoretical holism, as represented by Quine, treats the horizon or background of practices as a system of beliefs and rules, somehow epistemologically secured. Practical holism articulates the background as a tissue of habits, customs, and skills displayed in our everyday commerce with utensils, things, and other people. Furthermore, according to Heidegger, Dreyfus points out, this tissue of habits, customs, and skills already exhibits a noncognitive comprehension of the world as a totality of practical references *(Verweisungszusammenhang)* in the stance of *Vorhabe* (fore-having). The stance of *Vorsicht* (fore-sight), from which Quine's theoretical circle of belief-system and attendant rules emerges, is for Heidegger at best a relative latecomer to the scene. See Dreyfus's discussion in "Holism and Hermeneutics," *The Review of Metaphysics,* Vol. XXXIV, No. 1, Issue No. 133, 1980. Dreyfus's use of the distinction between

The related problem in Gadamer's hermeneutics has to do with his placement of method. As has frequently been observed, Gadamer's very important work *Truth and Method* is much ado about "truth" and little ado about "method." The reasons for this, however, are patently clear. Method is understood as a sterile preoccupation of modern and contemporary epistemology, nurtured by an obsession with positivistic principles of verification. Gadamer seems to have inherited from the thought of Husserl the idea that the protocols of positivism and the principles of method in contemporary science come very close to being the same thing. Husserl defines the crisis of the European sciences as a situation in which the positivistic ideals of science have eclipsed the vitality and intentionality of the life-world. Gadamer's invectives against method proceed from similar assumptions about the nature of scientific inquiry. The upshot of all this is a continuation of the state of alienation between the natural and the human sciences. The natural sciences deal with method; the human sciences are the custodians of truth.

The unfortunate consequence of this proliferation of oppositions— *Naturwissenschaft* versus *Geisteswissenschaft,* nature versus spirit, and method versus truth—is that it rends asunder the labors of understanding and explanation in their joint efforts of making sense together. Gadamer's bifurcation of truth and method registers its adverse effects on the definition of the proper roles of understanding and explanation. After method is given over to the positivistic models of explanation (which we would argue is precisely what should not be done), it is difficult for Gadamer to discern the play of method in the explanation at work in the interpretive labors of communicative praxis. We have sought to articulate this method as the analytical procedures of sorting out the constitutive elements of discourse and praxis. Explanatory analysis travels with the holistic comprehension of understanding in the odyssey of interpretation. Truth and method (when method is divested of its positivistic prejudices) are bonded by a genuine connective tissue rather than separated by a disguised disjunction.

Paul Ricoeur, whose contribution to the continuing discussion of explanation and understanding on this point is noteworthy, sees the matter as being very much involved with the issue of method that Gadamerian hermeneutics poses. For Ricoeur, however, method takes

---

theoretical and practical holism constitutes an ingenious strategy for distinguishing the projects of Quine and Heidegger and fixes the source of the *misplacement* of theory. What is not so apparent, however, is where Heidegger does place theory within the context of his practical holism, and whether or not a resituation of theory within the designs of his fundamental ontology of *Being and Time* does not reactivate the theory/ praxis conflict on another level.

on a less pejorative significance. He speaks of the "methodic moment" of explanation, which is dialectically bonded with the "nonmethodic moment" of understanding.

> Strictly speaking, only explanation is methodic. Understanding is rather the nonmethodic moment which, in the sciences of interpretation, comes together with the methodic moment of explanation. Understanding precedes, accompanies, closes, and thus envelops explanation. In return, explanation develops understanding analytically.[15]

In emphasizing the positive accomplishments of explanation as the methodic moment in interpretation, working in concert with understanding, Ricoeur is able to rescue method from the negativities to which Gadamer had condemned it. Further, Ricoeur's articulation of the labor of understanding as one of envelopment and that of explanation as one of analytical development provides another access to the interplay of the holistic and the elemental in the joint comprehension of understanding and explanation. Understanding and explanation appear on the scene not as competing epistemologies but rather as interdependent ways of responding to the solicitations of communicative praxis. They are located not at the opposite ends of an epistemological spectrum but rather, as Ricoeur suggestively puts it, "at two different stages of a unique hermeneutical arc."[16]

Ricoeur's incorporation of the methodic moment of explanation as an integral moment of the labor of interpretation opens up a more positive attitude toward the accomplishments of the particular sciences than either Gadamer or Heidegger are able to manage. Indeed, for Ricoeur, it installs the requirement for careful and sustained explorations of the terrain which the special sciences inhabit. Ricoeur submits this requirement as flagging a principal difference between his approach and that of Heidegger. Heidegger opts for the "short route" to the understanding of Being, whereas Ricoeur proposes to follow the "long route," which proceeds by way of a detour along the highways and byways of the special sciences—and particularly the sciences of linguistics, semantics, psychoanalysis, and the history of religion.[17] Now Ricoeur does

---

[15] "Explanation and Understanding," *The Philosophy of Paul Ricoeur*, p. 165.
[16] *Interpretation Theory*, p. 87.
[17] "The short route is the one taken by an ontology of *understanding*, after the manner of Heidegger. I call such an ontology of understanding the 'short route' because, breaking with any discussion of *method*, it carries itself directly to the level of an ontology of finite being in order there to recover *understanding*, no longer as a mode of knowledge, but rather as a mode of being . . . The long route which I propose also aspires to carry reflection to the level of an ontology, but it will do so by degrees, following successive investigations into semantics and reflection," *The Conflict of Interpretations*, ed. Don Ihde (Evanston: Northwestern University Press, 1974), p. 6.

not consult these special sciences for the purpose of finding in them the definitive rules of method which can then be universally applied across the spectrum of studies of human culture, nor does he gather their several accomplishments into an archetectonic of a final philosophy or a consumated *Weltanschauung*. The main purpose for taking the long route is to observe interpretation at work in each of these sciences in such a way that the methodic moment of explanation is highlighted, but not at the expense of the moment of understanding.

Ricoeur's emphasis on the need to explore the discourse and praxis of the special sciences, and particularly the sciences of linguistics and psychology, strikes us as being well-placed. Both Heidegger and Gadamer exhibit a tendency to short-circuit the contributions that flow from these areas of human endeavor and seem to be rather confident that the artist and the poet are in better position to educate us in the ways of seeing the world. Such neglect of the patterns of interpretation at work in the special sciences, we would maintain, leads to an unwarranted restriction of the manifold configurations of sense in the texture of communicative praxis.

Nonetheless, we are of the mind that Ricoeur's proposed long route through the pathways of reflection in the special sciences leads him into some conceptual difficulties along the way—not because he has chosen the long route but because of the way that he travels it. He encounters these difficulties because he has not fully succeeded in freeing himself from the epistemological paradigm in defining the methodic moment. Interpretation is recovered in the methodic moment as a "mode of knowledge," and the resources of the special sciences are tapped for the purposes of filling out the epistemological vacuum left by understanding in its hurried attempt to lay out the structures of being. In this recourse to the epistemological, Ricoeur buys into that very paradigm that produced the unhappy state of affairs in the traditional bifurcation of understanding and explanation in the first place. What we would suggest is that the use of the special sciences to solve epistemological quandaries, enlisting their services toward an answering of the philosophically incoherent problem of the "knowledge of knowledge," is a misuse of their resources. That the special sciences provide knowledge in their respective disciplines need not be called into question. The community of practitioners in the special sciences have the requisite resources to decide what counts as knowledge in their scientific conversation as they strive to work toward a consensus. What is placed into question in the shift to interpretation as the reciprocity of understanding and explanation is the epistemological effort to provide a reconstruction of knowledge as a universal feature of the human mind.

The reintroduction of the epistemological paradigm in Ricoeur's thought leads to a troublesome dissonance in his theory of interpretation, seen particularly in his use of linguistics and semiology as modes of explanation. The issue centers on the use of sign as a linguistic reference to other signs within a system of signs, combined with a reconstructed Fregean sense-reference couplet which Ricoeur believes can lead us out of a linguistic closure and direct us to an external reality.[18] In all this the sign stands in service of epistemological interests. But then it is difficult to see how the sign can fulfill the interpretive requirement, and Ricoeur is clear that the "hermeneutical arc" straddles the envelopment of understanding and the analytical development of explanation. How can the hermeneutical arc perform this function unless the sign is already interpretive? The hermeneutical demand requires a de-epistemologization of the sign and a tracking of its descent into the space of praxis, where the sign functions in tandom with the working of interpretation.

This internal problem in Ricoeur's theory of interpretation leads to a more general one. In working out from the linguistic and semiological paradigm of sign and the literary model of text, Ricoeur falls prey, particularly in his later writings, to an overdetermination of the metaphor of textuality and its questionable extension to the domain of action. To use the text of discourse, both as spoken and written, to illustrate commonalities in the reading of a text and the interpretation of an action, which Ricoeur does very well, is one thing; but to use the text as the *proton analogon* in the explication of an action is quite another. Ricoeur rather serenely embraces the latter, evidenced by his explicit statement that the theory of discourse, which culminates in the privileged status of the text, "governs all the subsequent developments of my interpretation theory."[19] Consequently action is itself conceptualized through the use of the linguistic exemplar of the text as work and object. This results in an amalgam of discourse and action within the dynamics of communicative praxis at the expense of a reduction to textuality. We have urged throughout a more cautious metaphorical play of "texture" in our elucidation of the texture of communicative praxis. Texture encompasses not only the texture of textuality but also the texture of the tissues of human action and the fibers of institutional life. These tissues of action and institutional fibers can be described, understood, and explained in multiple ways, not all of which are beholden to a textual paradigm.

In this chapter we have sought to continue the conversation on the

---

[18] See particularly his essay "The Hermeneutical Function of Distanciation," in *Paul Ricoeur: Hermeneutics and the Human Sciences,* ed. and trans. John B. Thompson (Cambridge: Cambridge University Press, 1981).

[19] *Interpretation Theory,* p. 72.

topic of understanding and explanation with some modern and contemporary philosophers who have spoken out on the issue, and principally with the two contemporary hermeneutical thinkers, Hans-Georg Gadamer and Paul Ricoeur. In our conversation with them we have tried to work out a posture of interpretation as illustrated in the life of communicative praxis. We have emphasized the reciprocity and interplay of understanding and explanation, detailing their movements within the context of a holism that does not forget the contributions of an analysis of partitive profiles and constitutive elements by the various human sciences. However, the whole-part intertexture that we have found fit to employ in carrying through our designs has been pruned of the epistemological and metaphysical constructionism, both of an empiricistic and rationalistic sort, that has informed the history of modern philosophy. In doing so we have liberated interpretation from the alien requirements of epistemological foundations and representational schemata, and from the wearisome search for brute facts that might correspond to clear and distinct ideas of them.

CHAPTER FIVE

The Illusion of Foundationalism

The topic for discussion in this concluding chapter of Part I is one to which we have intermittently alluded throughout our foregoing explorations. We have not had the occasion, however, to address it directly. The topic at issue has to do with the philosophical use of the metaphor of foundations. It would be difficult to find another metaphor in the history of philosophy that has been so ubiquitously employed, save possibly the metaphor of interior versus exterior. Close examination will show that these metaphors have often traveled together, serving the common cause of epistemological and metaphysical grounding. Although the antifoundationalist stance in our elucidation of the texture of communicative praxis should by this time have become apparent, what may not yet be clear is how our project avoids a gravitation into a new species of foundationalsm in which the unitary complex of discourse and action functions as a transubstantiated given and a refurbished necessary starting point. It is for this reason that a more concentrated and sustained discussion of the issue of foundationalism is required at this time.

It is particularly the voices of the canonized modern philosophers, in the rationalist and empiricist tradition alike, that have spoken most resoundingly about the importance of philosophical foundations. Descartes in detailing his procedure of systematic doubt impressed upon us the need to return to and build anew from the foundations, which he allegedly found to rest securely in an indubitable *res cogitans* and its clear and distinct ideas. Locke and his empiricist followers continued to use the metaphor of foundations in a revised fashion and coupled it with a new employment of the metaphor of interior versus exterior. In his well-known essay on human understanding, Locke appealed to the outer contents of sensation and the inner contents of reflection as "the fountains of knowledge, from whence all the ideas we have, or can naturally have, do spring."[1] Kant looked for foundations on another and supposedly deeper level, namely that of necessary transcendental conditions which he believed were always already at work in our experience of the world. To establish these conditions he had to invent a transcendental ego and a formidable procession of transcendental faculties and concepts. Although the philosophical positions of Descartes, Locke, and Kant were marked by significant differences, they exhibited a common quest for foundations.

This quest for foundations among these notable architects of the modern philosophical mind quickly congealed as a burgeoning epistemological enterprise. The ideal that informed the quest was the ideal of knowledge. Foundationalism thus took on in the early stages of modern philosophy an explicit epistemological design. The business at hand was that of getting to the foundations by way of epistemological excavations. Richard Rorty's statement on the issue of foundationalism would thus seem to be directly to the point.

> Philosophy can be foundational in respect to the rest of culture because culture is the assemblage of claims to knowledge, and philosophy adjudicates such claims. It can do so because it understands the foundations of knowledge and it finds these foundations in the study of man-as-knower, of the "mental processes" or the "activity of representation" which makes knowledge possible. To know is to represent accurately what is outside the mind; so to understand the possibility and nature of knowledge is to understand the way in which the mind is able to construct such representations. Philosophy's central concern is to be a general theory of representation, a theory which will divide culture up into areas which represent reality. well, those which represent it less well, and those which do not represent it at all (despite their pretense to do so).[2]

In this definition of foundationalism we see first of all a congenial fraternization of the metaphor of foundations with the allied metaphor of interiority versus exteriority. The "activity of representation" proceeds from a mental interior that yearns for an accurate reading of external reality. In chapter two we have already examined the philosophical mischief that ensues from a reckless use of the latter metaphor, producing a gloss on the expressive meanings displayed in communicative praxis. It now remains our task, in concert with our previous explorations, to restrain, if not to dislodge, the language of

---

[1] *An Essay Concerning Human Understanding*, abridged and edited by A. S. Pringle-Pattison (Oxford: The Clarendon Press, 1924), p. 43.
[2] Richard Rorty, *Philosophy and the Mirror of Nature* (Princeton: Princeton University Press, 1979), p. 3.

foundations in a philosophy of communicative praxis. The use of this longstanding metaphor in the interests of philosophical grounding promises more than it can deliver. It comprises an effort to achieve a godlike survey that surmounts the facticity and perspectivity of human finitude. It forgets the lesson that interpretation as a way of understanding and explanation bears the marks of our inherence in history.

Rorty's characterization of foundationalism provides us with the principal marks of foundationalist thinking as inaugurated chiefly by Descartes and Kant, and then pursued in the tradition of analytical philosophy from Frege and Russell onward. The principal intention in his recent *Philosophy and the Mirror of Nature* is to undermine the developing foundationalism in analytical philosophy by way of an internal critique, moving out chiefly from Wilfrid Sellars's attack on the given and Quine's critique of necessity.[3] A complementing challenge, invited by Rorty's reflections, is to expunge the foundation-metaphor in recent Continental thought from Husserl to its manifold contemporary varieties. Proceeding mainly from the context of this tradition, our effort is to diffuse the metaphor as a philosophical presupposition for phenomenological analysis and hermeneutical elucidation. The texture of communicative praxis can only be properly displayed after the search for foundations is abandoned.

Herbert Spiegelberg has appropriately described the elan of Husserl's phenomenology as a relentless search for "ultimate foundations."[4] These foundations, according to Husserl, were to be found in the depths of subjectivity—"transcendental subjectivity" is what he came to call it. After installing the requirement of a turn to the data themselves *(Zu den Sachen Selbst),* which initiated a turn to the object, Husserl's reflections led him to the roots of philosophical inquiry itself, i.e., the object-as-meant in the consciousness of the knowing subject as it intends its selected data. The epistemological interests guiding this return to the object via the subject, instrumented by the celebrated *epochē* and reduction, are obvious and explicit.[5] The regression to

---

[3] See chapter 4, "Privileged Representations" (pp. 165–212). This chapter in many ways is the pivotal chapter of the entire work.

[4] *The Phenomenological Movement: A Historical Introduction,* Vol. I (The Hague: Martinus Nijhoff, 1960), p. 82.

[5] Theodor Adorno is surely on target when he says of Husserl, "The claim to novelty and theoretical impartiality, the battle cry 'To the things themselves!' arises directly out of an epistemological norm." *Against Epistemology,* trans. Willis Domingo (Cambridge: The MIT Press, 1983), p. 125. However, Adorno quickly overstates his case against Husserl in the sentence that directly follows the above: "That is the positivistic norm which restricts thought to the practically technical procedure of abbreviation and attributes the substance of cognition only to what is supposed to exist without the supplement of thought, and what certainly ends up as the flimsiest and most abstract of findings." The rather facile attribution of a "positivistic norm" to Husserl's epistemology is surely a gloss on

transcendental subjectivity delivers a ratifying principle for the adjudication of claims in our predicative judgments about the world.

Now certain complexities enter the picture in the moment that one's attention is directed to the "later Husserl" and the shift of standpoint indexed by the substitution of "the going-back to the life-world" (*Rückgang auf die Lebenswelt*) for "the turn to the data themselves." Does not the introduction of the life-world motif in Husserl's later period make all things new with respect to his phenomenological program? Clearly, significant changes in the topical design of Husserl's phenomenological format are effected, and Husserl even speaks of a departure from the "Cartesian way" that he followed during his period of phenomenological idealism as developed in the *Cartesian Meditations*.[6] This departure, however, does not entail an abandonment of the transcendental ideal of unassailable foundations. Even the more concrete reflections on the language, historicity, and sociality of life-world experiences in the later corpus are guided by the principles of transcendental grounding. Admittedly, transcendental subjectivity becomes an intersubjectivity, and this does make a difference with regard to the breadth of phenomena included in the vision of intuitive seeing and in the range of intentional constitution. Yet, the salient fact remains that the life-world, as the ultimate horizon on which the phenomena of intersubjectivity and historicity appear, continues to function as an irreducible foundational substratum against which the success of the sciences and the viability of a general theory of judgment are to be measured. The life-world provides us with "the primal self-evidence" and "the source of verification."[7] The European sciences are seen as having gravitated into a situation of crisis because of the occlusion of

---

Husserl's spirited attack on positivism. Admittedly, a case can be made for the claim that in spite of his anti-positivism Husserl continued to buy into an epistemological framework of inquiry which positivism shared. But this does not provide a legitimate inference that the positivistic norm was the *telos* of Husserl's epistemology. Adorno's recurring accusation of Husserl as a positivist is one of the more discernible flaws in his otherwise interesting, and at times entertaining, broadside against Husserl's phenomenological program.

[6] *The Crisis of European Sciences and Transcendental Phenomenology*, trans. David Carr (Evanston: Northwestern University Press, 1970), p. 155.

[7] "From objective-logical self-evidence (mathematical 'insight,' natural-scientific, positive-scientific 'insight' as it is being accomplished by the inquiring and grounding mathematician, etc.), the path leads back, here, to the primal self-evidence in which the life-world is ever pregiven." *Ibid.*, p. 128. "But while the natural scientist is thus interested in the objective and is involved in his activity, the subjective-relative is on the other hand still functioning for him, not as something irrelevant that must be passed through but as that which ultimately grounds the theoretical-logical ontic validity for all objective verification, i.e., as the source of self-evidence, the source of verification." *Ibid.*, p. 126. Aron Gurwitsch succinctly summarizes the foundationalist impulse of Husserl's life-world concept when he writes: "All theoretical truth—logical, mathematical, scientific— finds its ultimate validation and justification in evidences which concern occurrences in

the life-world as a ratifying principle. The Galilean ideal, which Husserl is careful to distinguish from the specific scientific achievements of Galileo, has led to a *mathesis universalis,* applicable to all forms of theory and praxis. Husserl's vestigal phenomenological hope is that through a return to the life-world a displacement of this mathematization and objectivation of theory and praxis can be achieved and the original foundations reclaimed. That a species of privileged access to and accurate representation of the life-world is possible does not seem to come into question.

The impact of Husserl's life-world concept upon subsequent developments in phenomenology was notable and far-reaching. Even the existentially oriented phenomenologists who rejected Husserl's reinvention of the transcendental ego, his emphasis on theoretical act-intentionality, and his doctrine of essence wanted to hold on to the life-world motif, which they found to be unproblematic. Although some of the salvage efforts undertaken—and particularly that of Merleau-Ponty—exemplified a high degree of ingenuity, the fact remains that even in its existentialized version the life-world continued to function as at once a founding subject matter and a tribunal with the legislative power to somehow ratify the "truth claims" of existential descriptions.

The disassemblage of the phenomenological notion of foundations, used in the interests of epistemological underwriting, requires the resources of both an internal and an external critique. The internal critique has to with a dismantling of the notion by staying with the paradigm of knowledge interests that inform it, showing how it collapses under its own weight. The external critique proceeds by way of something like a paradigm-shift, undermining the foundation-metaphor by installing a different posture of questioning.

Two problems in particular surface on the level of internal critique. There is first the problem of locating that which is given by sorting it out from that which is not given. The notion of the "self-giving" of sense by the phenomena as experienced is a pivotal notion for Husserl, orchestrated throughout the stages of his philosophical development. But this self-giving of sense is characterized by a pervading elusiveness, ever escaping definitive determination. It is a fugitive given, perpetually deferred, never surmounting the perspectivity of interpretation. Furthermore, the conceptual net devised to capture the given, namely that of the interstructure of ego-cogito-cogitatum within transcendental subjectivity, is refashioned as one moves from the implied realistic require-

---

the *Lebenswelt.* If Husserl assigns to the evidences of the *Lebenswelt* a privileged status with respect to those of objective and scientific theory, it is in the sense of the latter being founded upon the former." *Studies in Phenomenology and Psychology* (Evanston: Northwestern University Press, 1966), p. 418.

ment of intuition to the implied idealistic requirement of constitution. The appeal to intuition, which propels the move to "the data themselves" in the early period, comes down heavy on the seeing of the data as they are given to consciousness. This defines the realistic requirement of Husserl's phenomenology. The appeal to constitution, which appears later and remains subsequently entrenched, emphasizes the importance of the activity of consciousness in shaping the sense of phenomena as intended. This is the idealistic requirement. This ambiguity, which appears to be built into the very project of Husserl's phenomenological analysis, is but a further illustration of the difficulty in neatly sorting out the given from the non-given.[8]

The second problem that surfaces in an internal critique of Husserl's programmatic has to do with the continued, although attenuated, employment of claims for necessity, inherited chiefly from his earlier ideal of apodicticity that he carried over into his phenomenological idealism. Although Husserl clearly recognized the need to attenuate the relevance of necessity as he moved away from the early influence of mathematical modes of thought on his philosophical construction to a more explicit phenomenology of experience, the ideal of apodicticity inhabits even the corridors of his later reflections. The life-world motif, which completes the long progression toward the *Letztebegründung,* is proffered as the unassailable and irreducible foundation of phenomenological analysis. Still positioned within the framework of transcendental philosophy, the life-world is the ultimate of transcendental conditions. It is at once the necessary starting point for and the necessary result of the myriad reflections on our inherence in language, time, and history. But in the moment that the life-world is shouldered with such an awesome responsibility it collapses under its own weight. It is difficult to see how it forestalls a regress to another level or domain—for example, a prehistorical world of nature which itself might contain the seeds for the intentional life of human history. Even more disconcertingly, if one sticks with the epistemological paradigm, it is difficult to see how an infinite regress might be forestalled. There appears to be more than a tincture of arbitrariness in Husserl's decision to stop at a particular cluster of evidence for the origin of human thought and action.[9]

These two internal critiques of Husserl's brand of foundationalism,

---

[8] For a discussion of some of the consequences of this ambiguity of intuition and constitution as it is operative in Husserl's method see particularly Paul Ricoeur, *Husserl: An Analysis of His Phenomenology* (Evanston: Northwestern University Press, 1967).
[9] These two internal critiques of Husserl's foundationalism would seem to exhibit some concerns common to Sellars's relentless attack on the given and Quine's attack on necessity. As the concerns of Sellars and Quine emerge within the context of a critique of

although they hold a strategical importance in our deconstruction of the philosophical use of the metaphor of foundations, are rather limited in what they can achieve. At most they present aporias and perplexities that arise within the epistemological space in which the issue of foundations is defined. They are continuations of the epistemological debate, but in such a manner that a dissatisfaction with the debate itself may begin to emerge. Nonetheless, the framework of inquiry still remains that of arguing and providing claims for and against a recourse to foundations. To the arguments that we have proposed, telling counterarguments by Husserlian philosophers might be provided, calling forth a rejoinder, and a rejoinder to the rejoinder, and so on. The mounting of arguments and counterarguments proceeding from agreed upon philosophical problems is surely an honorable practice, and one in which philosophers have been engaged since the beginning of the discipline. Indeed, this is what philosophers normally do. Extending Thomas Kuhn's distinction between normal and revolutionary science to the field of philosophy, as Rorty and others have recommended, one could speak of the continuation of the epistemological debate as the practice of "normal philosophy."

The crucial move in our project of a deconstructive reclamation of the texture of communicative praxis pertains not, however, to another step or strategy within the inquiry framework of epistemology. We proceed to another space of questioning. One can speak of this as a shift from "normal" to "revolutionary" philosophizing if one wishes. In any case, what is at issue is a radicalization of the critique of foundationalism. This radicalization, initiated by what we have called an external critique, involves a shift to another set of concerns, a move not only to a different way of asking questions but to a way of asking different questions, a new posture of thinking. Nietzsche, one of the trailblazers of deconstructionist thought, already invited us to entertain such a radicalization in his observation that " 'Thinking,' as epistemologists conceive it, simply does not occur: it is a quite arbitrary fiction, arrived at by selecting one element from the process of eliminating all the rest, an artificial arrangement for the purpose of intelligibility—."[10] A radicalization of the critique of foundationalism sets the requirement for a new way of thinking, attuned to the solicitations of discourse and action within the holistic space of communicative praxis.

The "illusion of foundationalism" is thus not a conclusion arrived at

---

another tradition, broadly defined as the empiricist tradition, the possibility of a consequential dialogue between the representatives of the analytical and the Continental traditions on these specific issues would seem to emerge.

[10] *The Will to Power,* trans. Walter Kaufman and R. J. Hollingdale (New York: Vintage Books, 1967), p. 264.

through epistemological disputation. It is not a new epistemological "truth." Indeed, the "problem" of foundationalism as it has surfaced in modern and contemporary epistemology needs to be therapeutically treated. It awaits a cure rather than a solution. Foundationalism, as a problem for epistemology, becomes a subject for disputation between those who claim that there is an unimpeachable substratum in our knowledge of the world—be it a direct perception of physical objects, acquaintance with sense-data, experience of "raw feels," incorrigibly intuited essences, or whatever—and those who argue that there is no such substratum. Within the parameters of the debate one may eventually be persuaded that the preponderance of evidence rests with the epistemological antifoundationalists. But there comes a time when the very *telos* of the debate is called into question. This questioning leads to a reassessment of the status of philosophy as a special discipline that holds a franchise for trafficking not only in logic and epistemology, but also in metaphysics, value theory, and the ever-expanding list of philosophy of . . . language, science, religion, politics, technology, medicine, etc., etc. The radicalization of the critique of foundationalism moves to a radical thinking in philosophy about philosophy. It probes the matter of philosophy's understanding of itself. And so it must, for one needs to be wary of borrowing foundation talk from the epistemologists and substituting founding concepts and givens from another subdiscipline, such as value theory, the philosophy of language, psychology, or even theology. To substitute value for knowledge, semantics for truth, or culture for sense-data, as the bedrock reality, may not help matters much in the end.

The new posture of questioning installed by a shift away from the knowledge paradigm of epistemology thus leads to a reflexive questioning about the status of philosophy itself and its putative division of labor. The deconstruction of epistemology cannot be separated from the deconstruction of value theory, and the self-styled philosophical approaches to this and that. This may, a la Heidegger and Rorty, presage the "end of philosophy"—at least the end of philosophy as a special body of knowledge, rules, values, and facts that provide foundations for the wider cultural forms of life. Not only is epistemology as a species of knowledge about knowledge or as a rational reconstruction of our knowledge set aside, every effort to uncover first principles—be they in the domain of ethics or aesthetics, logic or semantics, the natural or the social sciences—becomes suspect.

The ideal of philosophical foundations, variously formulated, is a prejudice that has been inscribed into the very definition of philosophy for some time. In the turn of modern philosophy it was boldly illustrated in Descartes's well-known metaphor of the tree of philosophy, in which the branches stand for the special sciences, the trunk signifies physics, and the roots are supplied by metaphysics. Now the substitution of metaphysics for critical epistemology (Kant), or phenomenology (Husserl), or logic (Russell), or more recently semantics and empirical psychology, simply continues to buy into the stock of the original Cartesian holding company. Indeed, Rorty has shown, and almost effortlessly, how this honorific chain of developments is simply a continuation of the epistemological paradigm that was already anticipated by Descartes and then made central in Kant's critical philosophy. Thus the only viable option open to Rorty is that of a radical shift from the "normal" discourse of epistemologically oriented reflection to the "abnormal" discourse of hermeneutical understanding, a shift which falls out as a generalization of Kuhn's distinction between "normal" and "revolutionary" science.[11] It is thus that Rorty is able to flag the final scenario of his philosophical odyssey as a move from "epistemology to hermeneutics," or in somewhat more general terms as a move from "systematic" to "edifying" philosophy.[12]

The heroes of Rorty's provocative and often unsettling radical critique of philosophy are Heidegger, Wittgenstein, and Dewey. Each in his own way, according to Rorty, abjured the pretenses of systematic philosophy, undermined the epistemological paradigm, had no truck with a quest for foundations, and cleared the way for a continuation of "the conversation of mankind."[13] As Rorty sees it, it is the latter that philosophy as the love of wisdom is all about.

We find it helpful to address the topic of foundation-oriented thinking by citing Rorty not simply because he has a lot to say, but more specifically because he is a friendly interlocutor for our discourse on communicative praxis. He cautions us about certain conceptual thickets in which we might become ensnared in our effort to situate the philosophical importance of the amalgamated phenomena of speech and action, language and social practices. Also, the prima facie similarity between the "conversation of mankind" and "communicative praxis" is so striking that it suggests a common space of shared interests. Finally, our common antipathies toward foundationalism are deepseated and explicit.

Communicative praxis, as the interplay of discourse and action, is

---

[11] *Philosophy and the Mirror of Nature*, p. 320.
[12] *Ibid.*, Part III.
[13] Rorty's new metaphor for understanding philosophy as conversation receives its inspiration from Michael Oakeshott's "The Voice of Poetry in the Conversation of Mankind." Philosophy as conversation, like poetry, with which it often mixes and mingles, is one of the many voices heard in the corridors of human history. Rorty consistently distinguishes "conversation" from "inquiry," principally because, as he sees it, inquiry in its philosophical dress is always bent on a discovery of foundations.

not a new philosophical foundation. It is neither a metaphysical *archē* nor an epistemological given, nor a founding value principle. It is thus that we are constrained to take issue with some of our respected colleagues in the phenomenological and hermeneutical traditions. Despite the congruence of certain themes in the phenomenological life-world literature with those in our elucidation of the texture of communicative praxis, the construal of communicative praxis as either an unspoiled realm of pure facts of human experience or an expanded noema of these pure facts as meant is to be avoided. One needs to be wary of an unmonitored reinsertion of the fact/essence dichotomy into the texture of communicative praxis and of the temptation to view the elucidation of the worlds of discourse and action as a procedure of epistemological justification which finally delivers the facts as they really are. It is precisely this pretense and illusory hope, we have suggested, that have made their way into the life-world thematic of phenomenological philosophy.[14]

Not only, however, has the phenomenological notion of the life-world been called upon to perform the service of a final philosophical grounding, certain key interpretive notions in the recent hermeneutical literature (such as "tradition," "culture," "historicity," and "linguisticality") have been charged with fulfilling a similar task. These tendencies may be the result of an unsuspecting appropriation of the inquiry framework from those philosophical positions that hermeneutics purports to attack. Simply to substitute tradition, culture, or even language itself for the more narrowly circumscribed fictions of sense-data or noematic structures used in the service of epistemological underwriting is of little consequence. What is required is a more persistent hammering away at the form of questioning that invites such a programmatic in the first place. It is this that Rorty's deconstructive strategy does very well.

Against this backdrop of common concerns in our respective projects, however, certain differences of some consequence appear within

---

[14] Victor Kestenbaum has isolated some of the inherent problems of the life-world concept, and particularly as it is used in the philosophy of the human sciences, in his essay "Life-World as Origin," in *Man and World*, Vol. 15, No. 3, 1982. Kestenbaum finds the recurring use of the life-world concept as a basis for solving the problem of the human sciences, their lack of self-understanding with respect to their origin and goal, to be peculiarly unproductive. In his view the life-world concept cannot be used as a basis for solving this problem, because it is still part of the problem. Within this new context of questioning Kestenbaum finds James's radical empiricism and urbane pragmatism considerably more satisfactory for dealing with the issues at hand than Husserl's phenomenology of the life-world. Reflection on the variegated postures of human thought and action, a responsibility which the several human sciences shirk at their own peril, "does not promise to take us closer to what James calls the 'bottom of being', but it can redirect us, as he says, 'fruitfully into experience' " (pp. 334–335).

the fabric. There are a number of worries that Rorty's appeal to the conversation of mankind and his recommendation for edifying philosophy occasion in us. We are worried in the first instance about his unbridgeable chasm between "normal" and "abnormal" discourse and between "systematic" and "edifying" philosophy. Making much of the distinction between the "commensurable" and the "incommensurable," a distinction borrowed from recent discussions in the philosophy of science, Rorty sees the two postures of systematic and edifying philosophy, normal and abnormal discourse, as incommensurable. There is no overlapping, much less a consummate reciprocity, between them. They jut out on the scene as ruptures in discourse and manners of thinking. The consequences of this are far-reaching; indeed, we are of the mind that they overreach the positive results of his skillfully engineered deconstruction.

Much of course depends on what one packs into such pivotal notions as the commensurable and the incommensurable, the normal and the abnormal, the systematic and the edifying. These oppositions can be fleshed out in such a way that they illustrate a cluster of complementing distinctions, or they can be viewed as a series of rigid dichotomies. Rorty is disposed toward the latter; and it should be remarked that he has some heavy-weights on his side—notably Thomas Kuhn, whose philosophy of scientific discovery Rorty appropriates rather uncritically, as well as Michel Foucault and his neostructuralist theory of discourse. Indeed, the backdrop of Rorty's reflections on the matter looks very much like a Foucaultian rupture of epistemes in the discontinuous history of culture in which each episteme is an archipelago severed from all others. For Rorty the abnormal discourse of edifying philosophy decisively puts behind it all language and concepts that figure in normal and systematic philosophy. In exploring the texture of communicative praxis, however, we find it difficult to isolate the cleavages in thought and discourse so definitively. There appears to be a bit of the incommensurable in each chunk of commensurability, and the commensurable seems to inform the new postures of discourse that are viewed as incommensurable. The languages of the normal and the abnormal not only slide into each other in our descriptions of psychological traits, they also mingle and mix in our more general discursive practices. Indeed, for the most part we understand the discourse of our interlocutor even though his grammar and concepts have their share of what we might take as incommensurables. Admittedly, these incommensurables point to new ways of seeing the world and new ways of speaking about that which we see, but the introduction of the postulate of discontinuity or rupture to account for this is a too hastily devised piece of legislation.

There are some specific problems with the very language of commensurability vis-à-vis incommensurability. The distinction buys into a suppressed *mathesis universalis* that guides the direction of discourse and outlines the proper scope of conversation. The ways of discourse continue to be defined by the ideal of "measurement." But this unduly restricts the dynamics of conversation at work in communicative practices, whether these practices be in science or in the literary arts. The play of discourse may indeed contain criteria of commensurability (and it is difficult to imagine the doing of science without them), but it is not bound by them. Commensurability is not the "standard" of discourse against which the abnormal and incommensurable is then seen as but a reaction. Discourse as "measured" is an offspring of its polysemic play rather than a standard and criterion for it.

We will stick with our foregoing critique of life-world talk in classical phenomenology to illustrate the inmixing of normal and abnormal, commensurable and incommensurable discourse. Heidegger (one of the heroes in Rorty's company of edifying philosophers) surely needs to be credited with being one of the first post-Husserlian thinkers to accomplish a deconstruction of the life-world as a foundational phenomenon. Heidegger sets the stage for this deconstruction, already in *Being and Time*, through a *deformalization* of the Husserlian concept of "phenomenon." This deformalization provides the strategy for a deconstruction both of Husserl's earlier transcendental-phenomenological idealism and his later transcendental phenomenology of the life-world. As a consequence of this deformalization, "phenomenon," whether applied to *Dasein* or to the life-world, is understood by Heidegger not as that which shows itself in the domain of transcendental subjectivity, but rather as "something that proximally and for the most part does *not* show itself."[15] The meaning of "phenomenon" is shifted away from its foundational status in the "object as meant" and its function in the service of epistemological grounding. But all of this proceeds within the context of a critical dialogue with the "normal" phenomenologizing of Husserl, thinking with Husserl beyond Husserl, effectively using Husserl against himself. J. N. Mohanty states the circumstances surrounding this issue very well when he writes:

> Heidegger's real overcoming of Husserl, then, lies—as Gadamer has correctly pointed out—not in overcoming idealism for the sake of a realistic ontology, not in undercutting the very realism-idealism controversy, not

---

[15] *Being and Time*, trans. John Macquarrie and Edward Robinson (New York: Harper & Row, 1962), p. 59. Heidegger's deformalization of phenomenology is of course more extensively developed in his work *The Basic Problems of Phenomenology*, trans. Albert Hofstadter (Bloomington: Indiana University Press, 1982).

even in overcoming the alleged universality of objectifying acts (for Husserl himself had been able to do so in his discovery of horizon intentionalities), but in rejecting the very possibility of a laying bare which is not also a concealing.[16]

A phenomenon, or more precisely the unitary phenomenon of discourse and action which limns the texture of communicative praxis, is at once a revealing and a concealing, a showing and a not-showing of itself (because of the insinuation of forgotten memories, moments of self-deception, unconscious motivations, and ideological intrusions). This unitary phenomenon is hardly a foundation in any respectable extended sense of the metaphor. Yet, the extraction of this insight is made possible only through a dialogue with the normal philosophizing that is brought into question and ultimately displaced. And for such a dialogue to proceed the normal and the abnormal must remain, if indeed we are to continue to use this language, on the edge of "commensurability." The normal and the abnormal, the systematic and the edifying, seem to fraternize more than Rorty appears to recognize.

A second worry, allied with the first, that we have about Rorty's resituation of philosophy as a voice in the conversation of mankind has to do with the fate of the philosophical notion of reference. According to Rorty the philosophical notion of reference falls away in the instrumentation of his strategy of deconstruction, and philosophers are urged to make better use of their time than pursuing answers to the dusty and dreary questions concerning identity, meaning, and reference. There is much in Rorty's critique of reference that we applaud, particularly insofar as the usual theories of reference are so tightly interwoven with an epistemological paradigm of representation and justification. However, it is not all that clear to us why we have to give up such a fine word in the English language to the epistemological constructionists. As commonly used in ordinary speech and everyday conversation the word seems to serve us quite well. There is admittedly a measure of slackness in its varied uses, but the contexts in which it is used seem for the most part to be adequate for guiding its range of meaning. Thus far, Rorty, if we understand him correctly, would agree. He does take time to distinguish "talking about" from "reference," and observes that it is only the latter that is properly to be understood as a form of "philosophical art."[17] Yet, it would seem that one can take up the slack in the

---

[16] "The Destiny of Transcendental Philosophy" in *Phenomenology in a Pluralistic Context (Selected Studies in Phenomenology and Existential Philosophy)*, eds. William L. McBride and Calvin O. Schrag (Albany: State University of New York Press, 1983), p. 240.

[17] *Philosophy and the Mirror of Nature*, p. 289.

elasticity of the conversational "talking about" in a philosophical manner without committing the foundationalist fallacy and thus salvage reference as a philosophically useful concept. Ricoeur has made this attempt with his notion of "displayed reference," and in an earlier chapter we have sought to articulate an allied notion of hermeneutical reference. Taking its cues from the metaphorical play of language, hermeneutical reference is the display of the work-being of textuality, patterns of human action, institutional designs, and historical trends in the performances of discourse and social practices. Reference as a philosophical term is indeed displaced from its epistemological space, but it returns transmuted and transfigured into the space of communicative praxis.

The need to find a philosophical space for reference arises from the very texture of communicative praxis, in which speech is the saying of something *about* something. Communicative praxis, as we have detailed it, involves a describing, an interpreting, an understanding, and an explaining of the various attitudes, processes, and forms of life that make up the panoply of human experience. The introduction of the term "experience" at this juncture leads us to our third critical concern about Rorty's project. "Experience," like "reference," need not be given over to the constructionists, be they of an empiricist or a rationalist persuasion. One of the more puzzling features of Rorty's radical turn—puzzling particularly given his admiration for Dewey—is his refusal to come to terms with a notion of experience that could be consonant with his reposturing of philosophy as a voice in the conversation of mankind. He may well have inherited his uneasiness with experience-talk from a strand in Heidegger's philosophy. Not only in *Being and Time* but also in his *Kant and the Problem of Metaphysics* Heidegger took a rather firm stand against any "philosophies of experience," leading him to make the somewhat outrageous claim that *Kant's Critique of Pure Reason* has nothing whatever to do with either "theory of knowledge" or "theory of experience."[18] Now behind Heidegger's claim is his dissatisfaction with what the neo-Kantians did with the first *Critique,* construing it as a treatise in epistemology that provided the foundations for scientific knowledge by securing the proper conceptual basis for experience. Rorty clearly shares Heidegger's antiepistemological dispositions, and it may be a fair inference that he avoids the language of experience because of its explicit historical associations with the traditional use of the term in the service of a theory of

---

[18] *Kant and the Problem of Metaphysics,* trans. J. S. Churchill (Bloomington: Indiana University Press, 1962), p. 21. Heidegger does, however, attenuate somewhat his critical attitude toward experience in his later works and speaks freely of the "experience with language." *Unterwegs zur Sprache* (Tübingen: Neske, 1965) p. 177.

knowledge. But surely Dewey, and particularly in his *Experience and Nature,* had already put us on the path to a more vibrant and less constructionist notion of experience than was ever anticipated by the representatives of either classical empiricism or classical rationalism. There is also James, himself a member of the company of pragmatists extolled by Rorty, who set as his explicit task the liberation of experience from its pulverization and atomization in the schemata of professional epistemologists.

Experience, as the speaking and acting within life situations rather than as a building block in an ediface of knowledge, is at once the performance of communicative praxis and the displayed reference of our discourse and action. Experience provides the various topics or forms of life which are described and redescribed, interpreted and analyzed within the conversation of mankind. Ever responsive to the findings of further experience, communicative praxis moves within an open texture through new and revisable perspectives. Experience, in its originative sense, tokens the "living-through" of communicative praxis as both *seeing into* and *acting from* a situation. If there is to be any talk of a new ontology that might accompany the displays of communicative praxis in the wake of the deconstruction of traditional epistemology and metaphysics, it would need to take the form of an ontology of experience.[19]

Finally, we have some concerns about Rorty's tendency to gloss the creative play in the art of hermeneutics. He overemphasizes its reactive function as a counterthrust to normal discourse and the designs of systematic philosophy.

> Great edifying philosophers are reactive and offer satires, parodies, aphorisms. They know their work loses its point when the period they were reacting against is over. They are *intentionally* peripheral. Great systematic philosophers, like great scientists, build for eternity.[20]

There is an important point made in this, but if this is all that is said the positive accomplishments of edifying philosophy and the abnormal discourse of hermeneutics remain unrecognized. Rorty is correct in his observation that edifying philosophers (such as Wittgenstein, Heidegger, Dewey, Kierkegaard, and Nietzsche) do not "build for eternity," and he is right in maintaining that there is no ultimate unification of

---

[19]The principal features that might comprise such a new ontology of experience have already been examined in the author's previous work, *Experience and Being: Prolegomena to a Future Ontology* (Evanston: Northwestern University Press, 1969). However, in this work the author was still too optimistic about a possible "reconstruction" of transcendental inquiry in approaching the experience of being.

[20]*Philosophy and the Mirror of Nature,* p. 369.

interpretive perspectives. But one is mistaken if from this one draws the conclusion that hermeneutics and edifying philosophy are merely "re-active," and hence simply parasitical upon that against which they react. Unfortunately, Rorty seems to draw this conclusion. He does at times appear to ascribe "more" to the task of hermeneutics, when for example he alludes to its contribution in providing new descriptions and new slants on what it means to be a person and what is involved in being moral.

However, this strategy of opening up new perspectives, which them-selves remain parasitic upon the sedimented perspectives of systematic philosophy, is still too limited as a definition of the task of her-meneutics. The play of description and redescription in the perform-ance of the hermeneutical art surely must be acknowledged. We need to describe and redescribe the forms of communicative praxis time and again, providing new perspectives on how we see perceptual phe-nomena, use language, and live through social and historical situations. But in the conversation of mankind we often encounter alternative descriptions and conflicting interpretations. Some descriptions are judged to be "better" than others. We accept some social practices to guide our lives; others we do not. The hermeneutical conversation of mankind, we would urge, has a responsibility to work out the dilemmas of alternative descriptions and the conflict of interpretations. It is in this way that we move fruitfully through experience, as James and Dewey would enjoin us to do. But this requires the positive resources of critical and creative understanding. It is particularly this important feature of hermeneutics that we find missing in Rorty's version of it. It was our intention in chapter three to show how these positive resources are occasioned by the reflection and critique at work in the interwoven fabric of distanciation, idealization, and recollection. In chapter four we expanded the interpretive requirement to include the bonding of under-standing and explanation. The hermeneutical task as we have developed it in our preceding discussion confers upon hermeneutics a consistently more positive and creative function than Rorty's restricted definition of the art would allow.

Somewhere lurking in the background of Rorty's narrow and re-stricted notion of hermeneutics is the failure to recognize the retrieval power of hemeneutical thought and its dialectic of conservation and invention, repetition and novelty.[21] Hermeneutical comprehension nur-tures a liaison with that which has been delivered by the history of

---

[21] John D. Caputo in his defense of Heidegger against Rorty has called our attention to the absence of the recollective requirement in Rorty's version of hermeneutics. "For I think that Rorty has taken up only the 'deconstructive' side of Heidegger, the critique of

communicative praxis, extant texts of discourse and congealed forms of action. Hermeneutics seeks to "reclaim" the sense of these texts and patterns of social practices. Now admittedly this cannot be achieved through some species of mirroring a glassy essence which these texts and actions have at times been alleged to represent. On this point Rorty's argument is persuasive. Reclamation or retrieval simply does not proceed thusly. Rather it proceeds by way of an interplay of participation in the delivered forms of communicative praxis and a distanciation from them. It is this interplay that first occasions the combined understanding and critique of a tradition. Both this understanding and this critique, as we have seen, move along through a projection and invention of new interpretive profiles. We are here no longer dealing simply with a reactive stance. We are comprehending that which has been said and done with the help of new possibilities for posturing its sense. Herein reside the resources for critical, discerning reflection and creative, inventive insight. This defines the joint critical and creative moment of hermeneutics as a voice in the conversation of mankind. All of this adds up to more than a simple standpoint of reaction.

In this final chapter of Part I of our study we have sought to clarify the nonfoundationalist feature of our philosophy of communicative praxis. Our format for achieving this end has taken shape as a detour through Rorty's vigorous antifoundationalist polemic. This has enabled us to highlight some of the salient characteristics of a nonfoundationalist stance, showing principally how foundationalism as an epistemological problem becomes a wider concern about the status of philosophy as a discipline and a profession, courting reflections on the "end of philosophy." We have also found Rorty's shift of metaphors from "foundation" to "conversation," extended to the performance of

---

metaphysics *(Destruktion der Geschichte der Ontologie, Überwindung der Metaphysik),* but that he remains quite hostile to Heidegger's project of retrieval *(Wiederholung, Andenken).* In the end we get from Rorty neither Heideggerian 'thought' nor Gadamerian 'hermeneutics,' but—if there is anything 'continental' here—Derrida's play of signs." "The Case of Heidegger and Rorty," *The Review of Metaphysics,* Vol. XXXVI, No. 3, 1983, p. 662. Caputo would seem to be right about Rorty's attenuation, if not outright dismissal, of the notion of retrieval in Heidegger's project of recollective thinking. And this clearly restricts the resources and range of hermeneutics. We would agree with Caputo that this points to a "problem" in Rorty's understanding and use of hermeneutics. However, we remain somewhat reluctant in accompanying Caputo in his wholesale appropriation of the way that Heidegger marks out the path of retrieval in hermeneutical thinking. For Heidegger *"die Sache des Denkens"* is the disclosing power of Being (or event of appropriation in his later thought) to which there is a direct route via poetical thinking. As will become more apparent in Part II of our study, the question of being needs to be raised somewhat more obliquely and circuitously as one weaves one's way through the global anticipations and solicitations of experience within the discourse and action of communicative praxis. One does not begin with the Being-question; one backs into it through an exploration of the forms of communicative praxis.

philosophy, helpful in our placement of communicative praxis as a philosophical topic. Along the way we have engineered some criticisms of Rorty's philosophical conversations and of his more general recommendations for philosophy as a species of edification. But this has been done not in the interests of staging a professional debate, but rather in the interests of continuing the conversation by showing why the body of communicative praxis needs to be fleshed out in such a manner as to encompass the hermeneutical intentionality of displayed reference, critical discernment, and creative insight.

Part II

The New Horizon of Subjectivity

CHAPTER SIX

Hermeneutical Self-implicature

In Part I of our study we have probed the texture of communicative praxis and have seen how it opens up to a hermeneutical space of discourse and action in which a world of shared language and social practices is displayed. In successive chapters we have attended to the expressive meanings embedded in the tightly woven fabric of communicative praxis, detailed the performances of participation, distanciation, and recollection as they labor for a comprehension of the facticity of our situated discourse and action, and located the interpretive moment of such a comprehension in the bonding of understanding and explanation. This journey in Part I of our extended exploration has enabled us to track the ongoing intentionality of hermeneutical reference which postures communicative praxis as discourse and action *about* something. Discourse and action, in their amalgamated ventures, display a world of praxis in which the texts of the spoken and written word and the tissues of human associations and institutional life conspire in the figuration of forms of meaning. One might speak of this as an intertexture of praxial intentionality, which nurtures multiple ways, some new and some old, of interpreting the world and acting within it.

In Part II of our explorations we effect a shift of focus or attention. Proceeding from the intertexture of praxial intentionality a new posture of questioning unfolds. The goings-on in communicative praxis invite us to address the "who" of discourse and the "who" of action. Who is speaking? Who is writing? Who is acting? The unitary phenomenon of communicative praxis thus not only delivers a hermeneutical reference to the world, it also yields a hermeneutical implicature of a situated speaking, writing, and acting subject. The tracking of this implicature defines the task in Part II of our project as we explore the opening up of a new horizon of subjectivity within the global field of communicative practices.

In entertaining the move to a new horizon of subjectivity we are of course duly aware of the widespread suspicion that permeates various quarters concerning the language of subject, self, ego, and consciousness. Philosophers who still consider it as part of their trade to traffic in these concepts are finding that their services are less and less in demand. There is considerable discussion today about the dissolution and death of the subject. Fred R. Dallmayr has titled his comprehensive study of current philosophic and social thought *Twilight of Subjectivity*.[1] This title is especially apt for characterizing the state of affairs not only in the formal philosophy of the day but also in the current sciences of man and in literary theory. Not only professional philosophers but also social scientists and theorists of literature tend to see subjectivity as something which has had its day.

In formal philosophy Martin Heidegger of the Continental tradition and Ludwig Wittgenstein of the Anglo-American tradition have played a consequential role in the demise of subjectivity as a fruitful philosophical concept. Heidegger started much of this, already in his *Being and Time*, with his proposal for the destruction of the history of Western metaphysics and epistemology, through which subject, self, ego, and consciousness lose their preeminence in philosophical discourse. In his essay "The Age of the World Picture," a somewhat more direct assault on the philosophical use of "subject" is engineered. He sees the root of the problem residing in the misapplication of the Greek notion of *hypokeimenon* (as that which-lies-before and grounds everything else— later rendered as *subiectum*) to man as primary subject understood as center and ground.[2] This subjectivizing of man as center and ground, according to Heidegger, proceeds in tandem with the objectivization of the world. Man as subject "pictures" the world as object through a species of representation. The world becomes world-picture *(Weltbild)* as man becomes subject *(subiectum)*.[3] In the process man and world alike are eclipsed.

Wittgenstein's concerns about the conceptual aberrations of subject and consciousness, although they arise more specifically from the use of these terms in the contexts of perception and introspection, are not

---

[1] Amherst: The University of Massachusetts Press, 1981.

[2] "When man becomes the primary and only real *subiectum*, that means: Man becomes that being upon which all that is, is grounded as regards the manner of its Being and its truth. Man becomes the relational center of that which is as such." *The Question Concerning Technology,* trans. William Lovitt (New York: Harper & Row, 1977), p. 128.

[3] "When, accordingly, the picture character of the world is made clear as the represented-ness of that which is, then in order fully to grasp the modern essence of representedness we must track out and expose the original naming power of the worn-out word and concept 'to represent' *(vorstellen):* to set out before oneself and to set forth in relation to oneself. Through this, whatever is comes to a stand as object and in that way alone receives the seal of Being. That the world becomes picture is one and the same event of man's becoming *subiectum* in the midst of that which is." *Ibid.,* p. 132.

all that different from those of Heidegger. The genuine bugbear in our use of subject, self, and consciousness, according to Wittgenstein, is the propensity to look for their referents amongst the furniture of the world's factual contents, mistaking them for queer sorts of observable entities. But the "I" of consciousness does not belong in the world in the way that beetles and boxes do. It is not an object there to be observed, pictured, and represented. Nor is it a subjective mental basement out of which perception and consciousness emerge. The grammatical function of the "I" is neither that of representing an object nor that of representing a subject. It is rather that of announcing the way that one's attention is situated *(eingestellt)*.[4]

From yet another quarter the philosophical cash value of the currency of subject and subjectivity has been decisively deflated. In Michel Foucault's archaeology of knowledge, in which he charts the discontinuous epistemes that have appeared and disappeared in the history of the Western world, the human subject is destined for displacement. Foucault becomes a spokesman for the "Death of Man," which he understands as an unavoidable sequel to the "Death of God" already announced by Nietzsche. Under the spell of certain Heideggerian influences, many of them unacknowledged (and probably unrecognized), Foucault works out his "Death of Man" motif through a critical engagement with the history of Western metaphysics and epistemology. Consulting this history Foucault finds the crucial development to reside in the anthropological turn of Kant's philosophy. "Anthropology," Foucault observes, "constitutes perhaps the fundamental arrangement that has governed the path of philosophical thought from Kant until our own day."[5] Although Kant roused us from our dogmatic metaphysical slumbers, he did so only at the expense of inducing an even more consequential "anthropological sleep." By giving primacy to the question "What is man?" Kant contributed to the development of a new episteme, proceeding from the epistemological space of an analytic of human finitude forged by an "empirico-transcendental doublet."[6] This left its mark upon the developing sciences of man, which sought to ground themselves in a philosophical anthro-

---

[4] *Philosophical Investigations,* trans. G. E. M. Anscombe (New York: The Macmillan Company, 1953), # 417. Cf. 404, 410, and 413. See also *Philosophical Remarks,* ed. Rush Rhees (Chicago: University of Chicago Press, 1980): "One of the most misleading representation techniques in our language is the use of the word 'I', particularly when it is used in representing immediate experience, as in 'I can see a red patch.' " # 159.

[5] *The Order of Things: An Archaeology of the Human Sciences* (New York: Random House, 1970), p. 342.

[6] "Man, in the analytic of finitude, is a strange empirico-transcendental doublet, since he is a being such that knowledge will be attained in him of what renders all knowledge possible." *Ibid.,* p. 318.

pology of human historicity and human finitude. But anthropology falls asleep within the hollow carved out by Kant's counterpositioning of the transcendental and the empirical. Jarred from their anthropological slumbers, the human sciences were eventually awakened to the recognition that neither psychoanalysis, ethnology, nor linguistics needs to speak about man himself. Psychoanalysis situates its *telos* in the domain of the unconscious, ethnology in the domain of historicity, and linguistics in the domain of semiology. In this archaeology of modern thought, effected principally by the new sciences of man, the destiny of the human subject runs its course and its fate is sealed. It is seen as "an invention of recent date . . . perhaps nearing its end," occasioning the "wager that man would be erased, like a face drawn in sand at the edge of the sea."[7]

Foucault's illustration of the archaeology of knowledge strategy, as a species of philosophico-historical critique leading to the "Death of Man," points us directly to the fate of the subject in the special sciences of human behavior. In the modern disciplines of psychology, sociology, and anthropology the concept of the subject has fallen under a cloud of suspicion. Freud had already exploded the subject as a center of consciousness with his discovery of the play of unconscious motivations within the wider parameters of the psyche. Claude Lévi-Strauss, the structuralist anthropologist and sociologist, who might well be considered to be the founder of the influential *"Sciences de l'Homme"* movement, is rather adamant about the expulsion of the subject. Indeed, for Lévi-Strauss a human science can become a science only after the human subject is dissolved. Writing in his book *The Savage Mind,* he boldly proclaims his structuralist article of faith: "I believe the ultimate goal of the human sciences to be not to constitute, but to dissolve man."[8]

Now one must not be misled by the syntactical similarities between Foucault's "Death of Man" and Lévi-Strauss's "dissolution of man" shibboleths. Lévi-Strauss's call for a dissolution of man is the result of a methodological decision, requiring the pruning of all vestiges of subjectivity in the interests of knowledge relationships determined by classification and codification. Binary oppositions and structural relations, rather than entities, of either an objective or a subjective sort, provide for Lévi-Strauss the epistemological grid for knowledge in the human sciences. Foucault's approach is more historicist in character, following the lines of a philosophico-cultural critique of the successive epistemes in Western thought. Yet, the space of subjectivity is effectively dis-

---

[7] *Ibid.,* p. 387.
[8] Chicago: University of Chicago Press, 1966, p. 247.

assembled by both, and the subject as philosophical and scientific construct is placed aside.

The most dissident of the dissidents who have voiced their opposition to the category of subjectivity in its philosophical, scientific, and literary use, however, is Jacques Derrida. Hailed by many as the contemporary guru of deconstructionist strategy, Derrida is seen as having provided the proverbial coffin nails for the burial of subjectivity. The principal target of Derrida's deconstructionist strategy is the "white mythology" of logocentrism and the metaphysics of presence, the fragile superstructure that has been a refuge and solace for the denizens of subject, self, ego, consciousness, and their filial descendants. In the venerated tradition of Western thought from Plato onward, the metaphysics of presence has provided that territorial space in which the subject has sought a center and staked out its claims for permanence, self-identity, self-evidence, and apodicticity. It is this metaphysical space of presence that Derrida purports to disassemble or deconstruct. In the aftermath of this deconstruction the subject is rendered homeless. The subject, as at once presence of consciousness and consciousness of presence, loses its place. The guiding motif in all this, if indeed one can here still speak of that which "guides" and that which functions as a "motif," is the play of *différance*. Older than either presence or absence, *différance* is that "unnamable" out of which presence and absence can first be thought.[9]

To observe this play of *différance* Derrida points us to writing *(écriture)*. The voice of speech, indissolubly tied to the immediate self-presence of thought *(logos),* is effectively set aside by the dismantling of the metaphysics of presence. The question "Who is speaking?" is thus a question in pursuit of that which remains forever deferred. So we are advised to stick with writing. And here we find only writing, more writing, and writing about writing. Now the question "Who is writing?" seems to suffer the same fate as does the question "Who is speaking?" Just as the presence of the speaking subject is perpetually deferred, so also the search for the presence of intentions in the mind of the author

---

[9] " 'Older' than Being itself, our language has no name for such a differance. But we 'already know' that if it is unnamable, this is not simply provisional; it is not because our language has still not found or received this *name,* or because we would have to look for it in another language, outside the finite system of our language. It is because there is no *name* for this, not even essence or Being—not even the name 'differance', which is not a name, which is not a pure nominal entity, and continually breaks up in a chain of different substitutions." *Speech and Phenomena,* trans. David B. Allison and Newton Garver (Evanston: Northwestern University Press, 1973), p. 159. Also see page 147: "We thus come to posit presence—and, in particular, consciousness, the being-next-to-itself of consciousness—no longer as the absolutely matrical form of being but as a 'determination' and an 'effect'. Presence is a determination and effect within a system which is no longer that of presence but that of differance."

is a quest for that which escapes all determination. Now to ask about the "meaning" in this profusion of writing about writing is but to betray one's cathexis to logocentrism. There is neither meaning in the object of writing nor meaning in the subject who writes. There is only writing, as the inscription and reinscription of the play of *différance*.

The confluence of the above destructions, dissolutions, and deconstructions (in the thought of Heidegger, Wittgenstein, Foucault, Lévi-Strauss, and Derrida) has occasioned a "twilight of subjectivity," if not indeed a veritable disappearance of it from the horizon. We applaud many of these strategies coming from the different quarters because the subject as an epistemological, metaphysical, scientific, or literary construct is indeed a vagary of reflection that had best be set aside. But to be done with the subject in these senses is not to be done with the subject in every sense you please. We thus need to consider whether a new portrait of the subject and a new horizon of subjectivity might make their appearance in the wake of the current, proliferating deconstructions and dissolutions, which have become so familiar to us all.

We begin our consideration by suggesting that any new horizon of subjectivity, from which a resituated subject might emerge, will be disclosed only through the exploration of a new space. This new space is not an epistemological space of a lonely ego seeking commerce with an external public world. Nor it is the space of an encapsulated, interior mind of an author, somehow in communion with itself, creating an exterior text, a delivered object—like a sack of potatoes in one's pantry or a bundle of firewood on one's hearth. As we have already seen in a previous chapter, it is the metaphorical overextension of the senses of interior and exterior that is the genuine culprit in all this. Particularly since the time of Descartes every philosophical schoolboy has been trained to sort out the furniture of the universe in terms of that which is inside and that which is outside. This lies at the source of the modern paradigm of epistemological space. Within this space the subject is positioned as a container of interior meanings and intentions, and the works of thought and art become exterior and inert objects, alienated from the creative process that gave them birth. The solidification of this epistemological space, as an uncontested paradigm, has been particularly mischievous in our efforts to see the world and read a text.

It is this epistemological space, with its graphics of interior minds and exterior realities, private thoughts and public knowledge, that the modern-day deconstructionists have so effectively disassembled. But we see this deconstruction of epistemological space not as an end in itself but rather as providing a clearing for the global hermeneutical space of communicative praxis. It is this wider space of communicative praxis that provides the proper parameters for a transvalued subjectivity. This transvalued subjectivity, we will attempt to show, is implicated in the discourse and action that limns communicative praxis. We will call this posture of implication *hermeneutical implicature* because the implication at work in discourse and action always rides the crest of interpretation. Hence, "implication" in our usage should not be confused with its putative modal operation in a propositional calculus. Hermeneutical implicature is an experientially oriented tracking of the "who" of discourse and action.

We have already shown how discourse and action are always *about* something. They effect a nonobjectifying, displayed reference to the work of discourse and the world of action. Now we shift our attention to the implicated subject, setting forth this discourse and action as discourse and action *by* someone. It should be kept in mind that there are two intertwined spheres in which this implicature is at work. There is the discursive sphere of speaking and writing implicating a *speaking* and *authorial* subject, and there is the nondiscursive sphere of action and social practices implicating an *agentive* subject. Speaker, author, and agent, it should be underscored, are not *foundations* of communicative praxis, either singularly or as a trinity, but are rather implicates of it, emerging within its history and modified by its changing scenes. What is at issue is not a subject as a zero-point consciousness, unalterable presence, or underlying substratum; such would achieve intelligibility only within an abstracted epistemological space. The subject is not a *pre*-given entity; so also it is not a *post*-given entity, simply the sedimented result of an objective convergence of the historical forces within discourse and action. It is not an entity at all, but rather an event or happening that continues the conversation and social practices of mankind and inscribes its contributions on their textures. In this continuation of the conversation and practices of mankind the speaking subject is not the inventor of language, the authorial subject is not the creator of textuality, and the agentive subject is not the producer of social practices. The speaking subject always speaks in and from a language; the inscriptions of the authorial subject proceed against the background of delivered forms of textuality; and the subject as agent is socialized by the communal patterns in which he acts. Hence, when the subject is announced he appears not as the singular base, ground, or center of discourse and action but rather as a concrescence of multiple forms and facticities of communicative praxis.

The intentionality of implication in hermeneutical implicature is measured at every stage by the determinations of praxis. It moves within the holistic space of customs, skills, habits, and social practices, which marks out its directions. The subject is implicated somewhat like the way that the street urchin implicates himself in his telltale behavior and the unfaithful husband implicates himself in his careless conversation. The implicature at issue is an illustration of praxis-oriented intentionality, to be distinguished from the various formalized and mathematized notions of implication. Through the occasioning of hermeneutical self-implicature the questions "Who is speaking?" "Who is writing?" and "Who is acting?" assume new traces and new markings. They are no longer place-holders for an elusive and fugitive epistemological subject. They are questions which address a different phenomenon within a different space.

This different space is the hermeneutical space of discourse and action. Let us now attend more specifically to the space of discourse, of both speaking and writing, and follow the self-implicature of the subject within it. One has to start somewhere, so let us start the conversation by moving out from a promising portion of the text in Émile Benveniste's comprehensive study *Problems in General Linguistics*. Benveniste, the Lebanese linguist, has already suggested, although somewhat obliquely, the implicature of subjectivity that we wish to recommend.

> It is in and through language that man constitutes himself as a *subject,* because language alone establishes the concept of "ego" in reality, in its reality which is that of the being.
>
> The "subjectivity" we are discussing here is the capacity of the speaker to posit himself as "subject." It is defined not by the feeling which everyone experiences of being himself (this feeling, to the degree that it can be taken note of, is only a reflection) but as the psychic unity that transcends the totality of the actual experiences it assembles and that makes the permanence of the consciousness. Now we hold that that "subjectivity," whether it is placed in phenomenology or in psychology, as one may wish, is only the emergence in the being of a fundamental property of language. "Ego" is he who *says* "ego."[10]

This is a rather dense passage, but when unpacked it offers some interesting possible moves. Benveniste here sets forth a strong claim for the linguisticality of the subject. It is through language that man constitutes himself as subject. Now "constitution" as used here should not be confused with "causality." Benveniste is sufficiently conversant with the phenomenological tradition so as not to confuse the distinction between constitution and causality. It is not that the "I" or "ego" is a causal effect of the act of speaking. So when Benveniste submits

---

[10]Trans. Mary Elizabeth Beek (Coral Gables, Florida: University of Miami Press, 1971), p. 224.

" 'Ego' is he who *says* 'ego' " he does not mean that in the episodical moment of speaking the pronoun "I" the subject is created as a causal effect of the utterance. Among other things, this would produce an unmanageable proliferation of subjects in that each episode of saying "I" would create a new subject. The constitution at issue is not that of causal production but rather that of the determination of sense—in this case the determination of the sense of "psychic unity that transcends the totality of the actual experiences."

To proceed further: as the "I" is not the causal result of a speech act, so also it is not a formal place-holder for a parade of particulars. "I" is not a class concept like "rock," "tree," "table," and "professor" are class concepts, waiting for particulars to instantiate them. "I" is an index and indicator that points to and makes manifest the "who" of the saying. The "I" as the one who is speaking is implicated in the saying.

As one needs to be wary about mistaking constitution for causality and misconstruing the personal pronoun "I" as a class concept, so one also needs to attend to the event and performance of *saying* when one *says* "I" or "ego." In his construction " 'Ego' is he who *says* 'ego'," Benveniste underscores the word "says." This signals the importance of saying as a peculiar intentionality of discourse. Saying is not simply vocalization, the physiological process of uttering sounds; nor is it simply the execution of an individual speech act. It is surely these—but it is more. It is the saying of something *by* someone *about* something. The occasion for saying is that one has something to say. Saying is the relating of a narrative or the telling of a story. The German *sagen* highlights this originative sense of saying more pointedly than does its English equivalent. *Sagen* is the activation of a *saga*. It is a story or a tale being told. In the saying of "ego" the story that is told has a double plot. It is a narration of that around which the saying turns, and it is a narration implicating the narrator. In the peculiar intentionality of saying "I," the two plots become one. The story narrated is the story of the narrator. It is the story of the speaking subject, immersed in the density of the life of praxis, embedded within a sociohistorical formation process in which the subject already understands himself, albeit prereflectively, as the one who is speaking.

It is important not to confuse the hermeneutical self-implicature of the speaking subject in the event of saying with the idealist concept of self-reflexive consciousness. The concept of self-reflexive consciousness, which reaches far back into the tradition of modern idealism, regulated the putative cognition of a prelinguistic datum of subjectivity, a pure presence of consciousness, present to itself. Hermeneutical self-implicature, although it does not as such entail a denial of the event of self-consciousness, does call into question a prelinguistic origin. Self-consciousness is mediated through language, understood as the performance of discourse fleshed out as the event of saying. The event of self-consciousness is inseparable from the history of saying "I."

We have moved out from Benveniste's portrayal of the constitution of the subject through language, attempting to unpack and excavate some of the interesting suggestions that he provides in his dense, general statement. Admittedly, we may have gone further in this regard than he himself would want to go, but this is itself, we would maintain, an intrinsic feature of hermeneutical explication. And we wish to go even further and submit some important consequences that follow from the setting forth of the subject within the wider space of language as discourse.[11]

The first important consequence is that it overcomes the opposition between language and speech, which became so much a part of the structuralist rendering of Saussurian linguistics. Although Benveniste recognizes, as we all must, the distinction between *la parole* (the event of speaking) and *le langue* (the spoken language as a linguistic system), he is careful to avoid a bifurcation of these two aspects into separate levels or domains—the infrastructural and synchronic domain of language versus the superstructural and diachronic domain of speech. The constitution of the subject is executed through language as saying. Language, thusly understood, is not simply *le langue* as a linguistic system, nor is it simply *la parole* as an episodical speech act. It is a third feature, a mediating event of concretion. Language as saying is the epiphany of discourse in which speech intersects with a linguistic tradition of sedimented social forms and grammatical rules. The word as being spoken in the occurrent speech act joins the word as already spoken. It is in this way that the intolerable opposition within the structuralist model is overcome. The structuralist model leaves us with an abstracted space of language as system (phonemic and lexical units and syntactical rules) in which quite understandably the question "Who is speaking?" has no place. Here one is concerned only with the linguistic play of signifier and signified within the formal determination

---

[11]It is important that the reader recognize that our appropriation of Benveniste's approach to the subject in his *General Linguistics*, if one is indeed here to talk of appropriation, is a critical one. We find his entrée to the subject through language fruitful and suggestive. Yet, we are troubled by the residual foundationalism and idealism that intermittently insinuate themselves into his thought. This is evidenced in his appeal to subjectivity as a *foundation*, "determined by the linguistic status of 'person'" (p. 224). Here language seems to assume the privilege of a new foundation, through which man "posits" himself as subject. Constitution construed as a positing belies a rather heavy cargo of idealism. We recommend a more praxis-oriented and less idealist notion of constitution.

of the sign. But this is not yet discourse. One has discourse only in the performance of a saying, in which the act of speaking and the system of language conspire as a unitary event. It is in and through this unitary event that the speaking subject is implicated. Here the question "Who is speaking?" is not only permissible—it is unavoidable.

There is a second consequence of our effort to resituate the subject within the tissues of discourse as we carry our analysis yet a step further. We have observed the implicature of the subject in the performance of discourse as saying. Now we wish to suggest that this space of subjectivity, in which this self-implication eventuates, is at once a space of intersubjectivity. The subject is implicated not as an isolated speaking subject but as a subject whose mode of being in discourse is essentially that of being able to speak with other subjects. Again, we work this out by attending to the intentionalities of discourse as event and performance. The conversational space of the "I" in discourse is coinhabited by the "you." In the dialogic transaction, which is if not a privileged surely a frequent posture of discourse, the "I" and the "you" slide back and forth within a common space. In the saying of "I," in submitting my thesis or contention in the form of "I believe . . ." or "I maintain . . .," the indexical posture of "I" is dialectically bonded with the posture of "you" as the one being addressed. I as speaker emerge in the presence of you as hearer. A speaker/hearer intertexture limns the space in which the speaking subject is implicated. The indexicality of "I" as speaker achieves sense only in relation to "you" as hearer. I am able to say "I" only because of an acknowledgment of you as my interlocutor within the dynamics of the dialogic encounter. The "I" and the "you" are as it were coconstituted, sharing a common, intersubjective space.

Indeed, within the density of the dialogic encounter the thoughts that are mine and the thoughts that are yours codevelop in a consummate reciprocity. I lend you a thought-experiment, a possible way of seeing things, and you respond. Your response is one of incorporating what I have said, by either acceptance, rejection, or modification. Then I respond by incorporating your response into my initial claims. Such is the ongoing dialectics of dialogue. Only after we do a postmortem on the dialogue, lay it out as an accomplished fact, are we able to sort out, and only with relative success, the episodical histories of that which was mine and that which was yours. The "I" and the "you" thus need to be seen as coemergents within a more encompassing intentional fabric of intersubjectivity. No "I" is an island, entire of itself; every subject is a piece of the continent of other subjects, a part of the main of intersubjectivity.

Using Benveniste's doctrine of the constitution of the subject through language as an appropriate topic with which to begin, we have followed the route of hermeneutical implicature back to a transvalued subject, resituated within a nonepistemological space of communicative praxis. Our directives have been provided by the intentionality of discourse, understood as the event of saying something about something by someone. However, our attention has focused principally on saying as the event of speaking, and even more specifically on the dialogic transaction as a telling illustration of this saying. But writing is also a form of saying, and like the saying of speaking so the saying of writing exhibits a hermeneutical self-implicature, raising the issue of the posture and bearing of the authorial subject. The question of the primacy of speaking versus the primacy of writing, which currently has been given so much attention, may in the end be just another one of those invented "weighty" problems, symptomatic of an obsession with primacy and necessary starting points. Whether the word that was in the beginning was spoken or written is a worry that exudes a speculative pointlessness. We would urge that communicative praxis, in its lived-through engagements, affords both patterns of speech and patterns of writing as complementary modes of discourse. The principal task in an elucidation and probing of the texture of communicative praxis is not that of divining how the one might be parasitical upon the other but rather that of describing what it is that goes on in the saying of each.

Our probing of the hermeneutical implicature of self in discourse leads into the region of writing. Written discourse poses the question of the self-implicature of the subject in another form. What place is to be accorded the authorial subject in the event of writing? How does one recognize the "who" of writing? What manner of interplay occurs between the intentions of the author, his inscriptions, and the meaning of the text? Wherein resides the authority of the author? Schooled as we all are in the ways of modern criticism, frightened in our formative years by the "intentional fallacy," we no longer look for the author's *Weltanshauung* behind the text but look rather straight at the text itself so as to discern its architectonic thematic and its intricate web of internal relationships. To engage in a reconstruction of the thought and experience of the author, we have learned, is to miss the point of what text interpretation and literary criticism are all about. Michel Foucault has succeeded in stating rather well what the consequences of all this are.

Writing unfolds like a game that inevitably moves beyond its own rules and finally leaves them behind. Thus, the essential basis of this writing is not the exalted emotions related to the act of composition or the insertion of a subject into language. Rather it is primarily concerned with creating an opening where the writing subject endlessly disappears.[12]

This disappearance of the writing subject, observes Foucault, has been a distinctive mark of the age particularly since the time of Mallarmé. The question "Who is writing?" achieves an answer only through its displacement by the word of the text itself. The writing subject, along with the speaking subject, has veritably entered the twilight zone in the landscape of contemporary criticism and theory of literature.

There is much that strikes us as being "right" in all this. Our instructors on the intentional fallacy have steered us away from the fruitless search for authorial intentions, inhabiting the corridors of a fugitive and recessed mental sphere of interiority. As we have seen in Part I of our study, the texts of speaking and writing deliver a surplus of meaning that outstrips the particular intentions of speakers and writers within their socio-psychological-historical situatedness. The admonition to avoid the intentional fallacy has provided us with a noble truth of literary theory. However, the limited services of this noble truth should not go unnoticed. Geared chiefly toward an avoidance of psychologism in matters literary and textual, the intentional fallacy principle simply reviews for us what we had already learned from Husserl's *Logical Investigations*—namely that you cannot chase down meaning by detailing a spate of psychological conditions. The meaning of a text cannot be delivered through an inspection of the intrapsychic goings-on within the mind of the author, and this is the case because the very notion of such intrapsychic goings-on is suspect. Meaning does not arise thusly. To get to the sources of meaning, textual or otherwise, we need to attend to the dynamics and history of communicative praxis. But the tracking of meaning within the sociohistorical interstices of the conversation and practices of mankind does no more than resituate, relativize, and decentralize the role of the author. It does not entail his displacement. It decentralizes the authority of the author and invites an examination of the contribution of meaning from other quarters. It points to the surplus of meaning from which every author borrows, and at times unknowingly. To dethrone the writing subject as an absolute

---

[12] *Language, Counter-Memory, Practice*, trans. Donald F. Bouchard and Sherry Simon (Ithaca: Cornell University Press, 1977), p. 116. Roland Barthes has promulgated a similar view on the role of the writing subject in his essay "The Death of the Author." According to Barthes, "Writing is that neutral, composite, oblique space where our subject slips away, the negative where all identity is lost, starting with the very identity of the body writing . . . it is language which speaks, not the author; to write is, through a prerequisite impersonality (not at all to be confused with the castrating objectivity of the realist novelist), to reach that point where only language acts, 'performs,' and not 'me.'" *Image Music Text*, trans. Stephen Heath (New York: Hill and Wang, 1977), pp. 142–143.

monarch, who exercises an unconditional sovereignty over the meaning of the text, is not tantamount to his banishment from the kingdom of literary, scientific, and philosophical creativity. Foucault, in his usual elliptical way, recognizes this much in his musing on the matter.

> Is it not possible to reexamine, as a legitimate extension of this kind of analysis, the privileges of the subject? Clearly, in undertaking an internal and architectonic analysis of a work (whether it be a literary text, a philosophical system, or a scientific work) and in delimiting psychological and biographical references, suspicions arise concerning the absolute nature and creative role of the subject. But the subject should not be entirely abandoned. It should be reconsidered, not to restore the theme of the originating subject, but to seize its functions, its intervention in discourse, and its system of dependencies.[13]

Foucault here goes on record calling for a "reconsideration" of the author as subject—clearly not as an originating agent but rather as a function of discourse. This emerging "author-function" motif in Foucault's thought appears on the scene as an overture toward the resuscitation of the corpse that he unveiled in his "Death of Man" motif. Having died as anthropologico-historical subject, man comes back to life as a function of discourse. Unfortunately, however, we have only scattered promissory notes on how this resuscitation of the subject as "author-function" is to be accomplished and how it might fit into the wider space of discourse which he sought to clear in his archaeological investigations in the *Order of Things*. Also, it should be noted that we experience some nervousness about his heavy emphasis on the language of "function," whose meaning appears to result from its opposition to the language of "substance" on the one hand and the language of "structure" on the other. It may be that neither the traditional conceptual framework of substance versus function nor the more recent language of structure versus function, both of which continue their investments in the stock of metaphysical and epistemological enterprises, is particularly helpful for the current requirement of resituating the subject.

We also have some concerns about Foucault's suppression of the creative power and role of the subject. In viewing the author as a variable function of discourse, he is forced to strip the author-subject of his creativity. Foucault brings this upon himself by construing "creativity," "profundity," and "original inspiration" as matters of psychological intention on the part of the author and psychological

---

[13] *Language, Counter-Memory, Practice*, p. 137.

projections on the part of the reader.[14] In the moment, however, that creativity, profundity, and inspiration as features of the author's individuality are placed into a psychologistic matrix, we have the intentional fallacy all over again and begin to look for a way of suspending the psychological dispositions of the author as an individuated subject. What is required is a nonpsychological rendering of creativity in which creativity is linked more directly with the process of creative sense-formation in which the author participates than with occurrent psychological states and dispositions, either on the part of the author or on the part of the reader. This process of sense-formation proceeds by dint of a releasement which frees the inscriptions of the author from the matrix of psychological causality. It exhibits a power to display new discriptions and mark out new perspectives, which the author achieves principally through the resourcefulness of the imaginative play of metaphor. Nonetheless, Foucault's call for a reconsideration and resituation of the author is a question that does not go away, even after the event of deconstruction. The "who" of authorial inscription, like the phoenix, perpetually rises from the ashes of its own destruction.

Jacques Derrida, like his fellow countryman Foucault, has suggested the need to reask the question about the subject after it has been decentered as the zero-point origin in a philosophy of logocentrism. In an interchange with Serge Doubrovsky, Derrida rather candidly confessed that one cannot simply be done with the subject as speaker and author after the fallout of deconstruction is assessed.

> First of all, I didn't say that there was no center, that we could get along without a center. I believe that the center is a function, not a being—a reality, but a function. And this function is absolutely indispensable. The subject is absolutely indispensable. I don't destroy the subject; I situate it. That is to say, I believe that at a certain level both of experience and of philosophical and scientific discourse one cannot get along without the notion of subject. It is a question of knowing where it comes from and how it functions.[15]

---

[14] "The third point concerning this 'author-function' is that it is not formed spontaneously through the simple attribution of a discourse to an individual. It results from a complex operation whose purpose is to construct the rational entity we call an author. Undoubtedly, this construction is assigned a 'realistic' dimension as we speak of an individual's 'profundity' or 'creative' power, his intentions or the original inspiration manifested in writing. Nevertheless, these aspects of an individual, which we designate as an author (or which comprise an individual as an author), are projections, in terms always more or less psychological, of our way of handling texts." *Ibid.*, p. 127.

[15] *The Languages of Criticism and the Sciences of Man: The Structuralist Controversy,* ed. Richard Macksey and Eugenio Donato (Baltimore: Johns Hopkins Press, 1970), p. 271.

Derrida's resituation of the subject as a function would appear, on the face of it at any rate, to have much in common with Foucault's retrieval of the "author-function." And as is the case of Foucault so also in the case of Derrida, we would question the accentuated dependence on the language of "function." Function as distinct from what? Apparently as distinct from "substance." The subject is "not a being—a reality, but a function," Derrida tells us. But does function here have a *sense* except in relation to the classical category of an *entia realia?* Functions are the manners in which real things are displayed in their functioning. Although distinct from substance, function has a sense only in relation to it. In all this the traditional metaphysical (and one might add "logocentric") categorial frame of inquiry seems to remain rather firmly intact. But this will hardly do if indeed the tradition of logocentric metaphysics is to be disassembled through the strategy of deconstruction. Apparently something takes the place of substance. And that which takes its place is *écriture.* The subject is a function not of a substance but rather a function of writing. It is in writing that the traces of the authorial subject are to be found.

It is within this context of ruminations on *écriture* that the event of the "signature" assumes such importance for Derrida.[16] The signature provides the trace of the imprinting by the authorial subject. But the signification of the signature, Derrida points out, lacks a definitive reference. This is the upshot of his somewhat entertaining exchange with John Searle, resulting from Derrida's critical discussion of J. L. Austin's *How To Do Things With Words.* In his response to Searle's rejoinder to the discussion, Derrida puzzles over Searle's signature in the copyright inscription—"copyright 1977, John R. Searle." What, asks Derrida, is signified by this signature? Matters become somewhat complicated because in the footnote to the title of his rejoinder Searle writes: "I am indebted to H. Dreyfus and D. Searle for discussion of these matters." So who is the author? Is it J. Searle? Is it J. Searle and H. Dreyfus? Is it J. Searle, H. Dreyfus, and D. Searle? Is it all of these, and possibly more? The signification of the signature appears to explode and pulverize into a multiplicity of authors, all of whom have some species of claim to authorship.[17]

The issue that Derrida here addresses, punctuated with the accents

---

[16] See particularly his essay "Signature Event Context" in *Glyph: Johns Hopkins Textual Studies,* Vol. I (Baltimore: Johns Hopkins University Press, 1977)

[17] "If John R. Searle owes a debt to D. Searle concerning this discussion, then the 'true' copyright ought to belong (as is indeed suggested along the frame of this *tableau vivant*) to a Searle who is divided, multiplied, conjugated, shared. What a complicated signature! And one that becomes even more complex when the debt includes my old friend, H. Dreyfus, with whom I myself have worked, discussed, exchanged ideas, so that if it is indeed through him that the Searles have 'read' me, 'understood' me, and 'replied' to me,

of levity, carries its own measure of weight. Every author who has written a book knows that the preface is the most difficult part of the book to write, for it is in the preface that one acknowledges those who in one way or another contributed to the embodiment of thought within the text. There are, of course, the immediate colleagues who have read and critiqued the manuscript and whose suggestions have been directly and indirectly appropriated. So they are summarily acknowledged. But there are also the remote colleagues, with whom one has dialogued and discussed the issues at professional meetings. And then there are one's students, from whom one always learns more than one either recognizes or is willing to tell. Sometimes one's spouse and one's children have offered suggestions that make a difference both in what is said and in how it is said. Hence, they too would seem to be part of the authorship. And then there is the matter of other authors, both living and dead, whom one applauds or critiques in the course of one's own writing. Without their authorship one's own authorship could not come to fruition. But within the confined limitations of a preface one simply cannot acknowledge all those, living and dead, who have made a difference for the composition of the text. A preface has to be concluded, so one brings it to a close—and signs one's name.

Derrida and Foucault have highlighted some of the consequences of the disappearance of the author as an event of our time. No longer invested with a sovereignty over the meaning of the text, the author more and more recedes in the textual scheme of things. He still signs his name, but this signature is fraught with an ambiguity and an indeterminacy of reference. Yet, Foucault and Derrida are of the mind that the author needs to be "reconsidered" and properly "situated," and they propose that we think of the author in terms of a function—a function of the text and a function of *écriture*. Insofar as the term "function" trades so heavily on its metaphysical/epistemological cognates of "substance" and "structure," we propose another route back to the subject, that of hermeneutical self-implicature. This self-implicature, it must be emphasized, is no facile movement of self-reference. The author cannot be picked out as an abiding, self-identical, interior mind of which writing the text is one of its attributes. The construing of the author as an interior mind producing an exterior text is at once an effacement of the author as principal contributor and a diminution of the text as a work or labor of creativity. The relation between the author and the text is more

---

then I, too, can claim a stake in the 'action' or 'obligation,' the stocks and bonds, of this holding company, the Copyright Trust. And it is true that I have occasionally had the feeling—to which I shall return—of having almost 'dictated' this reply. 'I' therefore feel obliged to claim my share of the copyright of the *Reply*." "Limited INC a b c . . . ," *Glyph*, Vol 2, p. 165.

that of a consummate involvement than that of an exteriorization of internal feelings and ideas. The authorial space of the writing subject is not a sphere of interiority. Like the space of the speaking subject it is at once a public space of intersubjectivity. No author, like no speaker, is an island entire of itself. This is why the trace of the signature is so serpentine, winding its way through a multiplicity of profiles, illustrating various vectors of indebtedness to other subjects and an appropriation of that which has already been spoken and written in the tradition. The author with his text remains embedded in the delivered tradition and the sense-sedimentation that it exudes.

The author, reconsidered and resituated, emerges within this wider fabric of meaning, implicated within a hermeneutical space of sense-sedimentation and sense-formation. The authorial subject is at the same time implicated as the "who" that receives and transmits the interplay of thought-speech-writing as already accomplished, and as the "who" that releases through his genius and creativity new configurations of sense. The latter should not be glossed, as is so often the case in the "Death of the Author" literature. Genius, creativity, and originality, although neither isolable dispositions in an author's mind nor psychological projections on the part of the reader, are nonetheless genuine moments in the life of the author and in the more global event of writing. Although one might be properly advised against having any truck with a "great author" theory of history based on selected writings in science, philosophy, and literature, it would be folly not to recognize a measure of creativity in the labors of someone like Newton, Kant, or Shakespeare. Their inscriptions offer new ways of understanding both the physical universe and the cultural life of man.

It is this implicated author, intersticing the reception of the tradition and the creation of that which has not yet been thought and written, that is indexed by the signature, by the signing of either a proper name or a pseudonym. Victor Eremita, Frater Taciturnus, Constantin Constantius, Climacus, and Anticlimacus—the pseudonyms of Kierkegaard, are also signatures. But they are signatures that illustrate a characteristic weave of intentionality. They announce the multifaceted posture of the author and illustrate the strategy of indirect communication as a mode of discourse. Pseudonymous signatures display the multiplicity of personifications and possibilities through which the author moves in shaping his discourse. Kierkegaard, whose skill and profundity in pseudonymous writing to this day remain unparalleled, is one of the few philosophical authors who have written about their writings. In his illuminating exercise in authorial self-reflection, "The Point of View for My Work as an Author," he tells the story of his pseudonymous authorship. "One will perceive the significance of the pseudonyms and why I must be pseudonymous in relation to all aesthetic productions, because I led my own life in entirely different categories."[18] Pseudonymity points us to the play of possibilities within the portrait of the subject as author. It announces an author-subject transcending the facticity of his point of view by way of thought-experiments that concretize alternative perspectives.

Our explorations of hermeneutical self-implicature have led us over the terrain of discourse as speaking and writing, enabling us to excavate traces of a speaking and an authorial subject. In doing so we have restored the relevance of the question as to the "who" of discourse. Discourse exhibits a displayed reference to an intersubjective world of interlocutors and a multilayered world of the text, which in turn implicates a speaking and authorial subject within these worlds. This is the story about one side of communicative praxis. But there is another side—that of purposive action, social practices, and institutional involvement. The story of this other side also must be told, for in doing so one provides a sheet anchor against the sublation of action into textuality, social practices into discourse. One of the trouble spots in Derrida's otherwise imaginative notion of textuality is the tendency to subordinate action to the text of discourse. Textuality takes the place of "world." It is this reduction of action to textuality, the nondiscursive to the discursive, that we have sought to avoid throughout our discussion. Now in attending to this other side of communicative praxis we can follow the hermeneutical vectors leading to another posture of the subject—the subject as actor and agent in the midst of social transactions. In following the intentionality of these vectors another profile in the drama of subjectivity is adumbrated as the "who" of action moves onto the set.

Paul Ricoeur has opened the parameters of inquiry for addressing this emergent profile of subjectivity in his eidetics of the voluntary and the involuntary in his comprehensive study *Freedom and Nature*.[19] Presenting an eidetic description of the will and human motivation, this work offers a phenomenology of human action, pivoting around an

---

18 *The Point of View, ETC,* trans. Walter Lowrie (Oxford University Press, 1939), pp. 85–86. Also cf. pp. 13–14, 39–40, and 146.

19 *Freedom and Nature: The Voluntary and the Involuntary,* trans. Erazim V. Kohak (Evanston: Northwestern University Press, 1966). There is also Alexander Pfänder's very important work *Phenomenology of Willing and Motivation,* trans. Herbert Spiegelberg (Evanston: Northwestern University Press, 1967). A full appreciation of Pfänder's contribution to the phenomenological movement, and particularly to the phenomenology of volition, is still wanting. He developed a critical version of phenomenology which retained certain features of Husserl's epochistic reduction, in modified form, but which jettisoned Husserl's transcendental reduction and its accompanying idealism. In this critical phenomenology the interdependent phenomena of willing and motivation are

analysis of the phenomenon of decision and the intentionality of willing. Situated between the involuntary forces of nature and the possibilities for human freedom, decision is cast in the role of mediation. In describing this role Ricoeur points us to what he calls the "prereflexive imputation of myself" in the act of decision. Decision implicates me in the act. *"Je me decide a. . . ."*[20] The English rendering of this French syntax falls out roughly as "making up my mind in the act of decision." The German on this point is closer to the French: *"Ich entsheide mich. . . ."* The point at issue is that decision summons the self as agent in the action to be undertaken, as actor in the project to be realized. This "self-imputation" is prereflexive in that it is not a matter of a theoretical observation by a present self explaining its presence to itself through a reflexive duplication. It is, as Ricoeur puts it, a self-imputation via action rather than an observation of a state of affairs.[21] The trace of subjectivity is manifested in the decision-action configuration of praxis, rather than in a tortuous self-reflexivity of an epistemological subject attempting to deliver knowledge of itself. The actional route to subjectivity follows a detour around the deconstructed site of idealist, epistemologically oriented self-constitution.

The subjectivity implicated in decision and action is not an isolated and episodical act of will, a *voluntas solus ipse*. The space of subjectivity of the acting subject is that of a field of projects, incorporating an agenda of action that has both its precedents and its new business to be enacted. The "who" of action is implicated in action as already accomplished and in the projection of tasks yet to be done. Implicated in his action as a moving synthesis of a history of decisions as already decided (congealed into a monadology of will of sorts) with an expanding field of possibilities yet to be decided (which relativizes and sublates every monadology), the deciding and acting subject is always on the way. However, in the mode of "being on the way," in its perpetual process of self-overcoming, as Nietzsche would have it, the acting subject is never a pure possibility. It is concretized in its destiny of a self already

given studied attention. Pfänder's purpose in these investigations is to show how the intentionality of willing is misconstrued if it is set within a matrix of representation. Herbert Spiegelberg is one of the few scholars of the phenomenological movement who have recognized the importance of Pfänder's contribution. See his work *The Context of the Phenomenological Movement* (The Hague: Martinus Nijhoff, 1981), and particularly chapter 4, "Husserl and Pfänder on the Phenomenological Reduction," and chapter 5, " 'Linguistic Phenomenology': John L. Austin and Alexander Pfänder."

[20] *Freedom and Nature*, p. 58.

[21] "Thus it is clear that the entire initial implication of myself is not a conscious relation or an observation. I behave actively in relation to myself, I determine *myself*. Once again French usage throws light on the situation: to determine my conduct is to determine myself—*se determiner*. Prereflexive self-imputation is active not observational." *Ibid.*, p. 59.

decided. The history of its decisions provides the material for its self-overcoming.

The space of subjectivity, however, encompasses not only the history of the individual, concretized as a self already decided and temporalized in such a manner that it is ever on the way, deciding time and again. It also encompasses, and from bottom up if you will, the social practices of other agents and actors and the formative influences that issue from them. This conditions every individual action by the acting subject as a response to a previous action upon him. The trace of subjectivity in individual decision and action thus furrows a path to configurations of shared experiences and joint endeavors rather than to solipsistic volitional intentions. Action is placed into the context of a response to prior action of other subjects and the acceptance of challenges afforded by this action. The understanding of an action by an individual actor, either prereflectively or reflectively, is inseparable from the reading of the actions of other agents, embedded in a holistic, hermeneutical space of interpretation of communal memories and communal goals. So again we see how the space of subjectivity is disclosed as a texture of intersubjectivity.

The recognition of this global interdependence of subject and other subjects in the social practices of mankind has occasioned in the phenomenological literature an alleged requirement for an "intersubjective constitution." We share the phenomenologists' motivation that moves them to emphasize the intersubjectivity of the life-world, but we are suspicious about the residual idealism that travels with the language of constitution. Both the subjective and the intersubjective constitution, as worked out by Husserl and his followers, proceed along the designs of a phenomenological idealism, guided by a search for epistemological foundations. All constitution proceeds from the "principle of all principles"—the self-presence and self-identity of consciousness. Through the instrumentation of the phenomenological-transcendental reduction the presence of this consciousness is *re*presented, first in a sphere of ownness as the proper region for the subjective constitution and then in a sphere of otherness which provides the site for the constitution of the other-as-meant.[22]

The difficulties that we encounter here are twofold, one intrinsic to the project as defined and the other extrinsic, involving a questioning of the project itself. The intrinsic problem has to do with delivering an adequate notion of being-with-the-other by proceeding from the solitary mental life of the constituting subject and then moving to the other-

---

[22] See particularly Husserl's discussion of this topic in his "Fifth Meditation" of *Cartesian Meditations*, trans. Dorion Cairns (The Hague: Martinus Nijhoff, 1960).

as-meant within the broader context of cultural life. This results in an aporia of phenomenological solipsism. The other appears not as *other-as-encountered,* with a reciprocating ontological claim on the constitution of subjectivity, but rather as *other-as-known* through a species of empathic identification and analogical projection coming from the side of the subject as knower. The other as encountered remains perpetually deferred. The other as content of knowledge is only other-for-my-consciousness. The encountering of the other in the sphere of praxis leads to an epistemological rupture, a questioning of the performance of constitution as an epistemological act, which in turn leads to a questioning of the phenomenological "principle of all principles" in the guise of a self-evident and self-identical presence of consciousness. In our exploration of the texture of communicative praxis we have set aside this project of epistemological grounding and have replaced it with the task of interpretation as a symbiotic event of understanding and explanation. With this task a new set of requirements is instated—requirements having to do not with the retrieval of the presence of the other within the folds of the presence of the subject, but rather with a discernment of the traces of the coemergence of the subject and the other within the discourse and shared activities of communicative praxis. Hermeneutical implicature of self-with-other supplants the epistemological constitution of the other.

Because of the considerable indebtedness of the language of constitution to the tradition of idealism it might be argued that misunderstanding is best avoided by jettisoning the language of constitution itself. Such a case has been presented by John O'Neill in his probing study on the philosophy of Merleau-Ponty, where he recommends a shift away from the language of transcendental constitution to that of "reflection as institution."[23] We applaud the contextualization of reflection within the fabric of the institutional life of man, but in the interests of maintaining at least a residual commensurability of discourse, thus keeping the lines of communication in the conversation of mankind open, we suggest not the displacement of the notion of constitution as such but rather its de-epistemologization and resituation within the holistic hermeneutical space of communicative performance. As we have urged in a previous study, "constitution" need not be given over to the practitioners of transcendental phenomenology. There is an ongoing process of constitution stitched into the praxis of shared projects and joint endeavors that guide the reflections of the community of in-

---

[23] *Perception, Expression and History: The Social Phenomenology of Maurice Merleau-Ponty* (Evanston: Northwestern University Press, 1970), chapter 5.

vestigators and interpreters.[24] This constitution of, by, and for praxis proceeds not via the legislations of a "mental act" representing mental contents, but rather by way of a communal and institutional reflection, bearing the inscriptions of habits, skills, and social practices which display their own insight and disclosure.

It is against this background of human action, as a configuration of habits, skills, customs, and institutions, that the question concerning the "who" of the subject takes on a peculiar relevance. The hermeneutical self-implicature of the acting subject follows the route marked out within the holistic space of praxis. The implicature at issue here is not that of a linear progression from proposition to inference against the background of a system of beliefs, but rather that of a circling back to actors and agents involved in a system of social practices. The terminus of the implicature is not a mental act as the source of beliefs and the condition for representational knowledge of the world, but rather an acting subject engaged with other subjects. The mind and its mental acts can always be bracketed out of a system of beliefs, which can be treated as a formal, theoretical body of propositions. On this level the spectre of skepticism, relative either to an objectively known world or a subjectively cognized subject, cannot effectively be dispelled. As Kierkegaard had already so perceptively observed, the skeptic is entrapped not by a system of beliefs but by an ensemble of practices, actions, and decisions.

> The real trap in which to catch the skeptic is ethics. Since Descartes they have all maintained that, during the period in which they doubted, they might not make any definite statement with regard to knowledge but they might act, because in that respect one could be satisfied with probability. What a tremendous contradiction! As though it were not far more terrible to do something about which one was doubtful (for one thereby assumes a responsibility) than make a statement.[25]

In this chapter our concern has been to formulate a notion of hermeneutical self-implicature as the first stage in the recovery of self within a new horizon of subjectivity. The proper site for such a recovery, we have urged, is the holistic space of communicative praxis, in which the performances of speech, writing, and action are situated. In exploring this space we have found that the questions "Who is speaking?" "Who is writing?" and "Who is acting?" take on a renewed urgency in

---

[24] Calvin O. Schrag, *Radical Reflection and the Origin of the Human Sciences* (West Lafayette: Purdue University Press, 1980), pp. 66–69.
[25] *The Journals of Søren Kierkegaard*, ed. Alexander Dru (New York: Oxford University Press, 1938), entry 426.

the aftermath of the deconstruction of the subject as monadological mind and epistemological origin. The subject as speaker, author, and actor is restored, not as a foundation for communicative praxis but as an implicate of it. Implicated within the dynamics of communicative praxis the subject emerges via its co-constitution with other subjects as the narrator, actor, and respondent within the human drama of discourse and social practices.

CHAPTER SEVEN

The Decentered Subject

In the preceding chapter we detailed the first stage in the recovery of the subject by probing the hermeneutical self-implicature at work in communicative praxis. Following the traces of this hermeneutical implicature we found it necessary to reinvent the subject as speaker, author, and actor in the aftermath of its deconstruction and decentering. The subject lost through the disassembling of the representational thinking of metaphysics and epistemology is regained through a hermeneutical restoration of the "who" of speaking, writing, and acting.

The central claim in our exploration of a new horizon of subjectivity in Part II of our study is that a deconstructing and decentering of the subject does not entail a displacement of the subject in every sense you please. The result is rather a *replacement* and *resituation* of the subject within another space—within the holistic, hermeneutical space of communicative praxis. This resituation, however, it needs be underscored, requires new descriptions relative not only to the texture of praxial space but also to the texture of subjectivity. It is not a matter of simply rearranging an old set of properties and attributes within a new context. Both space and subjectivity receive new inscriptions.

Our projected description of the restored and resituated subject carries the mandate to consider again the ontological problematic. Are all ontological inquiries about the subject set aside once and for all after the subject as metaphysical and epistemological foundation has been dismantled, or is there still a sense in which one can speak of the "being" of the subject? Does the question as to the "who" of speaking, writing, and acting still invite an ontological commitment, or is such a commitment itself somehow sublated into the events of "mere" speaking, "mere" writing, and "mere" acting? Do we still have available the resources of an ontology of subjectivity which might in some manner deliver the being of him who speaks, writes, and acts?

The history of ontology, as Heidegger and Derrida in particular have shown, is the history of discourse about being as "presence." According to Heidegger the fateful moment in this history was the metaphysical turn, in which presence was construed as a property of entities present-at-hand *(Vorhandensein)*. This turn brought about a forgetfulness of Being *(Sein)* as ecstatic temporality. The format in which this forgetfulness of Being by metaphysics was articulated by the early Heidegger was that of the ontological-ontic difference—a format which still employed the resources of transcendental reflection, but in such a manner as to enable a thinking beyond them. This thinking beyond metaphysics culminates in the later Heidegger's celebrated *Kehre* from reflection to language, meaning to truth, and Being to event of appropriation *(Ereignis)*. Derrida, failing to recognize the revolutionary questioning in *Being and Time* and the *Kehre,* continues to indict Heidegger for his logocentrism and metaphysics of presence. In the process of applying his deconstructionist strategy to the early Heidegger, Derrida lands upon the notion of *différance* as it bounces off Heidegger's "ontological-ontic difference." It quickly becomes evident, however, that for Derrida the proper context for *différance* is that of grammatological rather than ontological ruminations. It is within the space of grammatology that *différance* stakes out its claim for primacy. "Differance (is) 'older' than the ontological difference or the truth of Being."[1] Neither *logos* nor presence have a place in this grammatological sphere of primacy. They are displaced by *écriture*.

Now what is at issue in our current discussion is not so much Derrida's reading of Heidegger, which has its own rewards, but rather the concerns that are expressed in their respective projects of "destruction" and "deconstruction." Both Heidegger and Derrida are troubled by the elusiveness of presence. Heidegger has detailed the problems of picturing the presence of the subject as a "standing-in-itself" of an entity present-at-hand. This results in a metaphysical suffocation of subjectivity rather than an authorization of it. The turn to the epistemological subject, inaugurated by modern philosophy, does not change matters much. Epistemology, after all, is simply the stepchild of metaphysics, and the redefinition of the subject as epistemic center or locus of knowledge continues the determination of the presence of the subject as zero-point source or origin, either empirically or transcendentally construed. So long as the being of the subject is understood in terms of a metaphysics of presence and its postulations of an underlying metaphysical substratum and an epistemological punctuality it will remain perpetually deferred. On this general point there seems to be

---

[1] *Speech and Phenomena,* trans. David B. Allison (Evanston: Northwestern University Press, 1973), p. 154.

some agreement between Heidegger and Derrida. But it is precisely at this juncture, after the varied deconstructions have been accomplished, that the most critical questions arise. After the metaphysical and epistemological encrustations have been removed, what is there to see and say about the presence of the subject? Can one deploy a non-metaphysical description of presence? Derrida at best offers a promissory note. He recommends that we consider presence as an "effect" of *différance*.[2] Clearly this is not to be understood as an "effect" in a causal sense nor in an epistemic mode. But what posture such an "effect" has continues to elude the reader of Derrida's writings.

The persisting question in all this has to do with the resources and limitations of ontological questioning in the recovery of subjectivity. Is there anything worth preserving in a discourse about the "being" of the subject? Derrida and Heidegger are in agreement that such discourse will need to be pruned of any metaphysics of presence underbrush. However, whereas for Derrida such a pruning, if properly performed, will somehow displace the question of being itself, Heidegger strains for a retrieval of a sense of being through repetition and commemorative thinking. Heidegger's project of deconstruction is that of a deconstructive retrieval. Derrida's stance remains principally reactive. There is deconstruction but no retrieval. Heidegger provides a more positive stance, one that keeps open the possibility for a restoration of that which has been forgotten, covered up by the metaphysics of presence. Here Heidegger's deconstruction works hand in glove with his hermeneutics as a project of recovery and repetition. What is recovered is the "sense of Being" *(Being and Time)* and the "truth of Being" *(Letter on Humanism)*. But clearly this is neither "sense" nor "truth" construed along the lines of a metaphysics of presence. The sense and truth of Being reclaimed through a hermeneutical restoration is that of Being somehow transfigured and transvalued. It is Being hermeneutically understood rather than metaphysically represented.[3]

Our project of the recovery of subjectivity within the hermeneutical space of communicative praxis admittedly displays a measure of indebtedness to Heidegger's reformulation of the *Seinsfrage* at the end of

---

[2] "We thus come to posit presence . . . no longer as the absolutely matrical form of being but as a 'determination' and an 'effect.' Presence is a determination and effect within a system which is no longer that of presence but that of difference. . . ." *Ibid.*, p. 147.

[3] John D. Caputo has masterfully articulated Heidegger's notion of repetition as a recovery or retrieval of the truth of Being in his article "Hermeneutics as the Recovery of Man," *Man and World*, Vol. 15, No. 4, 1982. He distinguishes Heidegger's repetition, which he correctly sees in the context of its Kierkegaardian indebtedness, from Husserl's phenomenological return to beginnings, which falls out as a nostalgia for a lost presence. He then shows how Derrida effectively deconstructs the Husserlian notion of presence but mistakes Husserl's notion for that of Heidegger's and ends up confusing the critique

metaphysics. Also it is informed by Ricoeur's restorative hermeneutics, articulated as "the recollection of meaning and as the reminiscence of being," which he distinguishes from the "demystifying hermeneutics" as practiced by the "masters of suspicion"—Freud, Nietzsche, and Marx.[4] In our project hermeneutics restores not only the world as nonobjectified referent, but also the subject as implicated by the dynamics of communicative praxis. This restored subject, it should by now be clear, has nothing to do with either a metaphysics or an epistemology of presence. But the ontological question about the status of the subject and its peculiar presence returns to haunt us time and again. What about the "being" of the subject as speaker, author, and actor, and what sense of presence is displayed in these various modalities? Again, our response will be that this question of being makes sense only within the context of communicative praxis. If we are to permit ontological talk entry into the conversation of mankind it will be talk of an oblique and subdued ontology, slanting off our descriptions of communicative praxis. Never directly addressed, because what is at issue is not an investigatable datum, the question of being is auxiliary to the question of the "who" of the speaker, author, and actor. The being of the subject is an implicate of communicative praxis—not a foundation for it. It is here that we see that not only a metaphysics of presence but also a "*fundamental* ontology" founders—as Heidegger himself came to realize in his later thinking. Ontology is not an excavation of foundations. It remains a project of description rather than reconstruction, responding to the solicitations of praxis. Reminiscence of being is a recollection and restoration of a hermeneutically referenced world and a hermeneutically implicated subject.

Now what about the "presence" of the restored subject in such a reminiscence? Can reminiscence deliver presence? In what sense is the subject as speaker, author, and actor present? Clearly, the subject is not present as a bare substratum that takes on the imprints of attributes and qualities, nor is it present as a point of origin of centrifugal mental

---

of presence with a critique of retrieval itself. "For the recovery of the primal and primordial of which Heidegger speaks—whether in his early writings or late—is never the recovery of a primal presence. It is the recovery of a primordial *experience (Erfahrung),* but this is always an experience of finitude and absence. In other words, and here one can put our counterpoint to Derrida succinctly, *in Derrida the critique of presence tends to pass over surreptitiously into a critique of retrieval itself.* And that is what I deny. For the one is not the other. Retrieval can indeed take the metaphysical form of a retrieval of presence—that is what Platonic recollection, Hegelian *Erinnerung* and Husserlian *Reaktivierung* surely are. But a more radical doctrine of retrieval, such as we find in Heidegger, has given up this nostalgia for presence and has become instead a readiness for anxiety, an openness, a self-exposure to finitude, limit and negativity" (p. 363).

[4] *Freud and Philosophy: An Essay on Interpretation,* trans. Denis Savage (New Haven: Yale University Press, 1970), p. 35.

forces. The *anamnesis* of restorative hermeneutics is not the recollection of fixed essences, unchanging substances, invariant natural properties, and the like; nor is it the representation or rendering-present of intentional objects. The suggestive notion of *anamnesis,* which played such a dominant role in the thinking of the Greeks, needs to be divested of any "theory of forms" construed as a secure metaphysical foundation. And the reappropriation of this notion in the interests of epistemological grounding, in the guise of a theory of representation, is but a recharting of the prejudice of pure theory that continues to occlude the intentionality of praxis. A return to praxis demystifies the nostalgia for a "golden age" once present, and it matters not whether this golden age be construed metaphysically or epistemologically. *Anamnesis* restores the presence of the subject in the life of praxis as an ongoing event and achievement, displaying openness and negativity as features of its development. The presence at issue is a perpetual coming-to-presence, responsive to the unavoidable play of absence. The peculiarity of presence in an ontology of subjectivity is that it is nurtured by the interplay of presence and absence.

The ontological task in a recovery of subjectivity is that of concretely illustrating this interplay of presence and absence in the self-implicature of the subject as speaker, author, and actor within the space of communicative praxis. The subject, resituated within this space, comes to terms with its presence and absence not via the protocols of pure theory (categories, propositions, and beliefs) but rather by way of a shift to the interests and concerns of praxis. The background of these interests and concerns is not a system of categories and beliefs, geared to the designs of pure theory, but rather the background of discursive accomplishments, enactments of projects, habits, customs, social practices, and institutional obligations. The recovery of subjectivity is addressed from the context of a different space, a space in which the dichotomies of thought and action, theory and practice, have not yet staked out their claims.

The "I" who speaks, writes, and acts is present in his speaking, writing, and acting. Implicated in the forms of life of communicative praxis, the subject as speaker, writer, and actor is announced in the conversation and in the participatory social practices. The subject comes to presence in the performances of evaluation, criticism, affirmation, denial, confrontation, acknowledgment, refusal, and consent. In these performances the subject undergoes its birth and rebirth, manifesting its presence in and to a world of history and nature alike. But this presence is not that of a "being there" construed as a given, either of a metaphysical or epistemological sort. It is a presence pervaded by absence, permeated by fragility, time and again dispersed within the anonymity of public beliefs and practices. It is a presence that can be lost in the multiple forms of social conformism, crowd behavior, and in the disproportion of a self divided against itself.[5] But not only is this presence modified by the negativities of conformism and disproportion, there is also an authentic divestiture of self in the creative absorption at work in artistic creation, in the intimacy of interpersonal relations, and in forms of ritual and mystical experience. In these varieties of human experience, impoverished and enriched, it is necessary to speak of both presence and absence.[6]

These experiences, in which the subject is both announced and annulled, affirmed and effaced, point to the peculiar texture of presence that pervades the subject. The very texture of presence is qualified by absence. This absence invades the space of presence in such a way that it perpetually decenters the subject as a stabilized presence to itself. This absence cannot be sublated into presence, nor can both be taken up into a higher concept without loss of the concrescence made possible through the interplay of presence and absence. It was this that Kierkegaard saw so clearly in his untiring attack on Hegel's idealism. And it was Kierkegaard, in advance of both Heidegger and Derrida, who apprised us of the *interest* on which metaphysics itself, with its logocentrism and objectivism, founders.[7] Admittedly, Heidegger made the issue of the poverty of the metaphysical approach to being a central topic in a way in which Kierkegaard did not, and from this certain lessons can be learned. In his early period Heidegger confronted the issue from the standpoint of a critique of transcendental inquiry which still made use of the resources of transcendental reflection in an effort to surmount it. The distinction between Being *(Sein)* and beings *(Seiendes)* and the corresponding distinction between fundamental ontology and metaphysics were decisive in this effort. These distinctions themselves, however, were put under erasure in his later thought, where being as a philosophical concept is effaced and rethought as the "event

---

[5] Heidegger's descriptions of the dispersal of *Dasein* in the public phenomenon of *Das Man* and Kierkegaard's descriptions of the loss of the self within the crowd are particularly germane at this point.

[6] One of the limitations in Heidegger's otherwise trenchant phenomenological description of *Dasein* as given over to the leveling and alienating determinations of *Das Man* is his failure to make explicit the resources for an authentic divestiture of self. This limitation is part and parcel of the more general limitation in the philosophical project of his early writings—and particularly *Being and Time*—which accentuated the threats to individuality, self-affirmation, and resolute choice at the expense of a creative praxis of being-with-others.

[7] The interest of which Kierkegaard speaks in this context is the interest of repetition, directed at once backwards and forwards. This is "the interest upon which metaphysics founders." *Repetition,* trans. Walter Lowrie (Princeton: Princeton University Press, 1946), p. 34.

of appropriation" *(Ereignis)*. Presence as "eventful" and as "making one's own" can no longer be thought from the perspective of a fundamental ontology. It is our claim and contention throughout that the proper context for addressing this event-character of presence as it interplays with absence is that of communicative praxis. Only within the folds of communicative praxis can the interplay of presence and absence be experienced and detailed.

In searching for ontological descriptions that might effectively disclose the peculiar texture of this presence/absence interplay in the life of the subject as speaker, author, and actor, we land upon three in particular that seem to offer some promise for doing the job—temporality, multiplicity, and embodiment. These are not proposed as an exhaustive list of categories of subjectivity. Indeed, they are not proposed as "categories" at all, so long as "categories" are understood as either inventories of the nature of things or as organizing faculties of the mind. Temporality, multiplicity, and embodiment are descriptions of the praxis-oriented subject as it makes its way about in its discourse and action. And it is important to remember that at every juncture these descriptions have to be used "against themselves," negating the metaphysical sedimentations in their peculiar philosophical histories. In their new role of ontological description they stand, as it were, "at the end of metaphysics."

At the heart of the project of deconstructing and decentering subjectivity as the substantiality of a "standing-in-itself" is a radical critique of temporality. The metaphysics of presence, from the Greeks onward, prejudged time as a succession or flow of instants which are somehow coordinated with the movement of objects across a continuum of geometrical, spatial points. In its classical metaphysical formulation, based on the requirements of a theory of substance, time as a succession or flow of instants was anchored to the solidity and self-identity of bodies moving across objective and measured space. The presense of the self as subject was viewed as partaking of this solidity and self-identity.[8] This led to the subordination of time as a negativity, a threat to the permanence of presence. Presence understood from this perspective translates into the permanence of a subject standing-in-itself, somehow underlying the succession of instants, securely sheltered from the rancor and ravages that such successiveness might bring. Time can indeed

---

[8] This notion of presence continues to inform the existentialist philosophy of Sartre, who, in spite of intermittent protestations, remained a metaphysical thinker. The *pour-soi* borrows its being from the *en-soi*. Although the *pour-soi* achieves its freedom through a project of transcendence that places it at a distance from the solidity and impermeability of the *en-soi*, it has no other self-identity than that which is supplied by the plenum of being-in-itself.

function as an attribute of the permanent and perduring subject, but it cannot touch the "in-itself" of the subject's substantial being. Informed by the metaphysical oppositions of permanence and change, being and becoming, presence is understood in terms of the former, and time is seen as a coefficient of change and becoming, posited as a threat to the purity of presence.

The modern epistemological notion of presence, which purportedly effected a Copernican revolution on matters of metaphysical thought, nonetheless still remained within the orbit of traditional ruminations on presence. In modern epistemology presence provides the locus of knowledge, garnering certainty and stability either through the immediacy of sensation (empiricism) or the immediacy of thought (rationalism). Presence indicates the primordial beginning or center from which the act of knowledge proceeds. Defined as a locus of interiority, the epistemological subject is posited as an undivided unity of self-presence, lodged in a fugitive temporal succession. Modern epistemology inherits the metaphysical enclaves of permanence and change, being and becoming, interiority and exteriority in marking out the parameters of epistemological space. Within this epistemological space temporality is destined to remain an intruder, a factor of distortion for both the knowing subject and the object as known.

Our resituation of both the subject and temporality within the folds of communicative praxis at once suspends the search for a nontemporal metaphysical and epistemological center and divests temporality of its adversity. The presence of the subject is reclaimed as an event of temporalization. Within this "eventful" posture of the subject there is indeed a play of presence with absence. Derrida's notion of *différance* does succeed in articulating this play of presence and absence, but what is missing in Derrida's grammatology of *différance* is a full recognition of the communicative and praxial space which presence and absence inhabit. This is the space of the speaking, writing, and acting subject in which the interplay of presence and absence is illustrated. This interplay is occasioned and accomplished by a temporalization that both recalls the idealities and forms of life of already accomplished discourse and action and projects the possibilities for their retrenchment, redescription, and critique. The presence of the subject is a *living* present, coming from a past and projecting into a future. As such it is the enabling of repetition and anticipation, preservation and creation, conservation and invention.

Within this presence the absences of the "already" of the past and the "not yet" of the future remain ensconced. But the absence of the "already accomplished," in the form of a text already spoken or written and an action already performed, and the absence of the "not yet accomplished," in the form of new meanings of discourse and action, do not obtrude on the scene as indices of adversity. The restoration at work in praxis is the repetition or recollection of that which has been said and done, not through a representation that facilely mirrors a state of affairs that once had reality but now is gone by, but rather through a reclamation that continues to inform the living present, without which it would have no concretion. Repetition makes possible an understanding of the absence of that which is past as being constitutive of the moment of presence. In the subject's understanding of itself as past there is a praxial reduction, a rupture through distanciation, but this rupture, far from being an impoverishment due to a lost self-identity, is precisely that which enables the comprehension and interpretation of the past as the history of the subject as a presence that has been. Likewise, the subject as "deferred" into the future is not an absence to be lamented, but is rather the foreground of possibilities for invention through which the past is reclaimed. It is in this manner that the temporality of the subject, in which presence and absence interplay, occasions at once the twin moments of preservation and creation. But it must be clearly recognized that what is at issue here is a *temporality of praxis,* through which the subject, decentered as a metaphysical foundation and an epistemological locus, achieves a comprehension of its historical posture at the intersection of past and future in the life of discourse and social practices. It is in the context of praxis that temporality provides us with a useful ontological description. In attending to the posture of the subject as event of temporalization we can see how presence and absence interplay.

We suggested above, however, that there is another decisive feature of the decentered subject—multiplicity. Both classical metaphysicians of the soul and modern philosophers of mind were frightened not only by temporality but also by multiplicity. Historically there has been an obsession with the values of unity and identity in the boldly metaphysical reflections on selfhood and subjectivity. These reflections, as James Ogilvy has observed, have tended to congeal into a "monotheistic, monarchical conception of the personal self."[9] Metaphysical and epistemological space is a congenial abode neither for that which is temporal nor for that which is multiple. Temporality and multiplicity are

---

[9] *Many Dimensional Man: Decentralizing Self, Society, and the Sacred* (New York: Oxford University Press, 1977), p. 105. Drawing upon the resources of reflection in Herbert Marcuse's critique of "one-dimensional man," Jungian explorations in psychotherapy, and contemporary studies on physiology, Ogilvy challenges this monotheistic and monarchical paradigm as applied to the self and sketches a portrait of a "heterarchical," many-dimensional subject that displays a heterarchy of postures and interests.

unsettling for the prejudices of substantial self-identity and stable Archimedean points of epistemic certainty. They are unwelcome guests who threaten to disrupt the household with an unstructured becoming and an unmanageable plurality. In the hermeneutical space of communicative praxis, on the other hand, temporality and multiplicity are native citizens of the terrain, accepted as indigenous inhabitants of the historical life of discourse and action.

Nietzsche had already warned us about the prejudices against multiplicity and plurality that seem to be built into our notion of subjectivity.

> The assumption of one single subject is perhaps unnecessary; perhaps it is just as permissible to assume a multiplicity of subjects, whose interaction and struggle is the basis of our thought and our consciousness in general? . . . *My hypothesis:* The subject as multiplicity.[10]

This Nietzshean hypothesis can be quickly supplemented with reflections by the American social behaviorist George Herbert Mead in his ruminations on the social behavior of the self. Mead too speaks of "multiple personality" as a characterizing feature of the subject within the context of its social process.

> We carry on a whole series of different relationships to different people. We are one thing to one man and another thing to another. There are parts of the self which exist only for the self in relationship to itself. We divide ourselves up in all sorts of different selves with reference to our acquaintances. We discuss politics with one and religion with another. There are all sorts of different selves answering to all sorts of different social reactions. It is the social process itself that is responsible for the appearance of the self; it is not there as a self apart from this type of experience.[11]

These paths of inquiry opened up by Nietzsche and Mead might provide certain directions for a fresh assessment of the role of multiplicity in the life of the decentered subject within the space of communicative praxis. They point us to a portrait of the subject as an ensemble of *multiplex personae,* whose identity is an acquisition rather than a given, achieved within the play of difference. Discourse and action, as we have seen, assume different forms of language and life against the background of multiple social memories, variegated customs, habits, and institutional practices. The presence of the subject within this network of communicative praxis is that of a postured response to the

---

[10] *The Will to Power,* trans. Walter Kaufman and R. J. Hollingdale (New York: Random House, 1967), p. 270, #490.

[11] *Mind, Self, & Society,* ed. Charles W. Morris (Chicago: University of Chicago Press, 1934), p. 142.

ongoing conversation and to the prior action upon the subject. In this response there is a "responding center" in terms of an existential sphere of interest and concern, a base of operations "from where" something is said and something is done, a stance of critique and assent; but this is neither a metaphysical nor an epistemological center. It is a shifting center which grounds the response at different junctures in the history of the conversation and the practices of mankind. Different profiles of self answer to the differing contexts in which the conversation and the action of the other is acknowledged. The "who" that is speaking, writing, and acting emerges within the concretion of these multiple contexts. It is this that solicits the mosaic of interpretations and descriptions of the subject. Hermeneutical comprehension finds its material in the varying profiles of self and society, ever struggling for new descriptions to keep the conversation going. In this hermeneutical conversation any language about the subject as a center that somehow mirrors and represents the reality either of the world or self-reflexively of itself remains as fruitless as it is philosophically problematic.

The new description of the decentered subject as a multiplex phenomenon of varying profiles, temporally situated, weaves its way around the philosophical position-taking of realism and nominalism alike. The longstanding controversy about the status of universals and particulars as it applies to the being and behavior of the subject is suspended, put out of play, in an effort to resituate the question as to the "who" of discourse and action. Theorizing about the status of universals and particulars in the interests of finding the "right" belief about what the self somewhere at the bottom of its being *truly is,* is set aside with descriptions and interpretations of the praxis-oriented subject within the actual context of its practical concerns and discursive performances. Realism and nominalism, as theories of being and knowledge seeking justification, are bracketed out so as to permit a showing of the self in its praxis-oriented personal and social existence. There is a shift of questioning away from the search for a universal human nature which would unify the changing and multiple profiles from above, as well as a suspension of the quest for a "bare particular" which might ground the profiles from below. The "self-identity" of the subject that accounts for the presence of the speaker and the actor in his varied roles and relationships is anchored neither in a hovering universal form nor in an undergirding stable particular. The fate of identity theories of the self is that they have become impaled on the horns of a philosophically constructed dilemma that encourages us to look for a reality, of either a universal or a particular sort, above, below, or behind the phenomena. The phenomena of subjectivity are translated into appearances, and the stage is set for a construal of the multiple profiles of self as *mere* appearances, which are somehow anchored in a *real* presence, a knowable form or particular, or a something we know not what. Our new description of the decentered subject is intended to discourage this logic of questioning because it misconstrues "phenomenon," and by implication "presence," within an alien doublet of conceptual oppositions—the universal versus the particular, and appearance versus reality. Presence does not show itself within this pairing of conceptual opposites, but rather remains occluded within the hollow of the epistemological space that is created by them. The phenomenon of the decentered subject delivers its own presence in the communicative performances of discourse and action. As event and acquisition the decentered subject emerges from and sustains itself within these performances.[12]

A third general feature of the presence of the decentered subject is embodiment. The constructionism of classical metaphysics and epistemology alike resulted in a disparagement of the body. The classical metaphysician's lustrous essence of soul or mind cannot be found within the corporeality of the subject. The soul, we are told, inhabits the body like a pilot resides in a ship, and apparently is able to survive the dissolution of the body in a way that a pilot might survive the scuttling of his craft. In modern philosophy of mind, which developed in concert with the epistemological turn, the role of the body continues to be devalued. What does the body have to do with the representational act of knowledge? Where is its "place" at the epistemological center of things? What is its cognitive function? For the modern epistemologist these questions belie a category mistake of the most grievous order. The body lies outside the epistemological center, in the region of the external world, properly an object known rather than a subject that knows.

In these metaphysical and epistemological views of the human body a prejudice with far-reaching ramifications becomes readily discernible. The human body is pictured as an object in the physical world, part of the furniture of things and artifacts. In modern philosophy of mind, begun by Descartes and bequeathed to his successors in both the rationalist and the empiricist traditions, this objectivist approach to the human body takes a fateful turn. The human body, as an instance of

---

[12] If one persists in talk of oppositions here, we would suggest that the appropriate opposite of appearance is *disappearance* rather than reality. The presence of the self is its appearance qualified by absence, qualified by the profiles, roles, enactments, and possibilities which it has *not* appropriated, and which given its finite temporality it cannot appropriate, because in its choice of the enactment of one it delays and postpones the enactment of another.

nature generalized as *res extensa,* is portrayed as a machine. The rules of mechanics, which according to Descartes are the rules of nature, are applied to the human body. Now admittedly, the human body is viewed as a *soft* machine; but the principles of mechanistic explanation continue to apply. This prejudgment of the body as a machine quickly became the basis for a cyberneticist speculation that was eventually universalized to include the workings of the mind. It is rather amazing that this prejudice for so long eluded the critical reflection of modern and contemporary philosophers of mind. Within this framework of inquiry it is only mind that poses a "problem." What it means to have a body and to exist as embodied somehow remains unproblematic. Even in Richard Rorty's astute critique of modern philosophy of mind and epistemology in his *Philosophy and the Mirror of Nature,* reflection on the meaning of the human body does not become part of the conversation of mankind. He has provided a telling and consequential deconstruction of the invention of mind by modern philosophy. The required complement of this is a deconstruction of the invention of the body within the same tradition.

Nietzsche, again, was one of the first to recognize the need for a dismantling of the sedimented conceptualizations of the body as they traveled with the *speculum mentis* of modern philosophy, and he saw clearly enough the implications of this for a new description of the subject, decentered and contexualized.

> Everything that enters consciousness as "unity" is already tremendously complex: we always have only a semblance of unity.
>
> The phenomenon of the body is richer, clearer, more tangible phenomenon: to be discussed first, methodologically, without coming to any decision about its ultimate significance.[13]

Nietzsche's challenge for a concrete phenomenology of the body was accepted, as is well known, by contemporary phenomenology and existential philosophy.[14] Particularly Marcel, Sartre, and Merleau-

---

[13] *The Will to Power,* p. 270, #489. Cf. *Thus Spake Zarathustra:* "Behind thy thoughts and feelings, my brother, there is a mighty lord, an unknown sage—it is called Self; it dwelleth in thy body, it is thy body." Trans. Thomas Common (New York: The Modern Library), p. 33.

[14] Gabriel Marcel was one of the first to accept this challenge for a concrete phenomenology of the body in his existential reflections on embodiment, in which the body is addressed not in terms of relations of "having" but rather in terms of relations of "being." The human body is described not as a possession or adventitious property which the self has in addition to its essential attributes, but rather the self exists as embodied. "I *am* the body," concludes Marcel (*The Metaphysical Journal,* trans. Bernard Wall [London: Rockliff, 1952], pp. 332–33). Sartre picks up the theme of embodiment as a manner of existing in the world in his work *Being and Nothingness,* proposing that we think of the

Ponty have opened pathways for reflection on the existential posture of the human body as a project of existence, a manner and style of the subject's inherence in the world. This inherence decenters the subject as a locus of interiority. It displaces the subject as an interiorized mental chamber and transforms the notion of presence. What is at issue in the wake of such a displacement is no longer the impossible task of defining a mind-subject present to itself in a self-reflexivity of consciousness, but rather the recognition of a plurality of inscriptions through speaking, writing, and acting that issue from the behavior of embodied thought. The decentered subject as embodied praxis, as discourse and action that proceed from configurations of gestures, motility of head, hands, and feet, and a general bodily comportment—all of which are already expressions of thought and a comprehension of the world—requires descriptions that go beyond the confining schema of center versus periphery or interior versus exterior. The decentered subject as embodied is already *at* the world and already *in* the social practices.

The introduction of embodiment into our considerations of the space and posture of the decentered subject opens up new dimensions of the phenomenon of presence. The presence of the subject is a *bodily* presence. This immediately shifts the emphasis away from a preoccupation with an elusive seat of unification of mental contents and a fugitive epistemological point. It is precisely such a center, sought for in modern philosophy of mind and epistemology, that is decentered. This shift makes all things new with regard to the meaning of presence. Bodily presence announces a texture of spatialization that remains existen-

---

body not as an item in the realm of inert objects and things (the sphere of the *en-soi*) but instead as a "synthetic totality of life and action" (trans. Hazel Barnes; New York: The Philosophical Library, 1956), p. 346. Merleau-Ponty, who made the thematic of the "lived-body" *(le corpe vecu)* central to his existential phenomenology, continues the Nietzschean challenge for a richer and more vibrant description of the body by placing it directly within the context of praxis-oriented existence. "My body is wherever there is something to be done," *Phenomenology of Perception,* trans. Colin Smith (New York: The Humanities Press, 1962), p. 250. Often neglected in the literature on embodiment are Karl Jaspers's seminal suggestions on the integration of thought and activity in the concrete expressivity of the uses of the hand. "As all activities of the hand already contain a thinking within them, it behooves us to note that thought activity *(Denktätigkeiten)* is expressed through the use of the hands *(Handtätigkeiten).*" *Von der Wahrheit* (Munich: Piper Verlag, 1947), p. 329. There is another tradition in which the challenge for a new perspective on the body, liberating it from the prejudgment by traditional philosophy of mind, is taken up. This is the radical empiricism of William James. "The world experienced comes at all times with our body as its centre, centre of vision, centre of action, centre of interest." *Essays in Radical Empiricism* (New York: Longmans, Green and Co., 1942), p. 170n. For further discussions on the assessment of the literature on human embodiment see Richard Zaner, *The Problem of Embodiment* (The Hague: Martinus Nijhoff, 1964), and Calvin O. Schrag, *Experience and Being,* chapter 4, "The Embodied Experiencer" (Evanston: Northwestern University Press, 1969).

tially coordinated with the temporalization of the subject as a coming from a past and a moving into a future. The embodied presence of the subject integrates spatiality and temporality. To be present is at once an event of spatialization and an event of temporalization. It is thus that bodily presence restores the dimension of spatiality that has been suppressed in traditional philosophies of mind. In this tradition the presence of the subject is the presence of a cogito, construed variously as nonextended substantiality, a blank slate upon which experience writes, a bundle of perceptions, behavioral dispositions, or transcendental consciousness.

The reclamation of the spatiality of embodiment within the fabric of presence, however, is not to be construed as a reintroduction of the abstract determinations of space as extensive magnitude, geometrical points, and the locality of position. It is the lived space of praxis-oriented behavior, the space of communicative praxis, what Merleau-Ponty had already named the "spatiality of situation" as contrasted with the "spatiality of position."[15] It is the spatiality of gestures, the handshake, the caress, the grimace and the smile, the situation from which the spoken word and the projected action originate. The bodily presence of the subject is announced through the expressivity of this complex of gestures and bodily bearing, which are themselves events of hermeneutical disclosure. A praxial intentionality and an expressivity of meaning are ensconced within the bodily presence of the speaking and acting subject. The truth of behaviorism was that it recognized the inseparability of body and mind in behavioral events and rejected the presence of mind as a "ghost" in a machine. Its error was its continued misconstrual of the body as a machine, a neurological transmission system, that could be explained through cybernetic functions. It was thus that behaviorism was unable to recognize the praxial spatiality of embodiment, and so it became progressively removed from the phenomenon of bodily presence.[16]

No longer pictured as a collection of abstracted data within an abstract empiricism and reductive behaviorism, embodiment is illustrated in the involvements and practical concerns of communicative praxis, eliciting a play of metaphors in our descriptions of the subject as

[15] *Phenomenology of Perception*, p. 100.
[16] The decentering of the subject through a new description of the phenomenon of embodiment should not be construed as the replacement of a "mental center" with a "physical center." This was precisely the error of behaviorism in its prejudicial view of the body as a centralized soft machine. The body as lived indeed expresses a harmony and integration of concrete movement and neurological functioning, but this is not a harmony and integration issuing from a neurological or physiological center. Ogilvy has perceptively addressed this issue in his reflections on the relevance of contemporary physiology

speaker, author, and actor. The speaker is embodied in his gestures, which take on the form of a body language. The author is embodied in his text, present in the *corpus* of his writings. This embodiment of the author is revisited in every reading of his works. The subject as agent and actor is embodied in his projects, in his labor of economic production and his accomplishment of social reform. Embodiment in its multiple metaphorical senses informs our descriptions of the subject in the spheres of art, politics, and religion. "Guernica" embodies the genius, creativity, and inspiration of Picasso. The "New Deal" is properly described as an embodiment of the ingenuity and ideals of Franklin Delano Roosevelt. Since the time of the early Christian community the church in history has been described as the "body of Christ." In all of these extended metaphorical uses of embodiment we see the illustration of bodily presence not as an abstracted corporeal datum but as a web of polysemic descriptions of the speaker, author, and social agent within the space of communicative praxis.

The phenomenon of bodily presence in the space of communicative praxis is a phenomenon that both conceals and reveals. It exudes, as it were, its own absences. As such it can never become fully transparent to itself as a given datum. Neither substance nor signifier, it provides neither a metaphysical nor an epistemological function. Bodily presence does not congeal as a sign, functioning as an indicator of recessed meanings either behind or within it. It announces its presence *in person*.[17] This presence of the body-subject *in person* is posited neither as

---

for a heterarchical, many-dimensional description of the self. "The body is a model for the balance or harmony of many selves within the personal self—and not just a metaphor but a living, real, concrete part of the territory where one can read a heterarchical order in its physical manifestation. The body is not a straight cylinder devoid of differentiation, not a 'perfect answer' to the question of balance, but a complex juxtaposition of oddly shaped, ever different yet obviously symmetrical parts that have to solve among themselves some amazing problems of physics in order to keep from falling flat on that part known as the face. Precisely *how* the body solves such problems is interestingly enough still a mystery to the science of neurophysiology. *That* the body solves them is reconfirmed every time an infant learns to walk." *Many Dimensional Man*, p. 117.

[17] Emmanuel Levinas, in his concrete phenomenology of the experience of the Other, focuses his attention principally on the "face-to-face" phenomenon in the upsurge of bodily presence. Breaking forth simultaneously as expression and speech, the face-to-face encounter displays an integrative unity of seeing eyes and speaking mouth in which the Other is present as incarnate existence. "Absolutely present, in his face, the Other—without any metaphor—faces me" ("A priori et subjectivité"). *Revue de métaphysique et de morale*, 1962; quoted and trans. Jacques Derrida, *Writing and Difference*, University of Chicago Press, 1978, p. 100. According to Levinas, the proper context for the discernment of the bodily presence of the face-to-face is ethics rather than metaphysics or epistemology. More Kierkegaardian than Husserlian, Levinas approaches the encounter of the Other not as a problem of transcendental constitution but rather as an issue of ethical engagement.

a metaphysical nor as an epistemological self-identical foundation. Indeed, it is not "posited" at all, as having a "position," either in physical or mental space. Bodily presence is an event rather than a position, suffering both temporalization and multiplicity. As event the body-subject is an ensemble of *personae*. It is present in the changeable masks that it turns on to the world. The shift to theatrical metaphors is deliberate at this juncture, offering possible new descriptions of the theaterlike character of the presence of the decentered subject. The decentered subject moves through its varied *personae;* yet insofar as these *personae* are appropriated and made "one's own," the subject is present in each of them.

The use of theatrical metaphors, as Bruce Wilshire has masterfully shown in his recent book *Role Playing and Identity: The Limits of Theatre as Metaphor,* is peculiarly apt for displaying the "drama" of decentered subjectivity. Persons in actual life, like the *dramatis personae* of the theater, make their way about by assuming different roles, authorizing their identity, enacting various forms of behavior. Within this drama, onstage and off, everything turns on what Wilshire has perceptively named "the mimetic response."[18] The multiple *personae* that the speaking and acting subject makes its own in a mimetic responsiveness to others have their origin in the taking over of the other's gestures as well as his attitudes, his bodily comportment as well as his ideas. The phenomenon of embodiment in this play and display through mimesis remains decisive throughout the career of subjectivity. Wilshire instructs us well when he observes: "To be a self is to be a human body that is mimetically involved with other such bodies, but that nevertheless has a capacity to distinguish itself consciously from others and to regard its history and its prospects as its own."[19] The bodily presence of self and other is announced through the embodied communication of the mimetic response.

The intentionality of embodiment in the play of mimetic responsiveness provides that new determinant of subjectivity which contributes toward a decentering of an idealist philosophy of consciousness. The telling insight of Hegel's *Phenomenology of Mind* that presence of self is borne by an acknowledgment and recognition of other selves needs to be reformulated with the help of a phenomenology of embodiment. Recognition and acknowledgment of the other is never the result

---

[18] *Role Playing and Identity* (Bloomington: Indiana University Press, 1982); see particularly chapter XI, "Body-Self and Others: Cognition, Expression, Mimetic Response, and Transformation."

[19] *Ibid.*, p. 226.

of a vector of pure consciousness. It involves the mediation of a bodily mimetic response and the communicative resources of a language of the body, already shared with others.

We have used the theater as metaphor in an effort to articulate the presence of decentered subjectivity as body-subject. We will now suggest the need for supplementing the theatrical metaphor of the body-subject with the political metaphor of the *body politic*. This slide from the theatrical to the political metaphor is facilitated by the recognition that the wider arena in which the theaterlike play of the decentered subject occurs is the *polis* of interacting social subjects, patterned by institutional engagements and reflections.[20] The space of the embodied *persona* is at once the space of the body politic. The body politic, like the body-subject, exhibits a multiplex of forms of discourse and action. Insofar as the body-subject and the body politic mutually reinforce each other a decentering is effected on both the personal and the social level. The understanding of the wider cultural-historical life of man becomes ripe for distortion when a particular body within the *polis,* be it governmental, ecclesiastical, or economic, puts itself forward as the substance of culture and the center of history. All monolithic interpretations of history, because they move out from a particular collective or institution posited as the center, at once oversimplify and disfigure the interdependence, multiplicity, and contextualism of the body politic. A logocentrism of society falls heir to the same ills as does a logocentrism of the subject.

This shift from theatrical to political metaphor in our move from the body-subject to the body politic provides a lesson on the communicative function of metaphor. The theatrical metaphors of role, drama, plot, script, and enactment are strategic for disclosing various configurations of presence in the actual life of the existing subject. But this performance of disclosure suffers its own limitations in a description of

---

[20] John O'Neill has made the metaphor of body politic the guiding motif in his social philosophy of "institutional reflection" and the "incarnate speech community." Using this metaphor he shows how political reflection and action are inscribed in the corporate bodies of protest movements and social agencies of reform. He distinguishes three discursive levels of the body politic as they are coordinated with their respective institutional settings. The bio-body is situated within the institutional framework of the family; the productive body regulates the activities in the arena of the associations of labor; and the libidinal body is the situated spatiality of the person. In concert these three levels of the body politic comprise the incarnate speech community which embodies the discourse, deliberation, argument and consensus that occurs in social interaction. The momentous import of O'Neill's incarnate speech community is that it at once deconstructs and concretizes the abstract "ideal speech community" recommended by Habermas and Apel. See particularly John O'Neill, "Gay Technology and the Body Politic," in *The Body as a Medium of Expression,* eds. Jonathan Benthall and Tel Polhemus (London: Allen Lane, 1975).

the "drama" of everyday life as it is inserted into the folds of the *polis,* with its concrete ethical demands. The "enactments" of the decentered subject within the body politic resist complete fictionalization. The "script" of communicative praxis and the "textuality" of its inscriptions overflow their theatrical and artistic determinations. Human discourse and action, postured against the background of the *ethos* pervading the *polis,* can never fully be captured within the net of theatrical, poetical, and artistic metaphors. We may indeed, as Nietzsche maintained, need art so as not to die of truth, but the life of the subject is no more *simply* art than it is *simply écriture.* The texture of human action within the ethical demands of the *polis* resists reduction to the textuality of literary and artistic production. Political and ethical metaphors are needed to properly balance and situate the metaphors of the text and the theater. Kierkegaard's description of this truth of subjectivity in his dialectic of the aesthetical and ethical stages of existence has yet to achieve its parallel.[21]

Our portrait of the decentered subject has highlighted the features of temporality, multiplicity, and embodiment in an effort to reclaim the presence of the subject in the wake of its deconstruction as a metaphysical or epistemological foundation. In this effort the notion of presence itself is put under the scrutiny of a radical reflection. Derrida's reservations about the invested capital in a "metaphysics of presence" are appropriated, as also are Rorty's reservations about epistemological starting points that belie a claim for primacy and necessity. But the setting aside of presence in these senses does not entail a setting aside of presence in every possible articulable manner. We have sought to articulate a notion of the presence of the speaking, writing, and acting subject as an event or occasioning of experience within the praxial space of communicative performance. Within the events of discourse and action presence interplays with absence, mediated by temporality, multiplicity, and embodiment, all of which are understood in their praxial orientations. In dealing with the presence of the decentered subject it is mandatory that we stick with praxis. An ontology of the subject is possible only as an ontology of praxis.

---

[21] See particularly *Either/Or: A Fragment of Life,* trans. David and Lillian Swenson (Princeton: Princeton University Press), 1949. For a perceptive discussion of the limits of theater as metaphor see Bruce Wilshire, *Role Playing and Identity,* pp. 245–296. In this section of his volume Wilshire develops a critique of the overextension of the metaphors of the theater into the domain of the human sciences. Using Erving Goffman's "Role Theory" model as an illustration, Wilshire addresses the limitations of such a model and the inherent dangers of fictionalizing reality. The metaphor of role playing abruptly butts against its limitations when matters of life and death are at issue. Wilshire invites us to reflect on the incredible irony of a dying man, enacting his death as a fictional episode which he might survive.

CHAPTER EIGHT

Dialogical Consciousness

We began Part II of our study with an exploration of hermeneutical self-implicature, tracking the speaking, authorial, and acting subject within the praxial space of discourse and action (chapter 6). We then sketched a portrait of the implicated subject, decentered and decentralized, giving particular attention to the features of temporality, multiplicity, and embodiment (chapter 7). In these explorations the topic of consciousness was at times invoked, but no sustained discussion of the issue was offered. What is now required is a more detailed and concentrated examination of the grammar of consciousness than we have thus far provided. This comprises the topic of the current and concluding chapter of Part II.

Subjectivity and consciousness, particularly since the epistemological turn of modern philosophy, have traveled side by side as mutually reinforcing concepts. Our portrait of the decentered subject, at once temporalized and embodied, a multiplex *persona* by virtue of its manifold social roles and institutional involvements, provides a new challenge for dealing with an old issue. A decentered subject will display a decentered consciousness, if indeed the language of consciousness is still to be found useful for philosophical discourse. The philosophical concept of consciousness, like that of subjectivity itself, will need to be tested through the exercise of a critical hermeneutics and then reexamined in light of its prospects for a restoration. A stock category of traditional philosophy and psychology will thus need to be retrenched and rehabilitated if it is to find a place in the story of communicative praxis.

In its travels with the subject, and particularly since the rise of Cartesian thought, consciousness has provided the subject with its most distinctive attribute, and in turn the subject has provided consciousness with its foundational support. Consciousness supplied the acts; the subject supplied the agency. A more convenient marriage could not have been arranged. The cogito and the ego seemed to be destined for each other, united in the conjugal bond of an "ego-cogito." But in the course of time, as is so often the case with marriages of convenience, strains and stresses made their way into this conjugal bond and critical questions were raised about the distinctive contributions of each of the partners. Worries about the axiomatic primacy of consciousness developed and suspicions about the role of the subject as an egological foundation became commonplace. Clearly Marx, Nietzsche, and Freud had much to do with this.[1] But there were also other dissident voices. Kierkegaard had registered a dissatisfaction with the lonely epistemological ego of modern philosophy and urged that consciousness be considered in conjunction with the ethical life of the existing subject. Sartre provided a formidable attack on egological consciousness within the phenomenological tradition. Wittgenstein, in another philosophical lineage, made us aware of the philosophical puzzles that ensue if the language of consciousness goes on a holiday.

In summation it could be said that these dissidents and critics have effected a demasking of the pretense of consciousness as bedrock origin and a demystification of it as an elusive presence. In the burgeoning current literature of deconstruction, these programs of demasking and demystifying consciousness have multiplied and intensified. But as in our story of the subject as an implicate within the interplay of discourse and action, so in our narrative of consciousness our underlying claim is that the displacement of consciousness as an epistemological and metaphysical denizen of the deep does not entail its banishment from the global scene. It reenters, as it were, as an inhabitant of another space—the holistic and hermeneutical space of communicative praxis.

This reentry is effected through a critique of consciousness as a datum, as a self-given presence which can do duty in the service either of epistemology or of metaphysics as the particular standpoint of inquiry might dictate. The peculiar destiny of consciousness, within such a metaphysico-epistemological scheme of things, is that its speech

---

[1] We are immediately reminded of the oft-quoted one-liner in the Preface of Marx's *A Contribution to the Critique of Political Economy:* "It is not the consciousness of men that determines their existence, but their social existence that determines their consciousness" (New York: International Publishers, 1970), p. 21. Nietzsche saw the philosophy of consciousness as being of a piece with the "error of being" that infected the history of philosophy since the time of Plato. In his "discovery" of the unconscious Freud placed the role of consciousness within sharply restricted limits. Ricoeur has perceptively characterized Freud's position as an "antiphenomenology" which employs the *epoche* in reverse: ". . . what we are confronted with is not a reduction *to* consciousness but a reduction *of* consciousness. Consciousness ceases to be what is best known and becomes problematic. Henceforward there is a question of consciousness, of the process of becoming-conscious *(Bewusstwerden)*, in place of the so-called self-evidence of being-conscious *(Bewusstsein)*." *Freud and Philosophy: An Essay on Interpretation,* trans. Denis Savage (New Haven: Yale University, 1970), p. 424.

becomes that of a monological voice issuing from a monadological ego. Such becomes the role and position of consciousness within epistemological space. The move to the praxial and communicative space inhabited by the speaking, writing, and acting subject occasions an accompanying redesign of the texture of consciousness as dialogical rather than monological. The decentered subject, contextualized as a multiplicity of profiles, authorized through its mimetic responsiveness to others, lives in its discourse and action as dialogical consciousness. Subjectivity and consciousness retain their descriptive potential for philosophical discourse, but both take on a new comportment by virtue of their insertion into the body politic of language, history, and social practices.

The story of the destiny of monological consciousness traveling with a monadological ego is pretty much the story of modern philosophy of mind from Descartes onward, coming to its end in a somewhat unexpected "fulfillment" in the antiepistemological thought of Nietzsche and Freud, Heidegger and Wittgenstein, Derrida and Rorty. However, what has not been told in this story is the fate of consciousness after its de-epistemologization and deconstruction by the hands of the demaskers and demystifiers. It is this part of the story that we propose to tell, but it cannot be told without rehearsing some of the twists and turns in the modern history of the concept of consciousness.

In dealing with the history of a concept, or the life of thought more generally, it is always problematic to speak of absolute beginnings. If there are such, they are extraordinarily difficult to find. Yet, there is a beginning of sorts for the modern concept of consciousness in Descartes's epistemological turn, which resulted in what Rorty has suggestively named "the invention of mind." Consciousness appears in the guise of "the cogito" as a relationship of knowledge which has a privileged access to its own contents and to an ego which in some manner provides the support for these contents. The ego-cogito is the alleged underwriter of mental contents, the Archimedean point, the locus of certainty in matters of knowledge, functioning as the secure foundation upon which all knowledge is to be built. It is in this manner that an internal relation between knowledge and consciousness is posited. What would it be like to have knowledge without consciousness—without consciousness of the object as known and the subject as knower? It is thus that the complex of knower-knowing-known provides the space in which consciousness can be seen to be at work. In all this we witness the birth of "philosophy of mind" in concert with the rise of modern epistemology.

Within philosophy of mind as thus established the peculiar bonus of consciousness is that it provides us with the most distinctive of all the distinguishing marks of the mental. The considerations which initiate such an approach to consciousness would seem to be of a rather innocent sort. We commonly distinguish mind from matter and persons from things. "Consciousness" affords a convenient label for doing so. A person is conscious of the traffic signal, but the traffic signal is not conscious of being observed. As one proceeds, however, things become a bit more complicated. There are the troublesome marginal cases that come to the fore when one probes the "awareness" that seems to be characteristic of animal behavior. Porpoises seems to be acutely aware of their environment and in various ways react to it, and sometimes in a manner that exhibits a rather high level of intelligence. Staying with the paradigm of consciousness, it is often urged that porpoises, and animals more generally, although displaying intelligent behavior do not display the reflexivity of that distinctively human consciousness which is able to engage in acts of *self*-consciousness. Animals are incapable of experiencing consciousness as reflexively directed back upon itself. The additional property of self-consciousness is thus invented to account for the distinctive nature of human consciousness. But further puzzles lie along the way. The technology of artificial intelligence has brought into the world computers that seem to function very much like human minds. They can classify, calculate, and predict; and through the installation of voice boxes they are able to "speak." So what is needed are further distinguishing marks and properties that might deliver the distinctive features of human consciousness.

The above moves to salvage consciousness as a distinguishing mark of the human mind, although at times ingenious in their strategy of argumentation, nonetheless trade on certain presuppositions and prejudices that need to be exposed. Chief among these is an appeal to data and to givens, and the continued employment of a substance-attribute model for uncovering the peculiar properties of that which is given. The mind as ego-cogito is taken as a given, a given with two parts. There is the ego or the "I" and there is consciousness as its peculiar and basal property. But there is an elusiveness to the presence of the "I." It is perpetually deferred, ever escaping itself. And it is not clear in what sense an elusive given can be spoken of as a given at all. Furthermore, consciousness as the basal property of this given requires supplementary properties so as to deal with the marginal cases. We thus witness a rapid compounding of properties—for example, intentionality, self-consciousness, privileged access, linguistic capacity, independence from the body, and a host of others.[2]

---

[2] For an informative discussion of the traditional marks of the mental see Richard Rorty, *Philosophy and the Mirror of Nature* (Princeton: Princeton University Press, 1979), pp. 35ff.

At this juncture we would urge that what should be of concern is not the length of this list of supplementary properties, nor the question about their singular sufficiencies and insufficiencies, but the very language of attributes and properties in elucidating the presence of consciousness. The proliferating attributes and properties tend to take on the status of adjunct givens. They are givens that travel with that which is originally given, i.e., the ego. Thus the problem of givenness is compounded. With this compounding of the problem of the given there is the concomitant problem of the properties of consciousness externalizing themselves from the foundational ego. Properties are those features "possessed" by the ego. The doctrine of properties co-opts the metaphor of possession. The ego *has* consciousness. Consciousness becomes a "possession," something to which the ego makes its claim of ownership. But that which is owned or possessed can also be disposed of. One's property can be lost, abandoned, or bartered. The metaphorical play of property in a quest for the identification of the marks of the mental leads to a conceptual crisis that undermines the initial effort. It leads to an intensification of the problem rather than to a solution of it.

Such an intensification of the problem through an appeal to givens and the language of properties and attributes becomes particularly evident in the effort to isolate the phenomenon of self-consciousness. In egological theories self-consciousness is understood as a peculiar property of consciousness in general, borne by a movement of "self-reference" or "self-relatedness" whereby the ego grasps itself in the relational act of being conscious of itself. The epistemological problem within such a model of self-reflexivity and self-reference is that the self must have some prior knowledge that it is the relatum which the self-reflexive consciousness intends, or else it could not recognize itself as thusly intended.[3] Hence, the self must be posited as a given datum, the "I as conscious," before its deliverance through the movement of self-reflexivity in which the self becomes present to itself. This epis-

---

[3] Dieter Henrich has perceptively articulated this problem in the self-reflexive model of egological theory in his trenchant article "Self-consciousness, A Critical Introduction to a Theory," *Man and World,* Vol. 4, No. 1, 1971. "But, in general, any interpretation of consciousness as the 'self-reference' of an 'I' can be seen to be untenable on grounds totally independent of the circularities of the reflection theory in its narrower sense: in any case, regardless of how the 'I' comes into relation to itself, whether by an act of reflection or in some way, the 'I' must grasp itself in a self-consciousness. Since this grasping of itself must specifically be a *conscious* apprehension, the 'I' must have some *notion* that with which it becomes acquainted in self-consciousness is itself. To this end it is not requisite that it have any sort of *conceptual* knowledge of itself or that it be able to give a *description* of itself. But, in any case, it must be able to assert with certainty that it is *itself* with which it becomes acquainted in self-consciousness, whether this self-acquaintance results from reflection or some other manner." P. 11.

temological problem will remain with us so long as we persist in construing consciousness as a datum and self-consciousness as a peculiar property of this datum. This model of self/consciousness/ self-consciousness, which is at once linear and circular, leads to a compounding of givens and properties of givens. Consciousness is a property of the self, and self-consciousness is a property of consciousness. As the property of consciousness trades on the metaphor of possession, so also does self-consciousness. In self-consciousness the self "grasps" and "has" itself. Thus consciousness is externalized from the self, and self-consciousness is externalized from consciousness. The original datum of the ego-cogito, proffered as an epistemic solidarity of "I" with consciousness, suffers a dispersal and fragmentation, succumbing to a circularity of predication of properties.

Yet, there are those who would maintain that these problems of the given and the use of a property-based theory of predication are the result of the failure to purify consciousness from its attachments to the empirical world. What is required, it has been argued, is the transcendental turn, which will deliver the distinction between empirical and transcendental consciousness. This transcendental turn, since its invention by Kant, has had a considerable impact on modern epistemology and philosophy of mind. Issues in these related spheres of inquiry have been framed, either implicitly or explicitly, from the standpoint of what Foucault has named the "empirico-transcendental doublet." It has been the destiny of this doublet to regulate ruminations on the nature of consciousness and knowledge from Kant onward—to contemporary phenomenology (Husserl), analytical philosophy (Strawson), and critical theory (Habermas and Apel). The transcendental turn, it has been urged by its proponents, circumvents the problem in the datum theory of consciousness by moving beyond consciousness as an empirical given to a sphere of meaning in which the logical and epistemic conditions for empirical knowledge are first discovered.

Kant set the format for the transcendental approach to knowledge and consciousness in his general prescription: "I entitle *transcendental* all knowledge which is occupied not so much with objects as with the mode of our knowledge of objects insofar as this mode of knowledge is to be possible *a priori*."[4] The function of transcendental inquiry becomes that of tracking the judicative claims in bodies of putative knowledge, which in Kant's case were principally Euclidean geometry and Newtonian science. Proceeding with the assumption that mathematics and science do indeed afford reliable knowledge, Kant's tran-

---

[4] *Critique of Pure Reason,* A 12, trans. Norman Kemp Smith (London: Macmillan and Company, 1953), p. 59.

scendental philosophy probes the universal and necessary conditions which make such knowledge possible. The proposed goal is that of a justification of belief in our truth-claims, and the method is that of sustained argumentation. Toward the achievement of this goal the representational function of transcendental consciousness and the subjectivity of a transcendental ego, which accompanies all forms of representation, are invoked. But this transcendental cogito and the accompanying ego remain within the a priori sphere of meaning. Subjectivity remains an *abstract* and *purified* subjectivity. There is no existential interest in the ego and in consciousness. The ego-cogito remains a logico-epistemic condition of principles and rules operative in the syntheses of apperception, making knowlege of the phenomenal world possible.

The pervasive influence of Kant's transcendental method is illustrated by its appropriation within both the analytical and the Continental traditions. One of the clearer instances of the adoption of transcendental reflection in contemporary analytical philosophy is the descriptive metaphysics of P. F. Strawson, where the transcendental turn converges with the linguistic turn. Strawson's transcendental inquiry is directed toward the conditions for identifying particulars (material bodies and persons) within a speaker/hearer context. Here linguistic considerations come to the fore in a way in which they did not for Kant, particularly in Strawson's emphasis on the role of the speaker in identifying reference. Yet, these linguistic considerations remain concordant with a theory of logic, and Strawson's search for transcendental foundations takes on an explicit logico-linguistic format. His intent is to describe the conceptual structure of the human mind through which knowledge of particulars is made possible. The indebtedness of Strawson's linguistic philosophy to Kant's transcendental reflection becomes explicit when he writes:

> I can, then, indicate the line of enquiry I have in mind by posing two questions, reminiscent in form and partly in content of Kantian questions: (1) What are the most general statable conditions of knowledge of objective particulars? (2) Do these most general conditions involve the requirement that material bodies should be the basic particulars, or is this simply a special feature of our scheme for knowlege of the objective particulars? Or—to run the two questions into one—is the status of material bodies as basic particulars a necessary condition of knowledge of objective particulars?[5]

---

[5] *Individuals: An Essay in Descriptive Metaphysics* (Garden City, New York: Doubleday & Company, 1963), p. 53.

As Strawson appropriated Kant's transcendental method and sought to make it compatible with the designs of linguistic philosophy, so Husserl took over the transcendental method and incorporated it into his program of transcendental phenomenological idealism. However, also in Husserl's appropriation of Kant some significant modifications of the understanding and use of transcendental inquiry occurred. The guiding interest, particularly in Husserl's early works, remained that of securing the foundations of knowledge, and in this respect Husserl's philosophical motivation continues to be epistemologically oriented. But there is a shift away from the interrogation of the possibility of truth conditions to a concern with the possibility and genesis of meaning *(Sinn)*, accompanied by an emphasis on description over argumentation, the securing of evidence over the legislation of principles, and an appeal to the rationality of intuitive insight versus the rationality of logical demonstration.[6] The chief goal in Husserl's phenomenology is no longer that of simply accounting for the a priori conditions that make accepted bodies of knowledge possible, but rather that of elucidating the horizonal structure of meaning that occasions the conceptual understanding in our mundane experience of objects and persons. Kant's egological view of consciousness is kept intact in Husserl's account, but again consequential modifications are made along the way. The transcendental-phenomenological ego is no longer viewed simply as a formal condition within consciousness, functioning as a logical principle of unification. Consciousness becomes intentional and the ego takes on a breadth and thickness in its posture as a "substrate of habitualities" and a concrete "monad." In this respect the abstract subjectivity of Kant's transcendental ego is attenuated. As substrate of habitualities and concrete monad the ego is immersed in the density of "transcendental experience," in which a concretion and sedimentation of habits, beliefs, and decisions take place.[7] The ego-cogito undergoes a form of "transcendental life"; yet it must be made clear that this transcendental life itself unfolds only within the sphere of sense. The consciousness of the transcendental "I" has a history, but this is an essential history within the determination of *eidos* rather than an existential history. The ego and consciousness remain insulated from the existential problematic.

---

[6] For a trenchant discussion of these differences between Kant and Husserl's views on the transcendental the reader is referred to J. N. Mohanty's essay "The Destiny of Transcendental Philosophy," *Phenomenology in a Pluralistic Context,* eds. William L. McBride and Calvin O. Schrag (Albany: State University of New York Press, 1983).

[7] *Cartesian Meditations,* trans. Dorion Cairns (The Hague: Martinus Nijhoff, 1960), p. 27. The locution "transcendental experience" would clearly have been found unacceptable by Kant, suggesting an amalgam of the transcendental and the empirical, which Kant struggled to keep separate.

The tracking of the destiny of transcendental consciousness from Kant to Husserl affords a number of instructive lessons along the way. Moving out from a sharply inscribed transcendental-empirical "difference" in the epistemological constructionism of Kant, the ego-cogito in the phenomenology of Husserl struggles to overcome its double life as a logical condition on the one hand and an empirical reality on the other. The ego and consciousness are situated within transcendental *experience*. What is decisive here is the suggestion of a fabric of experience that is broader and richer than the unidimensional view of sensory experience as invented by traditional empiricism. Kant was still working with an empiricist notion of experience, which he accepted as a starting point but found to be insufficient in that it provided only percepts. Percepts without concepts, we are told in the first *Critique,* are blind. The transcendental forms, schemata, and categories are thus designed to provide the sanction and justification of percepts as being constitutive of knowledge. The transcendental is set in opposition to the empirical and functions as its epistemic ground. Husserl's momentous contribution was to question the empiricists' unidimensional view of experience. This was the radical moment in Husserl's thought. But its radicality was attenuated in the end. The transcendental-empirical difference of Kant was overcome, but another difference took its place—the opposition of the transcendental to the mundane. This new opposition, however, remained parasitical upon the former because of the common project of seeking an epistemological foundation in the judicative activity of transcendental consciousness. This led to the reification of consciousness in another guise and produced a doublet of another order. Consciousness becomes the "residuum" of the transcendental-phenomenological reduction and is enthroned as the primary datum in the sphere of sense. The ego is reinstalled as a monad, separable from the psychological self of mundane experience, and is confronted with the "problem" of the constitution of the Other. The ego is posited as a lonely monad, and the prose of consciousness continues to be that of soliloquy and monologue.[8]

It was thus that the destiny of transcendental subjectivity had to await yet further stages in its transformation, courting its displacement. These were to be realized in Heidegger's deformalization of phenomenology, in Merleau-Ponty's move to existential phenomenology, in Karl-Otto Apel's retrenchment of the transcendental in the interests of critical theory, and in Hans-Georg Gadamer's hermeneutical turn.

---

[8] The later development of Husserl's thought in the *Crisis,* although acknowledging a greater role played by language, community, and history, does not change matters all that much with respect to the transcendental positioning of consciousness. Even in the *Crisis* the project of laying the foundation (now seen as the foundation for science, history, and culture) proceeds within the formal determinations of transcendental phenomenology.

Heidegger deformalizes the ego and the cogito as transcendental-phenomenological givens. The result is their displacement by *Dasein* and *Sorge*. The strategy in this deformalization and disassemblage in *Being and Time* and in *The Basic Problems of Phenomenology* is the use of transcendental analysis against itself in such a way that it becomes existential analysis. But this strategy suffers its own limitations—as Heidegger himself was quick to discern. It continues to buy into the transcendental-empirical doublet in the process of existentializing it and transmutes it into an ontological-ontic difference. Thus, there arose the requirement for the celebrated *Kehre* in Heidegger's thought, through which a nontranscendental posture of questioning is installed.

Merleau-Ponty follows the path of revolutionary thinking opened up by Heidegger. Although the resources of transcendental reflection are acknowledged by Merleau-Ponty, he considers this reflection as inescapably qualified by a "direct and primitive contact with the world" that antedates and situates the movement of reflection.[9] Phenomenological philosophy as practiced by Merleau-Ponty is pointed more in the direction of an elucidation and description of *Existenz* than in the direction of epistemic grounding. Taking its cues from the phenomena of embodiment, language, and historicity, the *logos* of these phenomena follows the path of prereflective understanding (Heidegger) rather than logical demonstration (Kant) or reflective intentional analysis (Husserl). Here the facile counterpositioning of the transcendental and the existential is critically confronted, and the ineluctable limits of transcendental analysis are made visible. But more than that, the transcendentally signified is placed under erasure as it "descends into history."[10] This descent of the transcendental into history effects a transformation of the presence of the ego and the life of consciousness. The presence of the ego, resituated in *Existenz,* becomes a *historical* presence and consciousness takes on the texture of embodiment. The transcendental ego is supplanted by an incarnate consciousness shaped by embodiment, language, and history.

---

[9] "Phenomenology," Merleau-Ponty writes in the *Phenomenology of Perception,* "is a transcendental philosophy which lays in abeyance the assertions arising out of the natural attitude, the better to understand them; but it is also a philosophy for which the world is always 'already there' before reflection begins—as an inalienable presence, and all its efforts are concentrated upon re-achieving a direct and primitive contact with the world, and endowing that contact with a philosophical status." Trans. Colin Smith (New York: the Humanities Press, 1962), p. vii.

[10] "Now if the transcendental is intersubjectivity, how can the borders of the transcendental and the empirical help becoming indistinct? For along with the other person, all the other person sees of me—all my facticity—is reintegrated into subjectivity, or at least posited as an indispensable element of its definition. Thus the transcendental descends into history." *Signs,* trans. Richard C. McCleary (Evanston: Northwestern University Press, 1964), p. 107.

Moving to another tradition, we are able to observe how the fate of transcendental reflection on matters of consciousness and knowledge follows yet another direction. In the critical theory approach of Karl-Otto Apel the transcendental is given a new role to play as it is put into the service of a "transcendental pragmatics of communication." Here the transcendental is employed not to aid us in the securing of the foundational structure of intentional consciousness (Husserl) nor to provide the resources for a descriptive metaphysics in identifying the general logico-linguistic features of our descriptions of persons and things (Strawson)—although it would seem to be closer to the later than to the former. Critical of Husserl because of his inability to establish trustworthy norms of validation due to the privilege that he confers on the principle of subjectivity, Apel appeals to the ongoing argumentation in the community of interpreters and to a pragmatic version of the consensus theory of truth. This falls out as a "transcendental hermeneutics" and a "transcendental pragmatics of communication." In this project there is a renewed emphasis on the importance of language and communal association, coupled with a loyalty to the inquiry framework of transcendental philosophy and its search for the conditions that make knowledge and validation possible.[11]

At this juncture it may be desirable to do an inventory of the results of our rather general tracking of the destiny of transcendental inquiry in its colorful variations from Kant onward. In the variations of transcendental philosophy that we have sketched we can observe that the philosophical sedimentations of what counts as the transcendental method have been rendered more and more porous. Transcendental inquiry no longer congeals into a clearly defined method and a unified program, as it did for Kant. It selects its data from different regions of theoretical interests—the nature of intentional consciousness (Husserl); the logico-linguistic structure of the human mind (Strawson); and the community of speakers and investigators (Apel). Yet this diversity of theoretical interests is bonded by a common faith in the resources of philosophical reflection to provide an unimpeachable grounding for

[11] Apel makes his debt to the Kantian heritage explicit when he formulates his principal programmatic thesis: "1. In contrast to the now dominant 'logic of science' I am of the opinion that any philosophical theory of science must answer the Kantian question of the transcendental presuppositions for the possibility of and validity of science. 2. Unlike those who adhere to an orthodox Kantianism, I am, however, of the opinion that the reply to the question raised by Kant does not lead back to Kant's philosophy of a transcendental 'consciousness as such.' Rather, I believe that the reply to the question as to the transcendental subject of science must be mediated by the real achievement of twentieth-century philosophy, namely, by the insight into the transcendental importance of language and, thereby, of the language community." *Towards a Transformation of Philosophy,* trans. Glyn Adey and David Frisby (London: Routledge & Kegan Paul, 1980), p. 136.

knowledge of self and world. The metaphor of foundations continues to guide the several inquiries and provides the goal for philosophical investigation. Traveling with this metaphor are a cluster of givens, sometimes empirical and sometimes conceptual, and the firm conviction that to know self and world is to "represent" them. The inquiries, in short, continue to move within the confines of epistemological space. But such a standpoint of inquiry, we have seen above, is peculiarly unfruitful for dealing with matters of consciousness and self-consciousness. The requisite given data are perpetually deferred; there is no "datable" presence in the neighborhood. And the effort to represent an elusive presence with the help of an equally elusive network of attributes and properties leads to an intolerable conceptual crisis.

Yet, our interest in the destiny of transcendental reflection is not that of simply finding something to negate. We are not using transcendental philosophy as an example of a position and approach that is obviously wrongheaded, an untenable thesis negated by our praxeological approach to consciousness. What interests us in the destiny of the transcendental is the manifestation of its own internal critique of the epistemological model and its intermittent forays into the domain of praxis. Although Apel still rather heavily buys into an epistemological model of justification, his pragmatics of communication courts the solicitations of discourse and action in a way in which a more hard-line transcendental approach simply could not do. In the thought of Heidegger and Merleau-Ponty the internal critique of epistemological presuppositions within transcendental philosophy becomes accentuated and the push toward praxis becomes explicit. Heidegger exploits the resources of transcendental reflection by thinking beyond it, refashioning it as a hermeneutic of everyday, praxis-oriented *Dasein*. Merleau-Ponty enjoins us to observe the descent of transcendental consciousness into history, entering the praxial space of embodiment, labor, and social practices. It is this internal dynamics in the destiny of the transcendental that elicits our interest. The move to history and social practices provides an aperture to that space of communicative praxis in which consciousness is repostured as *dialogical* consciousness.

As we have seen, the root problem in the epistemological model (and particularly in its egological expression) is that it remains wedded to a monadological view of the ego and to a monological view of consciousness. The ego is conceived to be present as a monad and consciousness functions as an epistemic monologue. In our decentering of consciousness as epistemological zero-point origin we displace the ego as monadic self-givenness of presence and resituate consciousness within the praxial space of discourse and action. The datum theory of consciousness is set aside in the interests of freeing the play of praxis.

This in turn allows for new descriptions of the consciousness of decentered subjectivity as multidimensional and dialogical. The subject as hermeneutically implicated within communicative praxis shows itself as an intersubjective event of consciousness, displaying multiple profiles, dialogical rather than monological in its hold on the world.

The resituation of consciousness as dialogical event within the texture of communicative praxis and its dynamic interplay of discourse and action may appear to be reminiscent of Marx's intriguing one-liner: "It is not the consciousness of men that determines their existence, but their social existence that determines their consciousness." That Marx was here on to something we would readily agree. However, before appropriating this one-liner as the philosophical shibboleth of the future one would need to get clear on what Marx means by "determines" and what all he packs into "social existence." Our concern, like that of Marx, is to accent the context of social practices in which consciousness emerges and shows itself in its multiple forms of life. But this concern was hardly distinctive of Marx. It was already present in the thought of Hegel and has received its due regard in the contemporary thought of the likes of Dewey, Heidegger, and George Herbert Mead.

The principal lesson to be learned from the advocates of praxis is that little is learned from the project of tracking consciousness with the space of cosmological-metaphysical categories (substance and attributes) and epistemological conditions (cognition and justification). We do better in looking elsewhere—to the space of praxis. But this space of praxis, as we have seen, unfolds as a composite texture of discourse and action, in which communicative language is amalgamated with communicative activities. Marx, in his definition of "social existence," gave a proper emphasis to the side of social action but neglected the component of language within the societal fabric. On the other hand, linguistic philosophers interested in an interpretation of the forms of social behavior (like Peter Winch) tend to emphasize linguistic performance and subordinate the intentionality of human action.[12] More recent attempts, notably that of Paul Ricoeur, illustrate an aggressive move into the domain of action, but in such a way that action is understood through the metaphors of textuality.[13] Our continuing argument throughout has been that discourse and action within the dynamics of communicative praxis are nonreducible twin halves of an

---

[12] See particularly Peter Winch, *The Idea of a Social Science* (New York: The Humanities Press, 1958).
[13] See particularly his essay "Explanation and Understanding: On Some Remarkable Connections Among the Theory of Text, Theory of Action, and Theory of History," in

undivided history. The texture of communicative praxis is reducible neither to the textuality of discourse nor to the tissues of human action.

In bringing the thematic of consciousness into play against the backdrop of communicative praxis we are able to describe it as an *event* of praxis, at once discursive and actional. The language of event as applied to consciousness has its intrinsic merit in that it effects a shift away from the metaphysically laden language of substance and the epistemological grammar of sources and relations of knowledge. It enables a description of consciousness as a happening or an occasioning, whose birth is in concert with the upsurge of speech and action. Gadamer has called upon the resources of the language of event and happening in his elucidation of "the hermeneutical consciousness," which he distinguishes from the self-referential and self-transparent consciousness as defined within the idealist model of self-reflexivity.

> The hermeneutical consciousness does not compete with that self-transparency that Hegel took to constitute absolute knowledge and the highest mode of being. . . . In the last analysis, *all* understanding is self-understanding, but not in the sense of a preliminary self-possession or of one finally and definitively achieved. For the self-understanding only realizes itself in the character of a free self-realization. The self that we are does not possess itself: one could say that it "happens".[14]

In this shift away from the epistemological model of self-reflexivity, the problematic metaphor of self-possession and the quest for a perpetually deferred, stable, monadic center of knowledge are set aside. The new description of consciousness that is opened up by such a move attends to its multiple forms within the density of praxis-oriented existence. Within this density the dialogical posture of consciousness is energized through its responsiveness to the speech and action of the other. Consciousness is given birth in the dialogic and actional encounters with other subjects, and it is able to sustain itself only within such encounters. Sartre may well have been correct in designating "the other" as the "original fall" of consciousness, but he neglected the truth that "the other" is also and already at play in the "original creation" of consciousness. Without the presence of another self, consciousness can neither fall into the negativity of self-estrangement nor experience the positivity of creative self-realization.

At this juncture it might be argued that we have still not moved one

---

The Philosophy of Paul Ricoeur, eds. Charles E. Reagan and David Stewart (Boston: Beacon Press, 1978).

[14]*Philosophical Hermeneutics,* trans. and ed. David E. Linge (Berkeley: University of California Press, 1976), p. 55.

step beyond Hegel and his celebrated dictum that self-consciousness is itself only in its acknowledgment by another *(ein anderes)*.[15] That there is in this dictum a truth worthy of appropriation is not denied. But this appropriation is made possible only via a deformalization of self-consciousness as a structural element in the odyssey of absolute knowledge. Through such a deformalization self-consciousness is de-epistemologized and descends into the tightly woven fabric of discursive and actional performance. In doing so it encounters the phenomenon of embodiment, which we have seen in the previous chapter to be a salient feature of the mimetic responsiveness within the dialectic of self and other. Language and action interplay in this embodied mimetic responsiveness. Self-consciousness as a hermeneutical moment of understanding is enveloped by the linguisticality and the social practices which allow one to say "I" in concrete speech transactions. Embedded within a tradition of the already spoken, the already written, and the already accomplished social practices, self-consciousness breaks forth as a dialogic event within embodied and decentered subjectivity.

The consciousness at work in decentered subjectivity is both linguistic and actional, embedded in a history of social practices. It thus borrows its being from the praxial history of speaking and acting subjects as they respond to the speech and action of others. Through this borrowing consciousness is dialogically constituted. Admittedly, consciousness can be alone; it can fashion a soliloquy, and it can monitor an individual act in solitude. In all this, consciousness is experienced as "mine." Yet, being alone is itself a peculiar modality of being with others; soliloquy is carried by a language that belongs to the public; and individual acts have meaning only within the wider context of social practices. One can be alone only because one has already been in communal interaction with others; one can speak "by" and "to" oneself only with a grammar that has a social history; and one can act as an individual only as differentiated from others within the body politic. Surrounding all individual manifestations of discourse and action is the space of communicative praxis.

In further probing the linguistic and actional texture of consciousness we find that it displays vectors of understanding soliciting a comprehension of self and world. It is thus that one can speak of dialogical consciousness as hermeneutical. Consciousness as a hermeneutical event displays an *interpretation* of self and world through the twin

---

[15] "Das Selbstbewusstein ist *an* und *für sich,* indem und dadurch, dass es für ein anderes an und für sich ist; d.h. es ist nur als ein Anerkantes." *Phänomenologie des Geistes* (Hamburg: Felix Meiner Verlag, sechste Auflage, 1952), p. 141.

moments of understanding and explanation. But this is not to define consciousness in terms of an epistemological function, as a series of *cogitationes,* emitted from a recessed ego, bent toward the framing of judgments and the construction of beliefs which are designed to represent reality. The backdrop of consciousness, as always, is the backdrop of discursive and actional practices rather than a system of beliefs and theories of judgment. The history of the use of intentionality as a chracterizing feature of consciousness is itself a witness to the progressive deconstruction of the epistemological foundation and function of consciousness. Already in the later Husserl, but more explicitly in the existential phenomenology of Merleau-Ponty, the limitations of theoretical act-intentionality are exposed and the broader and more vibrant notion of "functioning intentionality" *(fungierendes Intentionalität)* is introduced. In the thought of Heidegger intentionality is further deconstructed and repostured as "concern" *(Besorgen),* which displays its own comprehension of self and world.[16] Consciousness is the hermeneutical event of comprehending the world.

However, there is another feature of the story of consciousness descending into history as hermeneutical event and becoming incarnate in embodied and dialogic discourse and action. There is the episode of consciousness interrupted and disturbed, marred by the distortions of language and action in communicative praxis. Transcendental consciousness, by virtue of its transempirical status, was insulated from the threats of derangement. The transcendental ego could not go mad. Matters are different for the hermeneutical consciousness, inserted into the density of lived-through communicative praxis. The understanding displayed by hermeneutical consciousness is not insulated from distortion. The dialogical texture of hermeneutical consciousness can be disrupted, and its structure of intentionality can be fractured. To account for the myriad deviations and fractures of consciousness Freud invented the unconscious, which exploded the concept of conciousness as a given, unitary datum. It is thus that we are required to take up a conversation with Freud, as has been urged by Ricoeur, Habermas,

---

16 This deconstruction of intentionality was already discernible in *Being and Time,* where Heidegger recognized the "insight" operative in *Dasein's* circumspective being-in-the-world: " 'Practical behavior' is not 'atheoretical' in the sense of 'sightlessness'. The way it differs from theoretical behaviour does not lie simply in the fact that in theoretical behaviour one observes, while in practical behaviour one *acts (gehandelt wird),* and that action must employ theoretical cognition if it is not to remain blind; for the fact that observation is a kind of concern is just as primordial as the fact that action has *its own* kind of sight." Trans. John Macquarrie and Edward Robinson (New York: Harper and Row, 1962), p. 99. In *The Basic Problems of Phenomenology,* trans. Albert Hofstadter (Bloomington: Indiana University Press, 1982), Heidegger makes the deconstruction of intentionality a more specific and more pivotal theme.

Lacan, Derrida, Deleuze, and others.[17] This need not require a re-hearsal and critique of Freud's metapsychology, but it does require an addressing of the "problem" of consciousness as it emerges in Freud's deconstructionist hermeneutics.

We propose that this problem can be most fruitfully addressed through a consideration of the unconscious as a distortion of dialogue issuing from disturbances in discourse and action. Lacan, we would submit, is moving in the right direction in his interpretation that "the unconscious is structured as a language," properly explicated as a *forgotten* language, a language which has escaped our vigilance.[18] Habermas moves along similar lines in recommending that disturbed consciousness be portrayed as "deviations from the model of the lan-guage game of communicative action."[19] The emphasis by Lacan and Habermas on the role of language in tracking the traces of the uncon-scious is well-placed. However, this emphasis on language needs to be balanced with a complementing emphasis on the role of action to avoid a linguisticism in which there is an overextension of linguistic models and textual analogues. The unconscious is also structured as a *dynamis* of human action, embedded within a horizon of social practices whose hermeneutical significations escape our monitoring. A hiddenness of significations pervades both our language and our action. Commu-nicative praxis is infected with forgotten speech acts and forgotten social practices. There are meanings that lurk behind that which is delivered up through the manifest memory of our linguistic and social practices. Hence, the hermeneutics of a "depth psychology" neces-sarily falls out as a "depth hermeneutics," probing that which is forgot-ten and distorted in the amalgamated personal and social history of dialogical consciousness.

It is at this juncture that traditional hermeneutics, modeled after the manifest meanings of the written text, founders. Overly confident about the resources and continuity of memory and unable to recognize the latent significations in the life of consciousness, traditional her-meneutics was able to retrieve only the surface and manifest meanings

---

[17] See particularly Paul Ricoeur, *Freud and Philosophy*, trans. Denis Savage (New Haven: Yale University Press, 1970); Jürgen Habermas, *Knowledge and Human Interests*, trans. Jeremy J. Shapiro (Boston: Beacon Press, 1971); Jacques Lacan, "Of Structure as an Inmixing of an Otherness Prerequisite to Any Subject Whatever," in *The Languages of Criticism and the Sciences of Man*, ed. Richard Macksey and Eugenio Donato (Bal-timore: The Johns Hopkins University Press, 1970); Jacques Derrida, "Freud and the Scene of Writing," in *Writing and Difference*, trans. Alan Bass (University of Chicago Press, 1978); and Gilles Deleuze and Félix Guattari, *Capitalisme et Schizophrénie: L'Anti-Oedipe* (Paris: Les Éditions de Minuit, 1972).
[18] "Of Structure as an Inmixing," pp. 188–89.
[19] *Knowledge and Human Interests*, p. 226.

of the spoken and written word. But the mutilations and distortions of dialogical consciousness are as much a part of the life of the speaking, writing, and acting subject as are its consciously intended meanings and its manifest understanding. The principal requirement of a depth hermeneutics is that of a broader notion of reason and understanding than that which is called upon to do service on the level of conscious intending. It requires a radical reflection that is able to track the play of forgotten memories and distorted motivations in the life of the decentered subject and to discern the opaqueness and concealment that remains embedded in the conversation and social practices of mankind.[20]

A recognition of the fringes of forgetfulness and the distortion and mutilation of meaning in the life of dialogical consciousness regulates the limits and possibilities for any proposed ontology of subjectivity. From one perspective it disseminates ontological analysis by exploding consciousness as a pure presence, a given datum, and a unity of manifest and transparent intended meanings. From another perspective, however, it opens the path to a "new" ontology, the only one possible for decentered subjectivity. This is an oblique and subdued ontology of the finitude of communicative praxis. The question of being is still addressed, but only within the context of the interplay of presence and absence. Dialogical consciousness, whose presence is always an event and an acquisition, can lose its presence as well as achieve it. It can lose its presence, become absent to itself in its forgetfulness, its self-deception, its unmonitored subordination to the play of political power and ideology—all of which indicate features of communicative praxis under the conditions of finitude and estrangement. Freud named this absence of a self-monitored and vigilant consciousness the unconscious. That his theory of the unconscious may have involved some scientistic misunderstandings of the life of the psyche is not denied. Indeed, we are inclined to agree with Habermas and Ricoeur in their critiques of Freud precisely on this point.[21] But there is a hermeneutical challenge that Freud's reflections have set into motion. This challenge requires a response from any future ontology of subjectivity and any project to fashion a new humanism. We have attempted to respond to this challenge with a new description of subjectivity, decentererd and de-

---

[20] For a discussion of the shape and dynamics of this expanded notion of reason and understanding see chapter 5 of the author's *Radical Reflection and the Origin of the Human Sciences,* "Understanding and Reason: Towards a Hermeneutic of Everyday Life" (West Lafayette: Purdue University Press, 1980).

[21] See particularly Habermas, *Knowledge and Human Interests,* chapter II: "The Scientistic Self-Misunderstanding of Metapsychology," and Ricoeur, *Freud and Philosophy,* Book III: "Dialectic: A Philosophical Interpretation of Freud."

centralized, and through a reshaping of consciousness as dialogical. Embedded in a history of language and social practices, dialogical consciousness is textured by presence and absence, reminiscence and forgetfulness, disclosure and hiddenness. An ontology of subjectivity cannot escape human finitude.

Part III

The Rhetorical Turn

CHAPTER NINE

Rhetoric, Hermeneutics, and Communication

Our explorations of the texture of communicative praxis (Part I) and the new horizon of subjectivity (Part II) have led us to the rhetorical turn (Part III). Our probings of the expressive display of meaning by discourse and action in the communicative practices of mankind delivered a notion of hermeneutical reference. Communicative praxis, as word and deed, is a network of inscriptions and intentionalities *about* something. Our foray into the new horizon of subjectivity delivered a hermeneutical self-implicature of the subject as speaker, author, and actor, marking communicative praxis as performances *by* someone. Our sketch of the rhetorical turn is designed to render explicit the intentionality of communicative praxis as the communication of something *for* someone.

It is principally the directedness of thought and discourse to the hearer, the audience, the reader, and the wider public, already emphasized by Aristotle,[1] that elicits our interest in a reposturing of rhetoric within the texture of communicative praxis. In this directedness of discourse in the play of communicative praxis the "other," whose place is already secured when the story of discourse and action begins, is decisively disclosed. In this disclosure the other is generalized to encompass the hearer in the dialogic transaction, the audience of a public assembly, the reader of a text, and the respondent citizen in the *polis* of praxis-oriented existence.

There is thus in the rhetorical turn an accentuation of discourse and action as *for* and *toward* someone. This accent is rather ubiquitously

---

[1]In our rhetorical discourse, says Aristotle, we must take pains "not to annoy our hearers" and remain attentive to "whatever it is we have to expound to others." *Rhetoric* 1404a 4–10.

illustrated in the self-definition of classical rhetoric as the art of persuasion. Rhetoric as persuasive discourse is directed toward the other as hearer and reader. Yet it behooves us in the early stages of our tracking of the rhetorical turn to make explicit the proper tense in this placement of the accent on the hearer and the reader. It would be unfortunate if the placing of this accent were construed as a mere supplement or an adventitious appendage to the expressive texture of communicative praxis and the hermeneutical implicature of self. The *for someone* feature of discourse and action comprises the last topic within the general design of our work, but it is a feature that informs the dynamics and structure of communicative praxis throughout. Rhetoric is an integral and inaugural moment in the life of communicative praxis. It is already operative in the expressivity of discourse and action and in the self-implicature of a speaking and acting subject. As we have seen, this self-implicature appears against a backdrop of discursive and social practices in which the insertion of the other is an accomplished event. A rhetorical consciousness is stitched into the very warp and woof of the multiple forms of discourse and action, which in concert occasion a hermeneutical reference to the world, a hermeneutical self-implicature of the subject, and a disclosure of the other.

It is thus that one need be somewhat cautious in sorting out persuasive discourse as having a modality and an aim separable from other forms of discourse, commonly classified as referential, literary, and expressive.[2] Persuasive discourse, in its directedness to the other, is of a piece with the intertextual intentionality of communicative praxis that envelops a multiplicity of modes and aims. Against the backdrop of this wider intentionality persuasive discourse accentuates the role of the hearer, reader, and audience, emphasizing their importance for the genesis and development of meaning within the intersubjectivity of social practices. It discloses the role and contribution of the other in the manifestation of meaning, intensifying the awareness that discourse is *for someone,* as well as by someone and about something. This being-for-someone is an indelible feature of the creation and preservation of meaning.

The implications of this intertexture of discourse for the situation of

---

[2] This is one of the dangers in James Kinneavy's otherwise illuminating discussion of the modes and aims of discourse in his comprehensive study *A Theory of Discourse* (New York: W. W. Norton & Company, 1971). Kinneavy identifies four modes (narration, description, classification, and evaluation) and four aims (reference, persuasion, literature, and expression) of discourse. Within the limits of model construction and classificatory procedures (limits of which Kinneavy is himself aware) this portrait of discourse is more tidy and more fruitful than most, but it tends to gloss the intertexture of discourse as a multiplex phenomenon.

rhetoric as a special discipline are pertinent and far-reaching. This intertexture invites a dismantling of rhetoric as a special field of inquiry and a recovery of the fabric of persuasive discourse in its commingling with other forms. It also registers a decisive indictment of the prejudices of academic philosophy against the function of rhetoric. In the halls of academic philosophy, rhetoric, serialized as a special discipline in an atlas of knowledge and skills, suffers the fate of being subordinated to the more aggressive disciplines of logic, epistemology, and metaphysics. The latter disciplines comprise the alleged "core" of the philosophical enterprise, in which one first gets things right on matters of validity, reference, meaning, and reality. The accompanying assumption is that only after one has attended to these matters in the core disciplines does one acquire the franchise to ruminate on matters of rhetoric, poetics, and aesthetics. And it is made clear to all that if indeed such ruminations are taken up it best be done on one's philosophical "free time." It is precisely this cluster of prejudices that comes under critical questioning in our reinsertion of the rhetorical consciousness into the meaning-laden fabric of communicative praxis.

Classical rhetoric taught that rhetoric is the art of persuasive discourse. This definition of rhetoric has stood for some time and may continue to stand. However, what needs to be asked, time and again, are the questions of what it is that counts as discourse, art, and persuasion. With regard to these questions we have already urged a measure of caution in the penchant for a taxonomic approach to discourse in which persuasive discourse is classified as an independent genre, sectioned off from referential, literary, and expressive discourse. In Part I of our study we have seen how discourse as expressive, liberated from its epistemological paradigm of an interior mind standing over against an exterior world, slides into referential and literary discourse and transfigures both along the way. Expressive speech and writing, epistemologically deconstructed, effect a hermeneutical reference and a hermeneutical self-implicature which are at once a narration of a story about the world and the subject's place in it. Expression, reference, and narration commingle as discourse *by* someone *about* something. But this discourse is also *for* and *toward* someone. Persuasive discourse is thus already inscribed into the wider text of discourse, in which world, self and other are reciprocally involved.

Rhetoric, thus, has to do with discourse. But it also has to do with art *(technē)*. Aristotle and the classical rhetoricians were clear about that. However, the Aristotelian notion of *technē* should not be confused with the modern notion of "technique" as an affiliate of technology. Rhetoric as an art is not a technique for control, an instrument for manipulation, a routine that can be mapped out in advance.[3] Such a construal of *technē* leads directly to a technification of discourse, inviting a gimmickry of emotional appeals, twists of language, if not outright deception, designed to win someone over in accepting beliefs and practices without regard either for understanding or for availability of evidence. This of course is an old story, going all the way back to Plato's disenchantment with the misuse of rhetoric by the Sophists. The widespread prevalence of technological consciousness in the modern age makes the threat of this distortion of the art of rhetoric all the more ominous. Ricoeur's final admonition on this matter should be well heeded: "Rhetoric cannot become an empty and formal technique."[4]

Now what about the moment of persuasion in rhetoric as the art of persuasive discourse? We have the resources to distinguish persuasion from propaganda, flattery, seduction, threats, and outright violence. To persuade someone through discourse presupposes a background of rationality, understanding, and discernment against which what is persuasive is articulated. It was this that made the historical alignment of rhetoric and argumentation so decisive. This alignment has been given a renewed emphasis by Henry W. Johnstone, who in recent years has worked out a new slant on both rhetoric and argumentation. The issue has also become a dominant concern in the critical theory approach of Jürgen Habermas and Karl-Otto Apel, in which persuasion is construed as argumentation struggling for agreement and consensus. Yet, persuasion is never simply and solely the art of argumentation. It also proceeds by dint of a showing, a making manifest through the evocation of new life styles and new ways of seeing the world. Persuasion should not be reduced to argumentation on matters of belief. Its movements are sketched against a broader background of the habits, customs, and social practices of the *polis*. Beliefs are themselves embedded within a more encompassing history and system of social practices. It is thus that rhetoric must be prepared to fight against its subordination to argumentative techniques of disputation (eristics) and its construal as a strategy of debating, the winning of points in an argument with the intention of obliterating the beliefs of an opponent.

Aristotle had already recognized this possible devaluation of rhetoric as the mere instrumentation of skills of disputation and saw fit to install

---

[3] Ricoeur speaks to the point at issue when he writes: "There are as many *technai* as there are creative activities. A *technē* is something more refined than a routine or an empirical practice and in spite of its focus on production, it contains a speculative element, namely a theoretical enquiry into the means of production. It is a method; and this feature brings it closer to theoretical knowledge than to routine." *The Rule of Metaphor*, trans. Robert Czerny (Toronto: University of Toronto Press, 1977), p. 28.
[4] *Ibid.*, p. 29.

a distinction between forensics and the deliberative rhetoric of political oratory.[5] The former is geared to the winning of points in an argument or a formal debate; the latter seeks to effect a common orientation among the hearers within a situation calling for responsible judgment and action. Deliberative rhetoric broadens the space of rhetoric to include the common good of the *polis,* the interests of the rhetor and the hearers alike, and the rationality of practical wisdom as a guide for deliberation and action.[6]

Our expansion of the performance of persuasion to include a showing of paths of reflection, deliberation, and action that is nonargumentative in design does not entail a displacement of the uses of argumentation. It resituates them. Argumentation is made to stand in the service of understanding and deliberative action. Concomitantly language itself is broadened to include nonargumentative usages. One of the limitations in Apel's theory of rhetorical discourse, for example, is that it restricts the space of agreement and consensus to the domain of argumentative competence and performance. Language as it operates in the strategy of argumentation takes on a privilege and a primacy. But this is to neglect the play of performative utterances, metaphorical deployment, mythopoetic elucidations, and experimentation with alternative styles of behavior in disclosing to the other new modes of thought and action. If argumentation is not tempered with nonargumentative forms of persuasion, rhetoric degenerates into a coercive technique.

Robert Nozick has called our attention to the plethora of coercive metaphors in the restrictive definition of philosophy as the art of argumentation.

---

[5] "Hence it comes that, although the same systematic principles apply to political as to forensic oratory, and although the former is a nobler business, and fitter for a citizen, than that which concerns the relations of private individuals, these authors say nothing about political oratory, but try, one and all, to write treatises on the way to plead in court. The reason for this is that in political oratory there is less inducement to talk about non-essentials. Political oratory is less given to unscrupulous practices than forensic, because it treats of wider issues." *Rhetoric,* 1354b 23–30.

[6] Michael Heim provides an illuminating explication of what is at issue in Aristotle's notion of political-deliberative rhetoric when he writes: "In political or deliberative rhetoric, the interests of the hearer cannot be merely objectified as states of the *psyche* to be handled by the trained speaker. Rather, in such public address, the speaker and hearers are joined in considering pros and contras of actions which will entail weal or woe for the common interest, the well-being of the body politic. The rhetorician must therefore take into account the sobriety of those judging his speech, because they are to make decisions affecting their own well-being. So uppermost in the parliamentary or deliberative context is not the question, Who will win? The question is rather, Which is the best course of action now proposed? And the public speaker who brings to this context only a bag of techniques will surely fail to convince others of the merits of the proposal he defends." "Philosophy as Ultimate Rhetoric," *The Southern Journal of Philosophy,* Vol. XIX, No. 2, 1981.

The terminology of philosophical art is coercive: arguments are *power-ful* and best when they are *knockdown,* arguments *force* you to a con-clusion, if you believe the premises you *have to* or *must* believe the conclusion, some arguments do not carry much *punch,* and so forth. A philosophical argument is an attempt to get someone to believe something, whether he wants to believe it or not. A successful philosophical argu-ment, a strong argument, forces someone to a belief.[7]

There are undeniable features of coercion in argumentation as an in-strument of persuasion. Left to its own resources argumentation as a technique of disputation postures its *telos* as the obliteration or demoli-tion of an opponent rather than as the achievement of understanding and mutual enlightenment. It is thus that the rhetorical moment needs be structured as an inmixing of argumentation and understanding in which each reinforces the other. It is not that argumentation is dis-placed; it is incorporated into a broader posture of address in the encounter with the other.

The intercalated moments of art, persuasion, and discourse in the rhetorical event should be liberated from recurring tendencies to re-strict the patterning of the rhetorical event by narrowing *techne* to technique, construing persuasion as a paradigm of argumentation, and binding rhetorical discourse as an independent genre. These recurring tendencies can be effectively avoided by resituating rhetoric within the texture of communicative praxis as an amalgam of discourse and action. This texture, as we have seen, is a display of meaning through the expressivity of speaking, writing, and acting. Communicative praxis as expression is a process of making something manifest through the hermeneutical displays of word and deed. Communicative praxis makes manifest the world of thought and action. This manifestation and show-ing of world, both as nature and as history, we have maintained, is borne by an intentionality of hermeneutical reference. This referential dis-course, embedded within the texture of expressivity, slides into dis-course as narrational. Descriptions of the world involve the telling of a story. In turn this story about the world of nature and social practices implicates a community of speakers and hearers, authors and readers, actors and respondents. The signal event of rhetoric as persuasive discourse, we have suggested, is its directedness to the other, thus

---

[7] *Philosophical Explanations* (Cambridge: Harvard University Press, 1981), p. 4. Some-what playfully Nozick suggests: "Perhaps philosophers need arguments so powerful they set up reverberations in the brain: if the person refuses to accept the conclusion, he *dies.* How's that for a powerful argument? Yet, as with other physical threats ('your money or your life'), he can choose defiance. A 'perfect' philosophical argument would leave no choice." *Ibid.*

placing persuasion within an intertextuality of multiple modes of discourse limning the texture of communicative praxis.

The sliding of rhetoric as the art of persuasion into the expressivity of communicative praxis has received some attention in the current programs of "expressive" and "hermeneutical" rhetoric. Michael Heim, working out a perspective on "philosophy as ultimate rhetoric," locates expressive rhetoric within the interstices of the dynamics of deliberation striving for a consensus on the common good of the *polis*. He identifies expressive rhetoric by contrasting the deliberative form of rhetoric with its forensic form.

> While forensic speakers can hide their genuine selves and still attain their persuasive ends, the deliberative rhetorician must *express himself*, viz., his own deepest interests, if he is to provide the strongest argument for convincing other participants in the deliberation. That is, fellow deliberants are more likely to be convinced if the speech of the rhetor has a dimension of self-involvement or self-implication. This is the sense in which I call deliberative rhetoric "expressive."[8]

Although Heim's project of situating rhetoric within the texture of expressivity is to be applauded, he is still working with a too traditional and too subjectivistic notion of expression. He does well to remind us that there is a moment of "self-implication" within the dynamics of rhetoric as expressive, but the fabric of expressivity extends beyond the determination of meaning by the rhetor. In the commingling of expressive and persuasive discourse there is a concomitant upsurge of meaning involving self and other, speaker and hearer, within a common intersubjective field. In this commingling there is also the moment of referentiality. This is poignantly articulated by Ricoeur when he remarks that "no discourse ever suspends our belonging to a world."[9] Expressive rhetoric thus needs to be inserted into a wider texture of communicative praxis, which falls out as discourse by someone to someone about something.

The situating of rhetoric within the more global field of the expressivity of communicative praxis makes possible a grafting of rhetoric onto hermeneutics. This grafting has been performed by representatives of the hermeneutical school of rhetoricians, who have worked out a theory of complementarity of hermeneutics and rhetoric. In their innovative article "Hermeneutics and Rhetoric: A Seen but

---

[8] "Philosophy as Ultimate Rhetoric," pp. 183–84.
[9] *The Rule of Metaphor,* p. 43.

Unobserved Relationship," Michael Hyde and Craig Smith have detailed some programmatic directions for their hermeneutical approach.

> From the hermeneutical situation originates the primordial function of rhetoric. . . . The primordial function of rhetoric is to "make-known" meaning both *to oneself and to others. Meaning is derived by a human being in and through the interpretive understanding of reality.* Rhetoric is the process of making-known that meaning.[10]

The background against which the views of the hermeneutical rhetoricians are sketched is principally that of the philosophy of Martin Heidegger. They are particularly intrigued by Heidegger's explicit reference to Aristotle's *Rhetoric* as the first disciplined discussion of the hermeneutics of everyday life.

> It is not an accident that the earliest systematic Interpretation of affects that has come down to us is not treated in the framework of "psychology". Aristotle investigates the πα'θη (affects) in the second book of his *Rhetoric*. Contrary to the traditional orientation, according to which Rhetoric is conceived as the kind of thing we "learn in school", this work of Aristotle must be taken *as the first systematic hermeneutic of the everydayness of Being with one another.*[11]

In this passage the linkage of hermeneutics with rhetoric is made explicit by Heidegger; and he finds the precedent for this already in the thought of Aristotle. What is of particular note in this context is the selection of the data of rhetoric from the region of human affects—Aristotle's πα'θη and Heidegger's *Befindlichkeit*. The making manifest of meanings of self and world is sketched against the background of the play of affects, feelings, and moods that infuse the rhetor and the audience alike. The manifestation of meaning in rhetorical discourse draws upon the disclosing power of the situated affects (fear, trust, antipathy, indifference, etc.) which display their own intentionality and in subtle ways present the rhetor as rhetor and the public as public.

Of particular consequence in this linkage of rhetoric with a hermeneutic of everyday life is the undercutting of the troublesome dichotomy of pure theory and affective states. Affectivity, which is a gestalt of concern or attitudinal posture rather than a state or condition, exhibits an intentionality that fashions its own mode of disclosure. The affects of fear, pity, love, anger, shame, and the like, before they become

---

[10] *The Quarterly Journal of Speech*, Vol. 65, No. 4, 1979, pp. 347–48.
[11] *Being and Time*, trans. John Macquarrie and Edward Robinson (New York: Harper and Row, 1962), p. 178. Emphasis mine.

objectified as discrete psychic data or mental states, are intentional vectors, disclosing a situatedness of world-involvement, concomitantly making manifest the self and the other in the context of everyday, praxis-oriented engagements. It was for this reason, Heidegger reminds us, that Aristotle saw fit to deal with the phenomenon of fear not in his treatise on psychology but rather in his *Rhetoric*.[12] Fear accomplishes a hermeneutical disclosure of being-in-the-world. Sartre came upon a similar insight with respect to the performative intentionality of shame. The affectivity at work in shame reveals the self to itself in a world invaded by another self. *I* am ashamed of *myself* in the presence of the Other.[13]

This intentionality of the affects, bent toward a disclosure of self and other, speaker and hearer, rhetor and audience, marks out a move from a rhetoric of expression to a rhetoric of truth. Admittedly, in this move the traditional epistemological theories of truth, coherence as well as correspondence, operating within a system of beliefs and epistemic rules for justification, are if not summarily displaced at least forced to recognize their derivative status. The truth at issue in a rhetoric of truth is not that of an epistemic correspondence of a reified proposition with an equally reified state of affairs, but rather truth as the disclosure of possibilities for agreed upon perspectives on seeing the world and acting within it. Rhetoric deformalizes truth as the manipulation of propositions and reinserts it into a hermeneutic of everyday life, where truth is more a matter of disclosure than correspondence, making manifest the dynamics of the social world as a web of human affects and interests.

The situating of rhetoric within a hermeneutically informed notion of truth, liberated from its traditional epistemological paradigm, has been entertained by professional rhetoricians in the recent past. In 1967 Robert L. Scott published a seminal and influential essay, "On Viewing Rhetoric as Epistemic."[14] In 1977 he published a sequel to his earlier essay which carried the title "On Viewing Rhetoric as Epistemic: Ten Years Later."[15] What strikes us as being of rather momentous import within this ten-year odyssey of rhetorical reflection is a progressive dissimulation of the epistemological model and a reinsertion of rhetorical knowing into the space of hermeneutical understanding. Writing in his "Ten Years Later" essay, Scott informs us of the shift that has taken place during the interval.

---

[12] *Rhetoric* B 5, 1382 a 20-1383 b 11.
[13] *Being and Nothingness*, trans. Hazel E. Barnes (New York: Philosophical Library, 1956), pp. 221-222.
[14] *Central States Speech Journal*, Vol. 18, 1967, pp. 9-16.
[15] *Ibid.*, Vol. 27, 1977, pp. 258-266.

Thus far I have used the terms "knowing" and "understanding" as if they were interchangeable. Although I may have been correct in respect to ordinary usage in doing so, still the words do carry somewhat different weights, or can be made to deviate somewhat from one another, and the nuances that seem to me to cling to "understanding" make me prefer it to ascribe to rhetoric as epistemic. By "knowing" we may stress a sense of from-the-outside-in, taking knowledge as an external anchor point that may bring one into a consistent relationship with the world that is more than oneself. By "understanding" we may stress the sense of from-the-inside-out, taking understanding as a human and personal capacity to embrace what is outside the self, creating rather than finding meaning in the world.[16]

Now one might indeed quarrel (and we would be so inclined) with Scott's reactivation of the metaphor of inside versus outside and the consequent split between creation and discovery in addressing the ways of understanding. But such a quarrel would consist basically of a family dispute. What we wish to call to attention is Scott's "deconstruction" and vitalization of knowing in the turning of his thought to matters hermeneutical as he works out the resources and limitations of rhetoric as epistemic. One could well characterize this as a shift from rhetoric as epistemic to rhetoric as hermeneutic, enjoining us to see rhetoric "more broadly as a human potentiality to understand the human condition."[17]

This move beyond epistemology to hermeneutics within the field of formal rhetoric is itself part of the wider story of the "end" of epistemology and the emergence of a new notion of philosophical truth. It may indeed be the case that this wider story tells a tale of an unexpected fraternization of philosophy and rhetoric, after a rather long history of having gone their separate ways. There are those who have discerned on the contemporary scene a merger of sorts between the two fields of inquiry, at times leading to the collapse of the one into the other. Henry Johnstone, for example, finds that "Heidegger conceives philosophy as basically rhetorical."[18] Ernesto Grassi, in his portrayal of "rhetoric as philosophy," observes that "metaphor lies at the root of

---

[16] *Ibid.*, p. 262.

[17] "If Gadamer is correct in saying that 'the experience of meaning which takes place in understanding always includes application' then rhetoric as a means of understanding social reality as well as a means of acting effectively within a community is assured. Put differently: rhetoric may be the art of persuasion, that is, it may be seen from one angle as a practical capacity to find means to ends on specific occasions; but rhetoric must also be seen more broadly as a human potentiality to understand the human condition." *Ibid.*, p. 266.

[18] "Rhetoric and Communication in Philosophy" (in *Validity and Rhetoric in Philosophical Argument,* University Park: Dialogue Press of Man and World, 1978), p. 68.

our knowledge in which rhetoric and philosophy attain their original unity."[19] These may all be pointers in the right direction. Yet, we would urge that this symbiosis of philosophy and rhetoric, if such is destined to be the case, not be construed as a meta-discipline geared to the unification of formal fields of inquiry. The binding of philosophy and rhetoric into a super-discipline, accompanied with a graphics of curricular design, can yield little more than a juxtaposition of strategies of inquiry and conceptual schemes. Philosophy and rhetoric alike need to be deformalized as special disciplines, and the texture of communicative praxis, which they intermittently exhibit, should become the common topic of concern.

In all this there is admittedly an "end" of philosophy as epistemological inquiry and an "end" of rhetoric as a technique of disputation. But the end of philosophy as epistemology is not simply another propositional "truth," describing a state of affairs in the cultural history of philosophy as a discipline. It is rather the articulation of a task to be performed time and again as a project of recollection which at once reclaims the resources of the tradition and points to the potentialities for its transformation. The dismantling of epistemology, it should be underscored, does not entail a displacement of "knowledge." It resituates knowledge within a plurality of modes of discourse and communicative practices. The scientist, the historian, the economist, the musician, and the painter will continue to offer knowledge in their varied pursuits and practices. But what will have been called to our attention as we attempt to think to the end of epistemology is the vacuity and incoherence of talk about the knowledge of knowledge. Scientists and artists, historians and journalists, will continue to talk about "truths," but this will be talk about truths in the plural, multiple rather than singular, making manifest the variegated topics of communicative praxis. Preoccupations with a unifying epistemological theory of truth, which seeks to lay the foundations with a platform of correspondence or coherence within a belief-system of propositions, will be set aside.

As an expressive rhetoric slides into a rhetoric of truth within the historical texture and structure of communicative praxis, so a rhetoric of truth slides into a rhetoric of communicative competence and performance. The separation of the discovery of truth from the communication of it has traveled as an uncontested assumption in the philosophical tradition stemming from the epistemological turn in the thought of Descartes. The discovery of truth, according to this tradition,

---

[19] *Rhetoric as Philosophy* (University Park: The Pennsylvania State University Press, 1980), p. 34.

is viewed essentially as a private affair, a judicative act of a solitary ego-cogito representing a state of affairs in the framing of a proposition. The communication of this truth is then seen as an ancillary event, as something that one chooses to do after one has discovered truth. This bifurcation of truth and communication is dismantled in our recovery of the inaugural texture of communicative praxis, which moves beyond epistemology to a critical and restorative hermeneutics. The discovery of truth as an achievement of praxis is a shared project and a joint endeavor by a community of investigators and interpreters, which through its institutional reflection opens avenues for agreement and consensus. Truth is the process of disclosure eventuated in the describing, arguing, explaining, and showing that goes on in our speaking, writing, and acting. Description and redescription, understanding and explanation, argumentation and showing are themselves displays of communicative praxis, involving an actual or a potential hearer and reader. This comprises the rhetorical conversation of mankind, setting forth and making manifest to the hearer and reader multiple perspectives of world, self, and other.

Henry Johnstone has given particular attention to the intercalation of truth, communication, and rhetoric in his new theory of philosophical argumentation. He speaks of a "collapse" of each into the other. "Not only do communication and rhetoric collapse together, but the result of this collapse collapses together with the act of discovering truth."[20] The context from which Johnstone addresses this mutual collapsing is that of the nature of argumentation—and more specifically the context of the move away from his earlier view on the subject to his recent position. In his earlier view, articulated most succinctly in his essay on "Argument and Truth in Philosophy,"[21] he sought to keep in force the distinction between finding the truth and finding the proper rhetorical devices for communicating it. This distinction was informed by the belief that whereas an argument is addressed to the reason of the hearer or reader, rhetoric is an effort to persuade the hearer or reader through the manipulation of beliefs. The appeal to reason was construed by Johnstone in his earlier position as an appeal to the abhorrence of inconsistency, assumed to be shared by everyone. This facile appeal to reason, Johnstone later recognized, was "rationalistic" and suffered from "a defect common to many rationalisms: It makes the unwarranted assumption that all humans reason in the same way."[22] This

---

[20] "Truth, Communication and Rhetoric in Philosophy," *Validity and Rhetoric in Philosophical Argument*, p. 73.

[21] *Philosophy and Phenomenological Research*, Vol 18, 1957, pp. 228–36.

[22] "Truth, Communication and Rhetoric in Philosophy," p. 75.

assumption, Johnstone continues, fails to pass the test of careful scrutiny. The interlocutor can straightway deny the alleged inconsistency; he can doctor it up with another distinction; he can submit another view on the nature of contradiction; he can refuse to acknowledge the role of contradictions; or he can assume a Hegelian or Marxist stance and find in every contradiction a disguised relation that leads to a new positivity.[23]

In his concern to surmount traditional rationalism and its facile appeal to consistency, which informed his earlier view, Johnstone broadens the scope and dynamics of argumentation to include an explicit evocative function. "My present view," announces Johnstone, "is that a successful argument in philosophy is intended to evoke, and does evoke, a response of a certain kind in the man to whom it is addressed."[24] He then quickly enlists some notables in the history of philosophy in support of this broadened concept of argumentation. There is Plato, with his talk of recollection; Spinoza, on blessedness; Wittgenstein, with his strategy of reminding his reader of something he already knew; and Heidegger, calling his interlocutors to authentic existence. In all these, and particularly in the thought of Wittgenstein and Heidegger, Johnstone discerns a move to rhetoric as the art of evocation and to truth as the communication of a morale; and it is precisely such a move that Johnstone recommends. The posture of rhetoric as a form of evocation, which is at once a form of life, involves a transvaluation of rhetoric, truth, and communication and an inmixing of their performative capacities. "At one and the same time I tell a truth

---

[23] "In fact, however, one of the hardest things to do in philosophical argumentation is to get another person to admit that he has been inconsistent. Pinning him down is like pinning down a droplet of mercury. For it is usually child's play for him to find a distinction that will resolve the contradiction. If I charge you with having said 'A and not-A,' you can always retort that you meant the first 'A' in one sense and the second in another. More fundamentally, however, your very view of the nature of contradictions may differ from mine. You may refuse to consider it important that your expression is syntactically a contradiction; or you may refuse to take seriously any alleged contradiction that cannot be expressed in the syntactical form 'P and not-P.' As a kind of Hegelian or Marxist, you may refuse to take contradictions seriously at all, so that my polemic leaves you altogether untouched." *Ibid.* One is here also reminded of Walt Whitman's embrace of contradictions as a testimony of the multitudinous and variegated richness of life:

> Do I contradict myself?
> Very well then I contradict myself,
> (I am large, I contain multitudes).

> Leaves of Grass,
> "Song of Myself,"
> Section 51

[24] "Truth, Communication and Rhetoric in Philosophy," p. 75.

and evoke a basis for morale. Hence discovery, communication, and rhetoric all collapse into a unitary philosophical act."[25]

A reinforcement of Johnstone's notion of rhetoric as a form of evocation, and of the general position that we are recommending, is provided by Walter R. Fisher and his "narrative paradigm" of rhetoric. Fisher's "narrative paradigm" is designed to provide an alternative to "the rational world paradigm," a paradigm that finds its philosophical grounding in a rationalistic epistemology of self-evident propositions and incontrovertible proofs. The narrative paradigm solicits the resources of a "narrative rationality" that deformalizes the criteriology of epistemological theory, remains attuned to the conversation and social practices of public life, and undergoes both a discursive and a non-discursive expression. In turn this narrative paradigm, informed by a broader and more vibrant notion of rationality than was ever dreamed of by philosophical rationalism, supplies the proper context for public, moral argumentation.[26]

Of particular importance in Johnstone's notion of rhetoric as the art of evocation and in Fisher's narrative paradigm is the recognition of the need for a new slant on the meaning of rationality. Johnstone's detailing of the triadic intercollapse of truth, communication, and rhetoric falls out as a counterplay against the rationalism of his earlier view, which celebrated propositional consistency as the bottom line criterion of philosophical argumentation. Through his dissemination of the rationalists' view of reason Johnstone forces us to readdress the claim of reason within the texture of communicative praxis, and particularly as this claim is heard within the intertexturing of truth, communication, and rhetoric. The question "What does it mean to be rational, relating to both our thought and our action?" is a question that is not easily suppressed. One can attack the garden varieties of rationalism and inveigh against the "logocentrism" of the tradition, but in these attacks and strategies of deconstruction the issue of rationality does not go away. What may be displaced is the "problem" of rationality as an epistemological worry, but this displacement itself proceeds from a desire to evoke in our hearers and readers a sense of that which is appropriate for our thought and conduct. And surely an evocation of that which is deemed appropriate or suitable displays some sense of the reasonable. The matter reduces to a new vision of rationality. The "logos" operative in this rationality does not pre-exist the world of

---

[25] *Ibid.*, p. 76.
[26] Walter R. Fisher, "Narration as a Human Communication Paradigm: The Case of Public Moral Argument," *Communication Monographs*, Vol. 51, March 1984.

communicative praxis but is fully incarnate in its embodied speech and action.[27]

The rhetorical turn makes explicit this incarnation of the logos within discourse and action in a hermeneutic of everyday life. Communicative praxis announces and displays reason as discourse. On this point Heidegger has been of some help in recalling the tradition of the ancient Greeks, and particularly that of Aristotle, in which the association of logos and discourse was already explicit.

> λόγος as "discourse" means rather the same as δηλοῦν: to make manifest what one is "talking about" in one's discourse. Aristotle has explicated this function of discourse more precisely as αποφαίνσθαι. The λόγος lets something be seen (φαίνεθαι), namely, what the discourse is about; and it does so either *for* the one who is doing the talking (the *medium*) or for persons who are talking with one another, as the case may be.[28]

Rationality as discourse is the making manifest of something to someone, letting something be seen by the speaker and hearer alike. It is in the rhetorical situation, as the working of argumentation and evocation, explanation and understanding, that rationality is displayed. There is, if you will, a presence of the logos in the rhetorical stance. But this need not congeal into a "logocentrism." In entering discourse the logos is decentered and situated within the play of speaker and hearer as they seek consensus on that which is talked about.

The mantle of rationality displayed in the rhetoric of the conversation of mankind is spread out over the various modes and aims of discourse, discernible in the interstices of explanation and understanding, description and evaluation, persuasion and narration. It is within these interstices that the scientist and the artist move about as they strive to make sense together. This making of sense proceeds within a horizon where the discovery of truth is indissolubly linked with its communication, and in which expression, reference, and persuasion unfold in a developing reciprocity. In short, it is a making of sense within the folds of communicative praxis.

---

[27] This incarnation of the logos in the *polis* of discourse and action, it should be stressed, does not lead to an abandonment of consistency as a desideratum for human thought and conduct. Consistency matters in the life of the polis, as does argumentation that continues to abide by its rules. However, this consistency is integrated into a wider patterning of rationality that moves by way of an understanding and comprehension that tempers consistency and places it into a more global space. Consistency for its own sake can indeed become, as Ralph Waldo Emerson remarked, "the hobgoblin of little minds," producing a rigid mind and a rigid character. But situated within its proper relativity it remains a mark of the reasonable.

[28] *Being and Time*, p. 56.

The inmixing of truth and communication in expressive rhetoric as hermeneutic, we have attempted to show, forges a new and expanded notion of rationality as this rationality descends into discourse. The rationality of rationalism, with its Enlightenment concept of reason, is destroyed. But from the ashes of this destruction the phoenix of a new form of rationality arises within the discourse of mankind. However, this new form of rationality is displayed not only in discourse but also in action. Here we discern a further broadening of the logos of rhetoric. The descent of rationality into the texture of communicative praxis occasions a broadening of the notion of the reasonable to include not only the genre of discourse but also that of action. The rhetoric of discourse slides into an explicit rhetoric of action. Rhetoric as the disclosure of configurations of meaning in the public life of man necessarily falls out as a complementarity of speech and action. There is a rhetoric of the deed that accompanies the rhetoric of the spoken and the written word. The logos is at once word and action, and this dissemination and diffusion of the logos across the expressive spectrum of communicative praxis is another indication of the destiny of its decentering. The play of rationality overrides its location within the matrix of a center which functions as its privileged and invariant source.

A rhetoric of action displays its own truth, and like the rhetoric of discourse it displays this truth through a communicative performance. Actions disclose a belongingness to a world of social practices whose meanings are made manifest in and through the action. The complementarity of rhetorical speech and action is most visible in the performance of gesturing. The gestures of the rhetor are not adventitious body movements on the edge of the rhetorical event. They are tissues in the display of meaning. However, because of their usual interwovenness with the verbal speech act they are still within the space of discourse. Within this space they provide, if you will, the first bridge to action. To render more explicit the rhetoric of action one needs to attend to some of the more obvious cases of nonverbal individual and institutional behavior in which this rhetoric is operative. As we have seen in our exploration of the expressive texture of communicative praxis, the activities of individuals and groups are performances of social and historical meaning. The deeds of mankind, no less than its conversations, conspire in the discovery and communication of meaning structures in the public life of man. A protest march, as a pattern of institutional action, is a rhetorical display or making manifest of social ideals and goals. A political rally is an endorsement of a candidate through the sheer presence of the gathered bodies. The performance of a religious ritual announces the inscription of sentiments of valuation that preserve a tradition. In all this there is a rhetorical expression of variegated forms of meaning within the body politic of communicative practices. This expressivity can at times be more consequential and more revelatory than the rhetoric of the spoken or written word.

The move to a rhetoric of action accentuates the requirement for an expansion of the workings of rationality. We not only discern the inscriptions of rationality in the events of speaking and writing but also in the behavior patterns of human action. We flag actions as "reasonable" or "unreasonable"; "thoughtful" or "thoughtless"; "sensible" or "senseless." In doing so we employ, either explicitly or implicitly, certain benchmarks for critique and evaluation. In all this there is an appeal to consistency, but this is no longer the consistency of propositions within a system of beliefs. It is the consistency of a coherence of practices and a harmony of speech and action. The consistency at issue is "ethical," in the originative sense of the term, rather than epistemic. It is the consistency achieved through the struggle for a coherence of discourse and action amidst the threats of discrepancies and disjunctions. Discrepancies within the play of discourse and action can operate either knowingly or unknowingly. If the discrepancy of discourse with action is intended and willful we have a situation of hypocrisy; if it is on the edge of explicit awareness we have a situation of irony. Irony is the discrepancy or disjunction of speech and action that escapes the vigilance of individual and institutional awareness. When President McKinley in 1898 offered his verbal rhetorical support for the annexation of the Philippine Islands with the proclamation that the Philippinoes were God's children for whom Christ also died, while at the same time freighters at American seaports were readied to leave for the Islands to load up with hemp, sugar, and wool, there occurred a profound illustration of irony in the posture of American foreign policy. The rhetoric of politico-religious discourse, uttered in good faith and with the voice of sincerity, abruptly collided with an accompanying rhetoric of action that gave expression to a quite different set of political motivations—based on national self-interest and imperialistic expansionism. It is the insinuation of irony into our amalgamated discourse and action that most decisively elicits our awareness of the ethical. Kierkegaard, as is well known, had already informed us about this in his probing discussion of irony as the mediating stage in the move from the aesthetical to the ethical mode of existence.[29]

---

[29] Our notion of the rhetoric of action exhibits a family resemblance to what Kenneth Burke has called "administrative rhetoric." Administrative rhetoric for Burke is a nondiscursive performance of persuasion, a display of meaning through a network of actions. "The concept of Administrative Rhetoric involves a theory of persuasive devices which have a directly rhetorical aspect, yet include operations not confined to sheerly verbal

A rhetoric of action thus at once extends the vigil of rationality over the global terrain of communicative praxis and in its peculiar mode of showing and making manifest calls our attention to possible discrepancies that threaten the unity of our thought and action, the concord of our speech and behavior. This resituated rationality invites a vigilance over the fittingness of our words and deeds, and points us to the phenomena of ideological intrusion and patterns of self-deception which from time to time invade our discourse and social practices. It is thus that the rationality of rhetorical discourse and rhetorical action, disseminated within the space of communicative praxis, slides into ethics. It is this alignment of rhetoric and ethics that provides the topic for our final chapter.

---

persuasion." *Language as Symbolic Action* (Berkeley: University of California Press, 1968), p. 301. Burke provides an example which, like ours, is also drawn from the sphere of political life. "One example will suffice. It is a variant of what I would call the 'bland' strategy. It goes back to the days when the German Emperor was showing signs of militancy—and Theodore Roosevelt sent our fleet on a 'goodwill mission.' Ostensibly paying the Emperor the compliment of a friendly visit, the President was exemplifying his political percept: 'Speak softly and carry a big stick.' His 'goodwill' visit was clearly rhetorical insofar as it was designed blandly to use a display of force as a mode of persuasion." *Ibid.* The main difference between Burke's Roosevelt example and our McKinley example is that the latter depicts the rhetoric of action under the conditions of irony, thus highlighting the ethico-moral space of the rhetorical event.

CHAPTER TEN

Ethos, Ethics, and
a New Humanism

Even a casual observer of the current state of the arts and the sciences is able to discern that humanism, both as a philosophical position and as a cultural attitude, is under suspicion. The project and language of humanism alike have fallen into disfavor and have become fashionable targets of critique. This widespread suspicion, we would suggest, is due only in part, if at all, to the recent accelerated advances in science and technology and the much discussed "problem" of technology and human values. The genuine threat to humanism comes not from the outside—from the global developments in science and technology—but from within the camp of humanism itself.

Traditionally humanism defined its role to be that of a custodian of values. In this custodial role it construed values as properties of a moral subject, whose duty is that of zealously guarding its "property rights" from disfranchisement. Now it is precisely this language of "value," "property," and "moral subject" that has been brought under suspicion by those who allegedly have been in position to know about such things. Nietzsche was one of the first critics of traditional humanism, calling our attention to the fact that there was something rotten in the modern republic of value philosophy, urging a transvaluation of all delivered values. These delivered values, according to Nietzsche, received their ultimate sanction in a theo-metaphysical grounding. Hence, it is not at all surprising that his celebrated transvaluation of all hitherto existing values was accompanied by a deconstruction of theistic metaphysics. Nietzsche's proclamation of the "Death of God" is at once an announcement of the end of a metaphysics of theism and the demise of a metaphysics of value. Humanism, as the custodian of values, is disassembled and seen as a broken myth of classical and modern metaphysics.

In the proliferating current discussions of the "post-modern age," the attack on humanism has become intensified through a wresting from Nietzsche's pronouncement of the Death of God its implied and unspoken sequel—the "Death of Man." Man, we are told, is "an invention of recent date," destined to "be erased, like a face drawn in sand at the edge of the sea."[1] That the collapse of a theo-metaphysical system of values should carry with it the dissolution of the recent portrait of the human subject should come as no surprise, for man in the guise of a reified moral subject was invented precisely as the repository of such values. But the deconstruction and decentering of the subject, as we saw in Part II of our study, entails not an elimination of subjectivity but rather a redescription of it within the space of decentered temporality and embodiment, from which the subject as the "who" of discourse and action emerges as a multiplex *persona*. This sets us on the path to a new humanism—the humanism of decentered subjectivity. It is now our task to explore the ethical demands of this new humanism as they arise from the ashes of traditional value theory.

We enter the conversation on the ethical dimension of the new humanism from the side of rhetoric. We first discover the question in the rhetorical turn. This will strike many, the learned and the vulgar alike, as somewhat odd. Should not a discussion of ethical matters issue from the already established domain of ethical theory, with ample support from the special areas of logic and epistemology? Does not a placement of ethical concerns within the space of ruminations on rhetoric lead us to a reduction of morality to "mere rhetoric"? Now it is precisely this prejudice against rhetoric as a special discipline on the fringe of honest to goodness philosophy, and the accompanying devaluation of rhetoric as "mere rhetoric," that our preceding discussion in chapter 9 has sought to expunge. Our portrayal of rhetoric as an integral moment of the dynamics of communicative praxis, unfolding as a hermeneutic of the conversation and action of mankind, has effected a double deformalization of philosophy and rhetoric as self-contained and competing disciplines.

The primary accent in this deformalized rhetoric is on its peculiar intentionality, its directedness to the other. The distinctive stamp of rhetorical intentionality is that it reaches out toward, aims at, is directed to the other as hearer, reader, and audience. This intentionality illustrates not the theoretical reflection of cognitive detachment but rather the practical engagement of concrete involvement. In the rhetorical situation the other is not set at a distance. He is "engaged," brought

---

[1]Michel Foucault, *The Order of Things: An Archaeology of the Human Sciences* (New York: Random House, 1970), p. 387.

into the space of praxial concerns. The rhetor seeks to evoke from the hearer a response to a particular situation. He calls for deliberative action and reasoned judgment. Within this intentionality of engagement the ethical issue is unavoidably broached. The elicited response is within a continuum of the moral and the immoral, the authentic and the unauthentic, the appropriate and the inappropriate. Rhetoric as the directedness of discourse to the other, soliciting a response, is destined to slide into ethics.

But what is this "ethics" that we are seeking to unite with rhetoric, and which is to play such an important role in the drama of the new humanism? The proverbial "every schoolboy" learns that ethics is the science of moral behavior. It is that special branch of philosophy that studies values, the notions of the good and the right, moral sentiments and obligations, and the accompanying criteria of justification. Textbooks on ethics teach that there are many types of ethical theory—teleological, deontological, egoistic, and utilitarian, to name but the most common. These types are defined with respect to the relative emphasis that is put on the ends of ethical behavior, the obligations attaching to moral duty, the maximization of personal satisfaction, and the greatest good for the greatest number. And within these more general types there are garden varieties of each. It is thus, through the identification of the data of ethical analysis and the schematization of types of ethical theory, that our proverbial schoolboy apparently learns something about ethics as the science of moral behavior.

In more recent times the investigation of the traits of moral behavior has been taken up by another specialized science of man—ethnology. Ethnology takes up the study of the formation of human character as it develops out of the folkways and mores of a given society which tend toward institutionalization. Aspiring to be a positive science, ethnology constitutes its data through the use of objectifying procedures, often employing mathematical models, wherewith to render determinate and definable the facts of character formation. In the short history of its development as a discipline, ethnology has sought the allied services particularly of psychoanalysis, with which it has conspired to establish a foundation for the human sciences more generally.[2]

Our task is not to trace the history of these two specialized sciences, ethics and ethnology. Such a task possesses its intrinsic merit, and if properly executed would show a gradual erosion of ethics as a special discipline, bit by bit selling its birthright to ethnological analysis and

---

[2] See Foucault's discussion of ethnology and psychoanalysis as positive sciences, and their assumption of privilege in the tracking of the archaeology of the human sciences, *ibid.*, pp. 373–386.

explanation. Ethnology achieves its genuine positivity by absorbing the ethical problematic. Questions about moral behavior become translated into questions about the formation of human character. This, it should be emphasized, is not a move that we sanction. Rather, we propose a shift to another posture of questioning, more radical in nature, probing the origins of both ethics and ethnology as positive sciences. Before ethics and ethnology assume the mantle of positivity we encounter the praxial space of discourse and action in which these alleged sciences are constituted. Prior to ethics as the science of moral behavior and prior to ethnology as the science of the formation of human character there is the rhetorical space of the self/other encounter in which the dynamics of deliberation on matters personal and social proceeds. This dynamics is always contextualized within the political and religious affairs of the *polis* and the wider sociohistorical formation process. The Greeks had a name for this originative and encompassing rhetorical space. They called it *ethos.*

Ethos is commonly translated as "man's character." Heidegger has reminded us of the restrictiveness of this translation and has suggested that this ubiquitous Greek notion, which played such a consequential role in Greek tragedy as well as in Greek philosophy, could be more felicitously rendered as "abode" or "dwelling place." Working out the sense of *ethos* from the Heraclitean fragment which reads *"ethos anthropoi daimon,"* Heidegger proposes that *"Ethos* means abode, dwelling place. The word names the open region in which man dwells. The open region of his abode allows what pertains to man's essence, and what in thus arriving resides in nearness to him, to appear."[3] In another context Heidegger speaks of *ethos* as comprised of "freely accepted obligations and traditions," of "that which concerns free behavior and attitudes," and of "the shaping of man's historical being."[4] It is this global sense of *ethos,* involving the traditions, attitudes, and historicity of man's dwelling in the world, that was later degraded into the ethical as an autonomous branch of philosophy. This degradation proceeded by way of an alignment of ethics with value theory, through which traits of moral character become objects of valuation. Hence, Heidegger, along with Nietzsche, urges us to "think against values." But this deconstruction of value is not to be understood as an appeal to nihilism, a pronouncement of human culture as at bottom purposeless and without meaning. It is intended to initiate a move beyond the reification of value as objectified traits of man's

---

[3] *Letter on Humanism* (in *Martin Heidegger: Basic Writings,* ed. David F. Krell; Harper & Row, 1977), p. 233.
[4] *An Introduction to Metaphysics,* trans. Ralph Manheim (New York: Doubleday & Company, 1959), p. 13.

character which achieve their worth through the self's project of valuation.[5]

The translation of *ethos* as moral character, in the traditional formalized disciplines of philosophy and rhetoric alike, has directed ethical inquiry toward preoccupations with a "theory of the moral self." Ethics, and particularly in the modern period, became an investigation of character-properties which attach to a moral subject. These character-properties, defined as "values," were viewed as having their origin in a valuing subject. This valuing subject, posited as the center in a moral theory of the self, had conferred upon it a position and function similar to the knowing subject of modern epistemological theory. Both the ethical and the epistemological subject took on a positionality which marked out a center, an ethical or an epistemological point, from which valuations and knowledge proceed. Value and knowledge became viewed as properties possessed by a subject. This subject functioned as a chamber or cabinet of ethical and epistemic consciousness. Ethical space and epistemological space were measured from the point on which the moral subject and the epistemological subject were respectively positioned.

Our decentering and resituating of the subject within the wider space of communicative praxis disassembles knowledge and value as properties of mind and character, attached to a lonely, monadic self, cut off from the world. The decentered subject loses its positionality as a center within an abstracted space of ethical and epistemological theory, but in doing so regains its subjectivity as multiplex *persona* within the hermeneutical space of praxis. The space of value properties attached to a moral subject or that of mental properties attached to an epistemological subject is displaced as the subject is decentered. But from this it does not follow that the decentered subject is either ignorant or immoral. What does follow is that both "theory" of knowledge and "theory" of ethics are rendered superfluous, if not philosphically incoherent. Knowing, as it proceeds within the communities of shared concerns (e.g., science, art, and religion) establishes its consensus against a background of practices which display their own patterns of discovery and disclosure. Theory is already ensconced in the practices. To speak of a "theory of knowledge" in the guise of unifying and

---

[5] "To think against 'values' is not to maintain that everything interpreted as 'a value'— 'culture,' 'art,' 'science,' 'human dignity,' 'world,' and 'God'—is valueless. Rather, it is important finally to realize that precisely through the characterization of something as 'a value' what is so valued is robbed of its worth. That is to say, by the assessment of something as a value what is valued is admitted only as an object for man's estimation. But what a thing is in its Being is not exhausted by its being an object, particularly when objectivity takes the form of value. Every valuing, even where it values positively, is a subjectivizing." *Letter on Humanism*, p. 228.

foundational criteria and principles of justification is to speak incoherently of a grounding of knowledge in knowledge. Correspondingly, moral action, as it arises out of the dialectic of conflict and consensus within the space of *ethos,* exhibits an operating intentionality of moral insight and self-understanding that antedates the construction both of value properties and of a monadic ethical subject that entertains them. The moral significations of actions are situated in the practices of the *polis* that shape the historical being of the decentered moral subject. If there is to be talk about a "theory" of these moral practices, it already permeates the fabric of discourse and action that limns the space of *ethos.*

It is within the space of *ethos* that we meet rhetoric. The intentionality of the rhetorical event, its directedness to the other as interlocutor and co-agent, discloses the space of *ethos* as the arena for moral discourse and action, as the abode or dwelling in which the deliberations about the morale of the community and the ways of authenticity take place. This elicited process of collaborative deliberation, it must be emphasized, proceeds not simply by dint of an appropriation of the delivered tradition of accepted mores, but exercises its moments of critique in the face of the abuse of power, the insinuation of ideology, and the intrusions of self-deception in thought and action.

It is at this point of intersection between rhetoric and *ethos* that value theory is transvalued and the ethical question is repostured. The ethical question is no longer an inquiry guided by theories of the moral subject and an inventory of the peculiar properties that constitute moral character, but rather becomes a question about the *fitting response* of the decentered subject in its encounter with the discourse and social practices of the other against the backdrop of the delivered tradition. The ethical requirement within the space of *ethos* is that of the fitting response.

The notion of the fitting response is one that goes back to the concept of *"kathokonta"* (καθήκοντα) in antiquity, which played such a dominant role in Stoic ethics particularly. The Stoic mandate to live according to nature is executed through a performance of actions that fit into the order of Reason *(Logos)* that pervades all things. Living according to nature is doing that which is proper or fitting.[6] The continuing relevance of this notion is discernible throughout the history of Western thought. Nietzsche's notion of style, particularly in his *Birth of Tragedy,*

---

[6]"So a man as long as he doth that which is proper unto a man, his labour cannot be against nature; and if it be not against nature, then neither is it hurtful unto him. . . . Fit and accommodate thyself to that estate and to those occurrences, which by the destinies have been annexed unto thee." Marcus Aurelius, *Meditations* (New York: E. P. Dutton, 1949), XXXI, XXXV, pp. 65–66.

is reminiscent of the requirement of propriety that was inscribed by the Greek concept of *kathokonta*. Nietzsche, the philologist, was certainly aware of the importance of this concept in the classical tradition. It would also appear that this classical concept of the fitting or proper response informs, although somewhat obliquely, Heidegger's notion of "authenticity" *(Eigentlichkeit)*, designating an existential comportment in which *Dasein* appropriates that which is distinctively its own. More recently, Hans-Georg Gadamer has gathered some of the pivotal notions in the humanistic tradition (culture, *sensus communis*, judgment, and taste) through a recollection of this ancient concept. "Both taste and judgment are evaluations of the object in relation to a whole in order to see if it fits in with everything else. Whether, then it is 'fitting'."[7]

Our principal interest resides not so much in a philosophical-historical retrieval of the notion of the fitting response from the archives of philosophical systems as in a hermeneutical reformulation of the notion within the context of our elucidation of the texture of communicative praxis. We have been led back to this notion in our encounter with rhetoric as the disclosure of *ethos*. In its directedness to the other and its call for collaborative discourse and deliberative action rhetoric enters the space of the fitting response; and it enters it in such a manner as to realign the placement of traditional ethical theory through a shift of questioning. This shift is a shift away from the primacy of teleological inquiry (What is the end of man in terms of his nature-conferred essence?), the primacy of deontological inquiry (What is the unconditional duty of man?), and the primacy of utilitarian inquiry (What is the greatest good for the greatest number?). The question "How does one perform a fitting response?" is, we submit, more originative than inquiry about ends, duties, and the good. It is only by addressing this question that ends, duties, and the good achieve a context for defini-

---

[7] *Truth and Method* (New York: The Seabury Press, 1975), p. 36. The classical notion of the fitting has also found a new expression in contemporary philosophy of communication. Michael Calvin McGee has formulated a "logic of figuration" in which one of the chief marks is *propriety*. According to McGee figures of discourse are appropriate when they fit the circumstances of the audience and exude a "sense of cultural authenticity." They are the *right* figures for the occasion, readily eliciting assent from the hearers because the figures are in accord with the pattern of beliefs and practices that inform their culture. An example of such an appropriate figure, provided by McGee, is that of John F. Kennedy's striking figuration "Ask not what your country can do for you, but what you can do for your country." In this figuration Kennedy hit upon the "right" locution at the "right" time. At once a skillful invention and a fit to the occasion, the figure solicited a tacit portion of wisdom from the existing doxic consensus and social practices. Michael Calvin McGee, "The Limits of Figuration: A Critique of the Inventional Base of Scientific Discourse in Communication," paper presented to the University of Iowa Rhetoric Colloquium, March 1983. See also Professor McGee's forthcoming book, *Rhetoric and Social Theory* (Carbondale: Southern Illinois University Press).

tion. As always, it is the logic and ordination of questioning that guides hermeneutical reflection.

The question "How does one perform a fitting response?" does not put us on a path searching for value-predicates that might be attached to a moral subject, defining its character. Rather it places us in the proximity of the *ethos* of our communicative praxis, and invites us to assume a posture toward the patterns of comportment which inform our thought and action. The question points us to the patterns of obligations that arise from our interactions with other selves, interactions which we have seen are constitutive of selfhood. It directs us to the requirement of *responsiveness*, without which the very notions of a moral self and a moral character would have no meaning. The language of morality is the language of responsiveness and responsibility, and if there is to be talk of "an ethics" in all this it will need to be an ethics of the fitting response.

In working out the context of decision for the performance of that which is fitting or proper in the ethical response it is important—indeed salient—that we keep our attention fixed on the space of *ethos* in which are gathered the social and political concerns of the ongoing community. This is a required background which has been largely ignored by modern ethical theory, inspired, as it has been, by an irrepressible fealty to the "Enlightenment" concept of reason. This background was not ignored by the early Greeks. Alasdair MacIntyre correctly points out that although Plato, Aristotle, and the Greek tragedians (and particularly Sophocles) sketched different profiles of the Greek doctrine of virtue, they shared at least one common feature. "All do take it for granted that the milieu in which the virtues are to be exercised and in terms of which they are to be defined is the *polis*."[8] We have already discussed the historical importance of the Greek notion of the *polis* in our elucidation of the dynamics of communicative praxis. Now we are in a position to see its direct relevance for an understanding of the inscriptions of ethical discourse and action within this communicative praxis. The rhetorical turn makes visible the horizon in which *ethos* and *polis* meet, providing the occasion for deliberative-political discourse and action, calling for responses that are fitting or proper. It is hardly an accident that Aristotle was motivated to utilize the notion of *kathokonta* in his work on politics.[9]

---

[8] *After Virtue: A Study in Moral Theory* (Notre Dame: University of Notre Dame Press, 1981), p. 127.

[9] "And the good lawgiver should inquire how states and races of men and communities may participate in a good life, and in the happiness which is attainable by them. His enactments will not be always the same; and where there are neighbours he will have to see what sort of studies should be practiced in relation to their several characters, or how the measures appropriate in relation to each are to be adopted." *Politics* 1325 a 7–13.

Our appeal to the Greek notion of the *polis* in seeking a context for the fitting response, however, is not without its problems. The Greek *polis* was informed by determinants that do not characterize the *polis* in other ages. It is precisely this that occasions the hermeneutical demand for an ongoing interpretation and reapplication. The Greek notion accentuated the element of destiny, courting a fatalism that is more subdued in the modern notion of the *polis*. This was the result of viewing the *polis* as principally an extension of nature. The categories devised for a comprehension of the world of nature were used in an understanding of the world of human affairs. The category of substance, within the frame of the eternal return of the same, was made normative for an explanation of social relations and social change. In this respect the Greek view of the *polis* was ahistorical. The advent of historical consciousness brought about a transubstantiation of the Greek *polis* into the composite of freedom, individuality, subjectivity, and uniqueness. Freedom rather than destiny, individuality rather than participation, subjectivity rather than objectivity, and uniqueness rather than sameness received the principal emphasis.

Kierkegaard's essay "The Ancient Tragical Motive as Reflected in the Modern" still stands as one of the most incisive depictions of the ancient and modern views with respect to their relative emphases on corporate destiny and personal freedom. His discussion centers on the consequences of the ancient and modern views for the meaning of tragic guilt. In the Greek concept of tragedy the hero moves within the confines of a destiny that structures the *polis*. "Even if the individual moved freely, he still rested in the substantial categories of state, family, and destiny. This substantial category is exactly the fatalistic element in Greek tragedy, and its exact peculiarity."[10] Within such a scheme of things, in which events are plotted by destiny, the guilt of the tragic hero is a corporate guilt. It is a result principally of his suffering rather than of his acting. In modern tragedy, where character rather than plot is predominant, the situation is reversed. "The tragic hero is subjectively reflected in himself, and this reflection has not only reflected him out of every immediate relation to state, race, and destiny, but has often reflected him out of his own preceding life."[11] In modern tragedy the hero's predicament is the result not of suffering but of personal action. Guilt is personal rather than corporate.

Kierkegaard's interpretive analysis of the concepts of ancient and modern tragedy is particularly helpful for highlighting the changing views on the relation between the *polis* and the individual throughout

---

[10]*Either/Or: A Fragment of Life*, Vol. I, trans. David and Lillian Swenson (Princeton: Princeton University Press, 1949), p. 116.
[11]*Ibid.*

history. As is well known, Kierkegaard himself was the staunchest of advocates for "the individual" (which he had hoped would be inscribed on his tombstone); yet, he recognized clearly enough the distortions ensuing from an *abstract* individuality and a *reified* subjectivity. The lesson to be learned from him is that neither a substantialist and objectivistic mapping of the *polis* nor a historicist and subjectivistic view of the individual actor affords proper descriptions of the stages along life's way. The texture of the relations between self and society, the individual and the collective, man and his institutions, becomes visible only after the *polis* has been desubstantialized and the subject has been decentered.

With the help of Kierkegaard, our hermeneutical reformulation and redescription of the significations of *polis* and *ethos* in Greek thought provides us with a suitable point of departure for addressing more directly the sense of the fitting or the proper in our communicative ethics. The determination of that which is fitting proceeds by dint of a social perception of the relation of rhetor and interlocutor, actor and respondent, to the holistic fabric and pattern of communal thought and action. The fitting or the proper is informed by a holism of social practices. The sense of the fitting is guided by a contextual holism rather than by an ordination of virtues and values construed as isolable attributes or "properties." Here one confronts a semantical perplexity. The "proper" appears not to be a "property." *Kathokonta* is not a *proprium,* and much less a property-predicate in the sense of modern epistemology. Philology and etymology provide limited resources in resolving this matter. In the end the distinction can only be worked out hermeneutically. The proper, as the fitting or the appropriate, has to do with a way of inhabiting hermeneutical space. Property-predicates are elements within epistemological space. The proper is delivered through praxis-oriented understanding. Property-predicates originate from a theory of judgment. Appropriateness is the manifestation of a form of life in which there is a discernment of what is timely in the responses of both speech and action. Properties in the guise of value predicates are the reified products of discourse and action already accomplished, abstracted from the holistic space of ongoing social practices which solicit ongoing responses at the right time and in the right place.

It soon becomes evident in working out a hermeneutical reformulation of the dynamics of the fitting response that it has much do with temporality, a notion that we have repeatedly encountered in our elucidation of the texture of communicative praxis. The fitting or proper response is linked with the "opportune" or "privileged" moment—the *right* time for deliberation and action. This link was already suggested in Aristotle's *Nicomachean Ethics,* where the "right time" figures as a condition for the actualization of virtue.[12] Kierkegaard made much of the moment as the "time for decision" in which the self first becomes a genuine self by choosing itself in its manifold concretion. Heidegger elevated the *Augenblick,* as the moment of vision and action, to a position of central importance in sketching his portrait of authentic existence. A fitting response grasps the moment as the proper time for deliberation and action. Responsibility, temporality, and decision conspire in the constitution of the ethical posture.

With the help of the notion of temporality, as it is at work in the fitting response, we can proceed to another hermeneutical level of reformulation and redescription. The fitting response preserves the *ethos* and the *polis.* It is stationed within them and always proceeds from them. The response is a *response to* the attitudes, behavior patterns, meaning-formations, and moral assessments that define the space shared by the rhetor and the interlocutor, the self and the other. In the language of Gadamer, the response always takes place within the context of the tradition, with its delivered prejudgments and assessments. It is a *fitting* response because it serves and preserves the tradition (as the conjunction of *ethos* and *polis*). It appropriates the tradition, even if only in a negative way. So there is the moment of appropriation which fosters preservation, keeping the tradition intact and serving its end. This we might call the hermeneutics of participation, a participation which conserves that which has been transmitted through the tradition. But there is another moment in the fitting response—the moment that occasions invention, novelty, the emergence of the not yet said and the not yet accomplished. This defines the fitting response as a *critical* response, through which the prejudgments of the tradition are amended, reassessed, or indeed displaced. This we would call the hermeneutics of distanciation and critique. It is this side of hermeneutics that has been given particular attention by the exponents of the school of critical theory (and particularly Jürgen Habermas), who have emphasized the need to ferret out the distortions of communication resulting from insidious ideologies and dehumanizing power relations that infect the tradition. The fitting response is thus enjoined to do double duty—to preserve the tradition, without which communication could not proceed, and to critique the tradition in search of a pharmakon that might remedy its conceptual and existential ills. Hence, that which is "proper" in the fitting response contains within itself a field of

---

[12] "Both fear and confidence and appetite and anger and pity and in general pleasure and pain may be felt both too much and too little, and in both cases not well; but to feel them at the right times, with reference to the right objects, toward the right people, with the right motive, and in the right way, is what is both intermediate and best, and this is characteristic of virtue." 1106 b 17–23.

tension and a play of opposition. It involves both the appropriate in the sense of taking over and preserving the tradition and the appropriate in the sense of critique, reassessment, and invention. Ethical behavior, as discourse and action, is a comportment within this field of tension of the play of propriety as it moves between preservation and invention.

Within this play of propriety and the different posturing of what is appropriate in the fitting response, temporality plays a crucial role, as it does in decentered subjectivity more generally. The comportment of the fitting response is regulated by specific attitudes toward the three modes of temporality—present, past, and future. The present is under-stood not as a punctual now but as the opportune moment for decision. The response to the past is one of recollection, occasioning a preserva-tion of the discourse and social practices of the *polis*. The response to the future is that of a projection and anticipation of new possibilities for redescription and reinterpretation, setting the stage for novelty and invention. Not only a hermeneutic of ethical discourse and action but also any talk of "normal" and "revolutionary" science (Kuhn) or "sys-tematic" and "edifying" philosophy (Rorty) moves within this horizon of praxial temporality, which is at once a preservation and an invention.

Temporality thus structures the fitting response as intercalated mo-ments of decision, recollection, and invention. Ultimately the fit-tingness in the fitting response depends on the success of the response in integrating the three modes of temporality. What needs to be kept clearly in mind is that this integration occurs within the inaugural space of communicative praxis. The moment of decision antedates any theory of the instantaneous and passing now; recollection is earlier than any theory of representation; and invention precedes prediction and fore-cast. It is within this praxial space that the fitting response deconstructs ethical theory and transvalues philosophy of value. Recollection, as a praxial comportment, is neither a pure, theoretical beholding of pre-existing essences nor a representation of values in the guise of value-predicates.[13] Indeed, recollection is already oriented toward future possibilities of invention and recreation. Or in the language of Kierkegaard, recollection becomes *repetition,* properly understood as that which is "recollected forwards."[14] That which is preserved is creatively transformed through the inventiveness of speech and action.

---

[13] Fred R. Dallmayr, winnowing the reflections of Adorno, Merleau-Ponty, and Heidegger, has adumbrated a recollective ethics in which the Greek notion of *anamnesis* is defor-malized and rendered more concordant with the dynamics of praxial understanding. See *Twilight of Subjectivity* (Amherst: The University of Massachusetts Press, 1981), pp. 250–254.

[14] *Repetition: An Essay in Experimental Psychology,* trans. Walter Lowrie (Princeton: Princeton University Press, 1946), p. 4.

"Recollection forwards" displays an appetition for novelty, a projection into possibilities, a foresight toward discourse not yet spoken and deeds not yet done. The fitting response grasps this "not yet" and appropriates it as the place from which new questions, new descriptions, and new assessments are launched. This space of inventiveness against the foreground of an open future provides the standpoint for critique and creativity through which distorted forms of communication are overcome.

The encounter with *ethos* in the rhetorical turn has engaged us in a hermeneutic of the fitting response. We have elucidated this emergent ethic of the fitting response against the background of a deconstruction of value theory in an effort to trace the genealogy of morality back to its source in the praxial space of *ethos,* textured as an integument of attitudes, social practices, and cultural memories. Within this *ethos* the ethical demand is recognized as the call for a fitting response, structured by the play of preservation and invention, participation in tradition and critique of ideology. The horizon of this play is supplied by a praxial temporality in which ethical attitudes toward the present, past, and future regulate the form and dynamics of the fitting response.

Our tracing of the genealogy of morality through an exploration of the slide of rhetoric into ethics now brings us to another level of hermeneutical elucidation and critique, and raises anew the question of the destiny of humanism. *Ethos,* as the dwelling of the decentered subject within the space of communicative praxis, displays both ethical and aesthetical forms of life. Nietzsche in his own "genealogy of morals," which proceeded in tandem with his rediscovery of the Greek tragedians, had already seen this with ample clarity. His transvaluation of value achieves its positive moment in an ennobling of the aesthetic response. "It is only as an *aesthetic phenomenon* that existence and the world are eternally *justified,*" writes Nietzsche in his *Birth of Tragedy.*[15] The fitting response for Nietzsche becomes a matter of "style." What is required is a stylizing of one's character, imputing form to both its strengths and its weaknesses.

One Thing is Needful.—To "give style" to one's character—that is a grand and a rare art! He who surveys all that his nature presents in its strength and in its weakness, and then fashions it into an ingenious plan, until everything appears artistic and rational, and even the weaknesses enchant the eye—exercises that admirable art.[16]

---

[15] *The Birth of Tragedy,* trans. W. Kaufmann (New York: Vintage Books, 1967), p. 52.
[16] *Joyful Wisdom,* trans. Kurt F. Reinhardt (New York: Frederick Unger Publishing Co., 1960), p. 223.

After the transvaluation of all hitherto existing values, which issue from
the play of instincts as regulated by the good and bad conscience, we
are left with the resources of style. Ethics is transvalued into aesthetics.

The issue regarding the relation of the ethical to the aesthetical is
readdressed, although in quite different ways, in the philosophies of
Sartre and Heidegger. Sartre in developing his "existentialism as a
humanism" comes close to simply taking over the stance of Nietzsche
on this matter. Ethics for Sartre (at least during his earlier and more
programmatic period) is understood in terms of analogies drawn from
artistic creation.

> It is clearly understood that there are no *a priori* aesthetic values, but that
> there are values which appear subsequently in the coherence of the
> painting, in the correspondence between what the artist intended and the
> result. . . . The same holds on the ethical plane. What art and ethics have
> in common is that we have creation and invention in both cases. We can
> not decide *a priori* what there is to be done.[17]

Ethical values, for Sartre as for Nietzsche, appear only in the process
of the creative stylization of our behavior. Heidegger is more radical in
his approach to the value question than is Nietzsche or Sartre, and he is
expressly critical of Sartre's project of an "existential humanism."
Nonetheless, his ruminations on the privileged role of poetics continues to move about within the space of reflection marked out by
Nietzsche. Admittedly, he radicalizes Nietzsche. He designs a deconstruction of *both* ethics and aesthetics so as to make visible a
symbiosis of *ethos* and *poiēsis* on a more originative level—the level of
originative, poetical thinking. In this move Heidegger, like Nietzsche, is
unable to conceal his profound respect for the Greek tragedians. "The
tragedies of Sophocles," says Heidegger, "preserve the *ethos* in their
sagas more primordially than Aristotle's lectures on 'ethics.' "[18] This
admiration for Sophocles is coupled with Heidegger's high regard for
Hölderlin, whom he credits for having reclaimed the originative *ethos*
of the Greek poets as a "poetic dwelling." Heidegger has provided
extensive interpretive commentaries on Hölderlin's poetry and has
devoted an entire essay to a discussion of Hölderlin's stanza:

> Full of merit, and yet poetically, dwells
> Man on this earth.[19]

---

[17] *Existentialism*, trans. Bernard Frechtman (New York: Philosophical Library, 1947),
pp. 50–51.
[18] *Letter on Humanism*, p. 232.
[19] ". . . Poetically Man Dwells . . . ," trans. Albert Hofstadter, in *Martin Heidegger:
Poetry, Language, Thought* (New York: Harper & Row, 1971). See also the essay "What

(Voll Verdienst, doch dichterisch, wohnet
Der Mensch auf dieser Erde.)

Hölderlin's restoration of the Greek tragedians' notion of *ethos* as a "poetic dwelling" provides Heidegger with a touchstone for his notion of authentic existence. The fitting or proper response is at bottom the response of poetical thinking and dwelling. Poetical thinking, distinct from representational thinking *(vorstellendes Denken)* as governed by the logic of predication, proceeds by way of the logos of disclosure at work in what Heidegger names "commemorative thinking" *(an-denkendes Denken).*[20] Indeed, for Heidegger poetical thinking is the paradigmatic exemplification of commemorative thinking. Poetical thinking "unconceals" and "commemorates" that which remains hidden to representational thought. Commemorating the poet Hölderlin and that which he thought, Heidegger invites us to think poetically about Lake Constance. To think poetically about Lake Constance is not to represent it metaphysically as an in-and-for-itself of nature, nor to represent it scientifically as a combination of hydrogen and oxygen, nor to represent it technologically as a source of hydroelectric power. It is not to represent it at all, but rather to disclose it through commemoration, to disclose it as that which we care for and cherish, as we care for and cherish the earth itself as man's dwelling.[21]

That Heidegger's elucidation of *ethos* as a poetic dwelling carries a power of self-recognition and a profundity of vision cannot be denied. But we are of the mind that in the end he no more escapes the threat of aestheticism than did Nietzsche. Both thinkers offer us the power of the poetical so as not to die of the prosaic. But the conversations and social practices of mankind have their share of the prosaic. Concerns with the material conditions of human life, the use and abuse of power in social institutions, and distortions of communication are also features of man's dwelling on the earth. *Ethos,* we have maintained, encompasses a manifold of concerns and deliberations on the destiny of the *polis* and on man's wider sociohistorical existence. This is why the requirement of the fitting response should never be reduced to a matter of stylized comportment (Nietzsche) or poetical dwelling (Heidegger).[22] The

---

are Poets For?" in the Hofstadter collection, and the two essays "Remembrance of the Poet" and "Hölderlin and the Essence of Poetry," trans. Douglas Scott, in *Existence and Being,* ed. Werner Brock (London: Vision Press Ltd., 1949).
[20] See particularly Heidegger's essay "The Way Back into the Ground of Metaphysics" for an elucidation of the distinction between "representational" and "commemorative" thinking (in Walter Kaufmann, *Existentialism from Dostoevsky to Sartre,* New York: Meridian Books, 1956).
[21] "Remembrance of the Poet", p. 275.
[22] Glen Gray has provided one of the more trenchant criticisms of Heidegger on this point

proper or the fitting has both a moral and an artistic posture, simultaneously solicited by the *ethos*. The new humanism will teach that man dwells rhetorically, and in this rhetorical dwelling the ethical and the aesthetical are taken up into a new relationship, in which there is a coincident cultivation of poetical perspectives and responsiveness to the socio-politico-economic needs of man.

There have been recurring perceptions of the threat of aestheticism throughout the whole history of philosophy. The threat has been perceived on different fronts–ontological, epistemological, and moral. Plato was unable to find a place for the artists in his ideal state because their productions and representations were at a third remove from reality. He saw the result of artistic production as but an image of that which is itself an image of the real. Aristotle's use of the Greek proverb "Bards tell many a lie" also issued from a suspicion that *poiēsis* did not mirror reality. Modern positivism, in its epistemological critique of the aesthetical, found aesthetics to be wanting because it seemed to be incurably poverty-striken in providing verifiable truth-claims. Poetic utterances, the positivists maintained, remain cognitively meaningless. Augustine criticized the arts, and particularly the theatre, from the standpoint of moral concerns because of the life-styles of the performers. Kierkegaard found in the aesthetical stage, or more precisely in the absolutization of it, an escape from the responsibilities of ethical commitment.

Now many of these perspectives of critique, as Heidegger would remind us, trade on arbitrary divisions and surface readings of the ontological, the epistemological, the moral, and the poetic. Yet, even in Heidegger's deconstructive retrieval of the originative posture of *poiēsis* a problem remains with respect to the proper placement of socioethical concerns. Although the aesthetical is transvalued through Heidegger's retrieval and reclamation of an inaugural poetic thinking (thus exonerating him from the charge of aestheticism per se), the dynamics of an originative ethical thinking escapes his philosophical vigilance.

It is, however, in the post-modern age of deconstructive criticism (which remains more beholden to Heidegger's iconoclastic philosophizing than it recognizes) that a new species of aestheticism is most clearly

---

in his essay "Heidegger: Poets and Thinkers" (in *Phenomenology and Existentialism*, eds. Edward N. Lee and Maurice Mandelbaum; Baltimore: The Johns Hopkins University Press, 1967). Using Hölderlin against Heidegger himself, Gray emphasizes Hölderlin's admonition that the poet's medium is also "the most dangerous of possessions." This danger, according to Gray, resides in a forgetfulness of man's prosaic involvements and commitments. "Man's first vocation is that of taking care of himself and his fellows in a moral and social way, and this, though not divorced from poetry, is frequently a prosaic task" (p. 110).

discernible. Deconstructive criticism, in its enchantment with the paradigm of discourse, has everything become text. The metaphorical play with "text" leads to an extension of textuality to the domain of human action and history and invites a fictionalization of the moral fabric that pervades the *ethos* of communicative praxis. Man's dwelling on earth becomes a text to be read through experimentations with various strategies of reading and writing. Both nature and history become textualized. But if everything becomes text, then nothing is text. The crucial distinction between the textuality of discourse and the moral space of human practices is erased, and the integrity of rationality in moral action is sacrificed. The discrimination of the proper and the improper, the authentic and the unauthentic, as it applies to human action, is glossed. Historical atrocities and injustices, the massacre of innocents, economic deprivation, and myths of ethnic superiority are read as textual inscriptions subject to the play of deconstructive interpretation, occasioning the irony of a discrepancy between strategies of reading and the requirements of moral action. *Ethos* is taken up into an ontology of textuality. The illuminating metaphor of textuality is overextended and stretched beyond its elastic limits.

The extolling of discourse and textuality in the so-called post-modern age has proceeded in tandem with talk about the end of humanism. The buzz phrases "Death of Man," "Death of the Author," and "dissolution of the subject" have been designed to distract our attention away from preoccupations with invariant essences, transcendental-empirical doublets, authorial intentions, and epistemic centers of consciousness. It should be clear from the preceding chapters that we consider this negative moment of deconstruction to be timely and well placed. It provides a corrective to the freewheeling constructionism of modern thought and its epistemological prejudices concerning the centrality of the subject and the primacy of consciousness. A humanism that seeks to found itself on a monadic and self-contained subject is no longer tenable. But we have also argued that a displacement of the subject as defined within the conceptual frameworks of traditional metaphysics, epistemology, and axiology does not entail a displacement of the subject in every conceivable fashion. Rather, it confronts us with the demand to explore the comportment of a restored and decentered subjectivity within the holistic space of communicative praxis. It is within the folds of this communicative praxis that a new sense of humanism can be found—one that will provide a sheet anchor against the recurring tendencies toward an aestheticism of textuality which pervade the discursive strategies of the post-modern age.

Our hermeneutics of the texture of communicative praxis supplies the space for the elucidation of this new humanism. Communicative praxis unfolds as an interplay of discourse and action which preserves the integrity of both. It is from this communicative praxis that the subject, decentered and multidimensional, is seen to emerge in the ineluctable play of the questions "Who is speaking?" "Who is writing?" and "Who is acting?" This hermeneutical self-implicature of the subject proceeds in tandem with the rhetorical turn, in which discourse and action are disclosed not only as being *by* someone but also *for* and *to* someone. Directedness to the other, eliciting collaborative discourse and action, supplies the linchpin of the rhetorical event. Rhetoric's decisive disclosure of the other, and of the situated *ethos* in which self and other dwell, points us to the ethical requirement of the fitting response. In our hermeneutic of the ethical as the fitting response we have emphasized the need to avoid aestheticism, both of the modern and the post-modern variety. The phenomenon of *ethos,* as the dwelling site of man, shows itself not only in an artistic-poetical but also in an explicitly moral horizon of concerns. The integrity of the moral texture of human action needs to be secured not only from the threat of a scientific-technological reductionism but from that of an aesthetic-textual reductionism as well.

So what is the destiny of humanism? Foucault may be right in his prediction that man as an invention of recent date will soon be erased like a face drawn in sand at the edge of the sea; but this visage soon to be erased is but a portrait composed of modern philosophical constructs. In the restored portrait of man as decentered subjectivity, sketched on the terrain of communicative praxis, a new humanism begins to unfold. This new humanism no longer promises invariant definitions of a foundational subject, but instead moves about in a hermeneutical play of perspectival descriptions of the life of discourse and action.

Index